monday.com

A Step-by-Step Guide to Better Organization

Kiet Huynh

Table of Contents

Introduction

1.1 What is Monday.com?

Monday.com is a cloud-based work operating system (Work OS) designed to streamline workflows, enhance team collaboration, and simplify project management. It is a versatile tool that adapts to various industries and team sizes, allowing users to create custom workflows tailored to their specific needs. Whether you're managing a large-scale project, tracking individual tasks, or coordinating team efforts, Monday.com provides the flexibility and tools necessary to boost efficiency and transparency.

A Versatile Work OS

Unlike traditional project management tools, Monday.com is not confined to a single use case. It serves as a platform for managing anything from marketing campaigns to software development projects, HR processes, or even personal to-do lists. The platform's modular nature means users can build their own workflows using a combination of boards, columns, automations, and integrations.

For example:

- A marketing team might use Monday.com to plan content calendars, track campaign performance, and manage design requests.

- A software development team can track sprint cycles, bugs, and feature releases.

- An HR department could manage recruitment pipelines, employee onboarding, and feedback surveys.

Core Features of Monday.com

At the heart of Monday.com lies a set of core features that make it a powerful tool for organization and collaboration:

1. **Customizable Boards**: Boards are the foundation of Monday.com. Each board represents a project or process and can be customized to track tasks, deadlines, and team responsibilities. Boards are divided into groups and rows, where each row represents a task or item.

2. **Dynamic Columns**: Columns add structure to your boards by defining the type of information you want to track, such as task status, deadlines, assigned team members, or progress percentages. Popular column types include:

    o **Status Column**: Track the progress of tasks (e.g., "To Do," "In Progress," "Done").

    o **People Column**: Assign tasks to team members.

    o **Timeline Column**: Visualize project timelines and deadlines.

    o **File Column**: Attach important documents or images directly to tasks.

3. **Automation Capabilities**: Automations reduce manual work by handling repetitive tasks. For instance, you can set up rules to:

    o Notify team members when a deadline is approaching.

    o Automatically move tasks to the "Done" group when their status changes.

    o Send email reminders when a task is overdue.

4. **Integrations with Other Tools**: Monday.com seamlessly integrates with popular tools like Slack, Zoom, Google Drive, and Microsoft Teams. These integrations allow users to consolidate their workflows, ensuring that information flows smoothly between platforms.

5. **Visualization Options**: To better understand your data, Monday.com offers multiple views, including:

   o **Kanban View** for workflow management.

   o **Gantt Chart** for project timelines.

   o **Calendar View** for scheduling.

The Role of Monday.com in Modern Business

In today's fast-paced business environment, Monday.com serves as a central hub for organization and communication. Its impact can be seen in several key areas:

1. **Improved Collaboration**: With team members often working remotely or across different time zones, Monday.com provides a shared space where everyone can stay updated on progress, communicate effectively, and contribute to the project.

2. **Increased Transparency**: Monday.com makes it easy to see who is responsible for what and how tasks are progressing. This transparency helps prevent bottlenecks and ensures accountability.

3. **Better Decision-Making**: By consolidating data and offering visualization tools, Monday.com empowers teams to make informed decisions based on real-time information.

4. **Scalability for Growing Teams**: Whether you're a startup or an established enterprise, Monday.com scales to meet the demands of your organization. Its flexibility allows teams to start with simple boards and expand into complex workflows as their needs evolve.

A User-Centric Design

Monday.com is designed with user experience in mind, making it intuitive for beginners while offering advanced features for power users. Its drag-and-drop functionality, pre-built templates, and comprehensive help center ensure that new users can quickly learn the platform.

- **Templates for Quick Setup**: Monday.com provides templates for a variety of use cases, including project management, sales pipelines, event planning, and more. These templates offer a great starting point for users who are new to the platform.

- **Mobile and Desktop Access**: With apps available for iOS, Android, and desktop, Monday.com ensures that users can stay productive from anywhere.

Real-World Examples

To better understand what Monday.com is, let's explore a few real-world examples:

- **Small Business Use Case**: A local bakery uses Monday.com to manage its supply chain, track orders, and schedule staff shifts. With visual timelines and status updates, they ensure timely deliveries and smooth operations.

- **Enterprise Use Case**: A multinational corporation leverages Monday.com to coordinate marketing campaigns across multiple regions. By integrating the platform with Slack and Google Analytics, they track performance metrics and streamline communication across teams.

Why Choose Monday.com?

Whether you're an individual looking to organize personal tasks or a large team seeking a comprehensive project management tool, Monday.com offers several compelling reasons to choose it:

- **Ease of Use**: No technical expertise is required to set up or use the platform.

- **Flexibility**: Adaptable to various industries and team sizes.

- **Collaboration Tools**: Features like comments, updates, and notifications keep teams connected.

- **Cost-Effectiveness**: With plans for individuals, small businesses, and enterprises, Monday.com caters to a wide range of budgets.

Conclusion

In summary, Monday.com is more than just a project management tool—it's a dynamic Work OS that empowers individuals and teams to organize, collaborate, and succeed. By offering a balance of simplicity and advanced functionality, Monday.com has established itself as a valuable asset for businesses and individuals alike.

1.2 Who Can Benefit from Monday.com?

Monday.com is a versatile work operating system (Work OS) that caters to a wide range of individuals, teams, and organizations. Its flexibility and adaptability make it a tool suitable for various industries and roles, providing value to users who seek to streamline workflows, improve collaboration, and enhance productivity. In this section, we'll explore the key groups of people who can benefit from Monday.com, illustrating its broad appeal across different use cases.

Small Business Owners and Entrepreneurs

Small business owners and entrepreneurs often juggle multiple responsibilities, from managing teams to handling finances and customer relationships. Monday.com provides a centralized platform where they can:

- **Track projects and deadlines**: Entrepreneurs can create boards to manage tasks, set priorities, and ensure timely completion of projects.

- **Organize client relationships**: By using customizable templates, business owners can maintain a CRM system to track client interactions, sales pipelines, and follow-ups.

- **Optimize limited resources**: With its automation features, repetitive tasks such as follow-up reminders or status updates can be handled without manual intervention.

Example Use Case: A bakery owner could use Monday.com to schedule production timelines, monitor ingredient inventory, and coordinate with delivery staff, ensuring a seamless operation.

Project Managers

Project managers rely on tools that allow them to effectively plan, execute, and monitor projects. Monday.com provides the perfect environment for:

- **Detailed project planning**: Managers can break down complex projects into tasks, assign team members, and set due dates using visual timelines and Gantt charts.

- **Collaboration and updates**: The ability to tag team members, add comments, and share files ensures that everyone stays aligned.

- **Real-time progress tracking**: Dashboards offer an overview of project statuses, helping managers identify bottlenecks and make data-driven decisions.

Example Use Case: A project manager at a software company can use Monday.com to organize sprints, track bug fixes, and manage product launches.

Marketing Teams

Marketing teams often handle multiple campaigns and creative projects simultaneously. Monday.com is a valuable tool for:

- **Campaign planning**: Teams can map out content calendars, assign tasks, and ensure timely execution of deliverables.

- **Creative asset management**: By attaching files directly to tasks, team members can keep all creative assets in one place for easy reference.

- **Performance tracking**: Using custom dashboards, marketing teams can track campaign metrics such as ROI, click-through rates, and engagement levels.

Example Use Case: A digital marketing agency can manage social media content creation, email campaigns, and ad performance all within Monday.com.

Human Resources Teams

Human resources (HR) professionals often handle processes that require organization and coordination. Monday.com helps HR teams by:

- **Managing recruitment pipelines**: HR can track candidates, schedule interviews, and collaborate with hiring managers.

- **Onboarding new employees**: Create workflows to ensure a smooth onboarding experience, from setting up IT accounts to completing training modules.

- **Employee engagement**: HR teams can use Monday.com to plan events, collect feedback, and track employee satisfaction metrics.

Example Use Case: An HR manager in a mid-sized company can create a recruitment board to streamline job postings, applications, and candidate evaluations.

Remote Teams

With the rise of remote work, distributed teams need tools that enable seamless communication and collaboration. Monday.com serves as a virtual office by offering:

- **Centralized communication**: Team members can communicate directly on tasks, reducing the need for back-and-forth emails.

- **Time zone management**: Boards and timelines help teams operating in different time zones stay aligned.

- **Shared file storage**: Teams can attach documents, spreadsheets, and presentations directly to their tasks, making information easily accessible.

Example Use Case: A remote customer support team can track inquiries, assign tickets, and monitor response times to ensure customer satisfaction.

Creative Professionals and Designers

Creative professionals often manage multiple projects and clients, requiring tools that keep them organized. Monday.com caters to their needs by:

- **Streamlining client workflows**: Designers can create boards for each client, tracking revisions, deadlines, and deliverables.

- **Tracking creative assets**: By attaching files and linking them to tasks, creatives can maintain a clear record of project materials.

- **Collaborating with clients**: Shareable boards allow clients to view progress, provide feedback, and approve designs.

Example Use Case: A freelance graphic designer can use Monday.com to manage client projects, communicate revision requests, and deliver final assets.

Software Development Teams

Monday.com is an ideal tool for software development teams, offering features that cater to Agile and Scrum methodologies. Developers can benefit from:

- **Sprint planning and tracking**: Boards can be customized to manage sprints, backlog items, and bug tracking.

- **Integration with developer tools**: Monday.com integrates with tools like GitHub, enabling seamless tracking of code changes.

- **Cross-department collaboration**: Developers can collaborate with product managers, designers, and QA teams on one platform.

Example Use Case: A software development team can use Monday.com to plan releases, track feature development, and monitor test results.

Nonprofit Organizations

Nonprofits often operate with limited resources and need tools that maximize efficiency. Monday.com supports nonprofit organizations by:

- **Managing volunteers**: Track volunteer schedules, roles, and tasks in a centralized system.

- **Event planning**: Plan fundraising events, coordinate with vendors, and monitor budgets.

- **Grant tracking**: Keep records of grant applications, deadlines, and outcomes.

Example Use Case: A nonprofit working on community development projects can use Monday.com to plan events, coordinate volunteers, and track donations.

Educators and Students

Educational institutions and students can leverage Monday.com for academic and organizational purposes. Benefits include:

- **Course planning**: Educators can design lesson plans, manage schedules, and track student progress.

- **Group projects**: Students can collaborate on assignments, delegate tasks, and meet deadlines.

- **Event coordination**: Schools can use Monday.com to organize events such as parent-teacher conferences or extracurricular activities.

Example Use Case: A high school teacher can create a board to track class assignments, student submissions, and grades.

Event Planners

Event planners need tools to juggle vendors, timelines, and budgets. Monday.com provides:

- **Vendor management**: Track communication, contracts, and deadlines with multiple vendors.

- **Budget tracking**: Use customizable columns to monitor expenses and stay within budget.

- **Task coordination**: Assign tasks to team members and monitor progress in real time.

Example Use Case: An event planner organizing a corporate retreat can use Monday.com to manage schedules, coordinate with vendors, and track RSVPs.

Conclusion

From small businesses to global enterprises, Monday.com provides an adaptable platform for anyone looking to improve organization, collaboration, and efficiency. Whether you are managing a team, working independently, or coordinating complex projects, Monday.com offers the tools you need to succeed. The next chapter will guide you through the basics of getting started, ensuring you can unlock the full potential of this powerful Work OS.

1.3 How to Use This Guide

Monday.com is a versatile platform with a wide array of tools, features, and customization options designed to help individuals and teams organize their work better. Whether you are completely new to the platform or looking to deepen your understanding of its advanced capabilities, this guide is structured to serve as your companion in mastering Monday.com.

This section will walk you through how to make the most of this book and customize your learning journey based on your specific needs. By the end of this chapter, you'll have a clear roadmap for using this guide effectively, allowing you to navigate Monday.com with confidence.

Structure of This Guide

This book has been thoughtfully divided into chapters that cater to users at different levels of familiarity with Monday.com, from beginners to advanced users. Here's an overview of what each chapter covers:

- **Introduction**: Provides a brief overview of Monday.com, who can benefit from it, and how this guide will help you.

- **Getting Started**: Walks you through the basics, such as creating an account, understanding the interface, and setting up your first workspace.

- **Boards and Basic Functionality**: Introduces you to the core features of Monday.com, including creating boards, managing items, and collaborating with your team.

- **Collaborating with Your Team**: Focuses on team features such as assigning tasks, sharing files, and managing permissions.

- **Automations and Integrations**: Explores how to streamline your workflows by setting up automations and integrating Monday.com with other tools.

- **Views and Visualization Tools**: Covers how to customize views, create dashboards, and use reports for better data visualization.

- **Advanced Features**: Delves into time tracking, workload management, and other advanced tools to optimize your workflows.

- **Troubleshooting and Best Practices**: Offers solutions to common problems and provides tips for maximizing efficiency.

- **Real-Life Use Cases**: Provides examples of how Monday.com can be used for project management, marketing, and personal productivity.

- **Continuous Learning and Resources**: Directs you to additional resources, tutorials, and community forums to continue your growth.

Each chapter builds on the previous one, allowing you to progress from basic to advanced levels at your own pace.

How to Navigate This Guide

To ensure that you get the most value from this book, here are a few tips on how to navigate it effectively:

1. **Start Where You Are**:

   o If you're completely new to Monday.com, begin with the "Getting Started" chapter and work your way through the basics.

   o If you're already familiar with Monday.com, feel free to skip to the sections that address your current challenges, such as automations, integrations, or dashboards.

2. **Use It as a Reference**: This guide is designed to be user-friendly for both sequential readers and those who prefer to jump directly to specific topics. Use the detailed table of contents and index to find the information you need quickly.

3. **Follow Along with Examples**: Many sections include step-by-step examples and practical use cases. Whenever possible, replicate these examples in your own Monday.com account to reinforce your understanding.

4. **Focus on Your Goals**: Tailor your learning based on your specific objectives. For example:

   o If you want to improve team collaboration, focus on the "Collaborating with Your Team" chapter.

   o If your goal is to automate repetitive tasks, explore the "Automations and Integrations" section.

5. **Leverage Visual Aids**: The book includes screenshots, diagrams, and visual guides to make learning more intuitive. Pay attention to these aids, as they highlight key features and functionalities.

Hands-On Learning Approach

Monday.com is a platform best learned by doing. This guide encourages you to adopt a hands-on approach as you read through it. Here's how you can integrate learning with practice:

- **Create a Sandbox Workspace**: Set up a workspace in Monday.com specifically for testing and practicing the features you learn in this book. Experiment with creating boards, adding items, and setting up automations without worrying about disrupting actual work.

- **Complete Practice Exercises**: Each chapter includes small exercises to help you apply what you've learned. For example, after reading about "Adding and Managing Items," you can create a board with mock tasks to practice organizing and grouping them.

- **Test Advanced Features Gradually**: Once you're comfortable with the basics, move on to advanced features like integrations and dashboards. Practice with real-life scenarios to see how they can improve your productivity.

Learning for Individuals vs Teams

Whether you're using Monday.com as an individual or part of a team, this guide has you covered:

- **For Individuals**: Focus on chapters that address personal productivity, such as "Using Monday.com for Personal Productivity" or "Managing Tasks and Deadlines." Learn how to use Monday.com as a powerful to-do list or project tracker.

- **For Teams**: Dive into chapters like "Collaborating with Your Team" and "Automations and Integrations." These sections provide insights on assigning tasks, communicating effectively, and automating workflows to enhance team efficiency.

Key Features Highlighted in This Guide

This book emphasizes the following Monday.com features that are crucial for better organization:

1. **Boards**: Learn to create and customize boards to organize your projects, tasks, and workflows effectively.

2. **Columns**: Understand how to use different column types (status, timeline, numbers, text, etc.) to track and manage data.

3. **Automations**: Discover how to save time by automating repetitive tasks and processes.

4. **Integrations**: Learn how to connect Monday.com with tools you already use, like Google Drive, Slack, or Zoom.

5. **Dashboards**: Visualize your team's progress and overall project health using dashboards and widgets.

6. **Permissions and Roles**: Set up roles and permissions to ensure data security and effective collaboration.

Using This Guide as a Long-Term Resource

Monday.com is constantly evolving with new features and updates. This guide not only equips you with the skills to use the current version of Monday.com but also teaches you how to adapt to future changes. Here's how:

1. **Stay Updated**: Follow Monday.com's update logs and announcements to keep up with new features.

2. **Refer Back to Specific Sections**: As your needs evolve, revisit relevant chapters to refresh your knowledge.

3. **Combine This Guide with Online Resources**: Use this book in conjunction with Monday.com's online tutorials and community forums for deeper insights.

Final Words on Using This Guide

The goal of this guide is to empower you to become confident and efficient in using Monday.com. Whether you're organizing personal tasks, managing a team project, or scaling workflows for a large organization, the strategies and techniques covered here will set you up for success.

Remember, the key to mastering Monday.com is consistent practice and exploration. Use this book as your roadmap, and don't hesitate to experiment with the platform's capabilities as you learn. Let's get started!

CHAPTER I
Getting Started with Monday.com

1.1 Creating Your Monday.com Account

1.1.1 Free vs Paid Plans

When you start using Monday.com, one of the first decisions you'll need to make is selecting the right plan that fits your needs. Monday.com offers various pricing tiers, ranging from a free plan for small teams or individuals to advanced paid plans designed for larger teams with more complex workflows. In this section, we'll provide an in-depth guide to help you understand the differences between free and paid plans, and how to choose the best option for your goals.

Understanding the Free Plan

The free plan, also known as the "Individual Plan," is designed for freelancers, solopreneurs, or small teams that are just getting started. This plan is ideal for those who want to explore Monday.com's features without committing to a subscription.

Key Features of the Free Plan

- **Up to 2 Users:** The free plan supports a maximum of two users. If you're working alone or with a single collaborator, this is sufficient for basic project management.

- **Unlimited Boards:** You can create as many boards as you need to organize your projects, tasks, or workflows. This flexibility is great for keeping your projects separated and visually organized.

- **200 Items Per Month:** The free plan allows you to add up to 200 items (tasks, rows, or data points) per month. This limit may be enough for simple workflows but can be restrictive for more complex projects.

- **Basic Columns:** You can use essential column types like status, text, date, and numbers to structure your boards. These columns help you track task progress, deadlines, and other key details.

- **File Storage (500MB):** The free plan provides 500MB of file storage, allowing you to attach documents, images, or other files to your tasks. However, this space can fill up quickly if you're working on media-heavy projects.

Limitations of the Free Plan

While the free plan is great for getting started, there are notable limitations:

1. **Automation and Integrations:** Automation and third-party app integrations are not available on the free plan, meaning you'll need to handle repetitive tasks manually.

2. **Advanced Features:** Features like timeline view, calendar view, and dashboards are not included.

3. **Team Collaboration Tools:** The free plan offers limited collaboration tools, which may hinder team communication for larger groups.

When to Choose the Free Plan

- You're exploring Monday.com for the first time.

- You have a small, straightforward project or a personal task to manage.

- You don't need automation or integrations at this stage.

Exploring Paid Plans

Monday.com offers several paid plans, including Basic, Standard, Pro, and Enterprise, each tailored to meet the needs of different users and teams. Let's explore these options in detail:

1. Basic Plan

The Basic plan is the first tier of paid plans and is ideal for small teams that need more functionality than the free plan but don't require advanced features.

- **Unlimited Users:** Unlike the free plan, the Basic plan allows unlimited team members, making it a great option for growing teams.

- **5GB Storage:** You'll get 5GB of storage, which is enough for teams that need to upload larger files or store more data.

- **Priority Support:** Basic plan users receive priority support, ensuring quicker responses to any issues.

- **Limited Views and Features:** This plan still lacks advanced views (e.g., timeline) and automations but provides a solid foundation for collaboration.

2. Standard Plan

The Standard plan is the most popular option for small to medium-sized teams.

- **Timeline and Calendar Views:** Visualize your tasks in a timeline or calendar view, making it easier to track deadlines and dependencies.

- **Automations and Integrations:** Access to 250 automations and integrations per month allows you to streamline workflows by connecting with tools like Slack, Zoom, or Google Drive.

- **Guest Access:** Invite clients or stakeholders as guests to view or collaborate on specific boards.

- **Dashboards:** Create dashboards that pull data from up to five boards for high-level overviews.

3. Pro Plan

The Pro plan is ideal for teams managing complex projects or needing more customization.

- **Unlimited Automations and Integrations:** Remove limitations on how many automations and integrations you can use each month.

- **Advanced Reporting and Insights:** Generate detailed reports and analyze team performance.

- **Time Tracking:** Use time tracking columns to monitor how long tasks take, which is great for resource management.

- **Private Boards:** Create private boards for sensitive projects.

4. Enterprise Plan

The Enterprise plan is designed for large organizations with advanced security, compliance, and customization needs.

- **Enterprise-Grade Security:** Enjoy features like Single Sign-On (SSO), HIPAA compliance, and audit logs.

- **Tailored Onboarding:** Receive personalized onboarding sessions to get your team set up efficiently.

- **Advanced Permissions:** Manage access and permissions on a granular level to protect sensitive data.

- **Custom Features:** Work with Monday.com's team to develop custom features tailored to your business.

Free vs Paid: Side-by-Side Comparison

To help you decide, here's a quick comparison of the key differences between the plans:

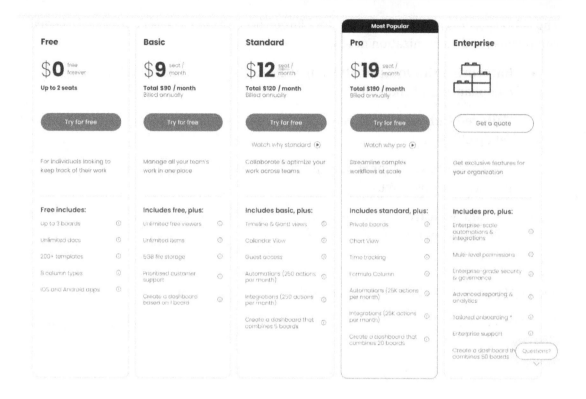

How to Choose the Right Plan

Here are some tips for choosing the best plan:

1. **Assess Your Team Size:** If you're working solo or with one other person, the free plan is sufficient. Larger teams will benefit from paid plans.

2. **Identify Your Workflow Needs:** Do you need automations, advanced views, or integrations? If so, look beyond the free and Basic plans.

3. **Consider Future Growth:** If your team or project scope is likely to grow, it's better to invest in a scalable plan like Standard or Pro.

4. **Try Before You Buy:** Monday.com offers free trials for its paid plans, allowing you to test features before committing.

This section equips you with everything you need to know about Monday.com's pricing plans, empowering you to make an informed decision. Up next, let's dive into **1.1.2 Signing Up and Setting Up Your Profile** to get started with your chosen plan!

		Free	Basic	Standard	Pro	Enterprise
		Get Started	Get Started	Get Started	Get Started	Contact sales
monday work management						
Essentials						
Maximum number of seats	ⓘ	Up to 2 seats	Unlimited	Unlimited	Unlimited	Unlimited
Items	ⓘ	Up to 1000	Unlimited	Unlimited	Unlimited	Unlimited
File storage	ⓘ	500 MB	5 GB	20 GB	100 GB	1000 GB
Activity log	ⓘ	1 week	1 week	6 months	1 year	5 years
Unlimited boards	ⓘ		✓	✓	✓	✓
Unlimited docs	ⓘ		✓	✓	✓	✓
Over 20 column types	ⓘ	✓	✓	✓	✓	✓
200+ templates	ⓘ	✓	✓	✓	✓	✓
iOS and Android apps	ⓘ	✓	✓	✓	✓	✓
Unlimited messages & updates	ⓘ	✓	✓	✓	✓	✓
Integrations	ⓘ			250 actions/month	25,000 actions/month	250,000 actions/month
Automations	ⓘ			250 actions/month	25,000 actions/month	250,000 actions/mo
Unlimited free viewers	ⓘ		✓	✓	✓	✓

Questions?

		Free	Basic	Standard	Pro	Enterprise
		Get Started	Get Started	Get Started	Get Started	Contact sales
Collaboration						
Embedded documents	ⓘ	✓	✓	✓	✓	✓
Updates section	ⓘ	✓	✓	✓	✓	✓
Zoom integration	ⓘ			✓	✓	✓
Guest access	ⓘ			4 guests billed as 1 seat	✓	✓
Productivity						
Shareable forms	ⓘ	✓	✓	✓	plus custom branded forms	plus custom conditional logic forms
Customizable notifications	ⓘ	✓	✓	✓	✓	✓
Custom fields	ⓘ		✓	✓	✓	✓
Premium integrations	ⓘ					✓
Time tracking	ⓘ				✓	✓
Formula column	ⓘ				✓	✓
Dependency column	ⓘ				✓	✓
Workload	ⓘ				✓	✓

Questions?

		Free	Basic	Standard	Pro	Enterprise
		Get Started	Get Started	Get Started	Get Started	Contact sales

Views & reporting

		Free	Basic	Standard	Pro	Enterprise
Activity log	ⓘ	1 week	1 week	6 months	1 year	5 years
Unlimited dashboards	ⓘ	1 board per dashboard	1 board per dashboard	Combine up to 5 boards	Combine up to 20 boards	Combine up to 50 boards
Kanban view	ⓘ	✓	✓	✓	✓	✓
Timeline view	ⓘ			✓	✓	✓
Calendar view	ⓘ			✓	✓	✓
Map view	ⓘ			✓	✓	✓
Chart view	ⓘ				✓	✓

Support

		Free	Basic	Standard	Pro	Enterprise
Self-serve knowledge base	ⓘ	✓	✓	✓	✓	✓
24/7 customer support	ⓘ		✓	✓	✓	✓
Daily live webinars	ⓘ		✓	✓	✓	✓
Dedicated customer success manager ^	ⓘ					✓
99.9% uptime SLA	ⓘ					✓

Security & privacy

Questions? ⌄

		Free	Basic	Standard	Pro	Enterprise
		Get Started	Get Started	Get Started	Get Started	Contact sales

Security & privacy

		Free	Basic	Standard	Pro	Enterprise
SOC 2 Type II Compliance	ⓘ	✓	✓	✓	✓	✓
Two-factor authentication	ⓘ	✓	✓	✓	✓	✓
Private boards and docs	ⓘ				✓	✓
Google authentication	ⓘ				✓	✓
Single Sign On (Okta, One login, Azure AD, Custom SAML)	ⓘ					✓
HIPAA Compliance	ⓘ					✓
Integration Permissions	ⓘ					✓
IP restrictions	ⓘ					✓
Content Directory	ⓘ					✓

	Free	Basic	Standard	Pro	Enterprise
	Get Started	Get Started	Get Started	Get Started	Contact sales
Administration & control					
Board administrators				⊘	⊘
SCIM provisioning					⊘
Audit log					⊘
Session management					⊘
Panic mode					⊘
Private workspaces					⊘
Advanced account permissions					⊘
Enterprise reporting & analytics					
Work performance insights					⊘
Dashboard email notifications					⊘
Pivot analysis & reports					⊘

1.1.2 Signing Up and Setting Up Your Profile

Getting started with Monday.com begins with signing up for an account and customizing your profile. Whether you are new to project management tools or transitioning from another platform, this section will guide you step by step to ensure a seamless setup.

Signing Up for Monday.com

The sign-up process for Monday.com is straightforward and user-friendly. Follow these steps to create your account:

Step 1: Visit the Monday.com Website

- Open your browser and go to www.monday.com.

- Click the **"Get Started"** button located prominently on the homepage.

Step 2: Choose a Sign-Up Method

Monday.com offers several sign-up options:

1. **Using Your Email Address:**

   o Enter your work or personal email address in the designated field.

   o Click **"Continue"** to proceed.

2. **Using Google or Microsoft Accounts:**

   o Click on the **"Sign up with Google"** or **"Sign up with Microsoft"** option.

   o Log in with your credentials, and Monday.com will automatically link your account.

Step 3: Verify Your Email Address

- If you signed up using your email, you will receive a verification email.

- Open the email and click on the verification link to confirm your account.

- If you don't see the email in your inbox, check your spam or junk folder.

Step 4: Set Your Password

- After verifying your email, you'll be prompted to set a secure password.

- Choose a password that is at least 8 characters long, including a mix of uppercase, lowercase, numbers, and special characters for maximum security.

Step 5: Select Your Account Type

- Monday.com will ask you to specify whether you are signing up as an individual, part of a team, or for an organization.

- Select the option that best suits your needs. This will help Monday.com tailor its features and recommendations to your goals.

Exploring the Initial Setup Wizard

After signing up, Monday.com launches an **onboarding wizard** to help you get started quickly.

Step 1: Answer Key Questions

The onboarding wizard will ask a few questions to personalize your experience, such as:

- **What will you use Monday.com for?**(e.g., Project Management, Personal Tasks, Marketing Campaigns, etc.)

monday.com

Hey there, what brings you here today?

◯ Work   ◯ Personal   ◯ School   ◯ Nonprofits

- **What is your role?**(e.g., Manager, Team Member, Freelancer, etc.)

- **What size is your team?**(e.g., Just Me, 2–5 people, 6–20 people, etc.)

Answering these questions helps Monday.com customize your workspace and suggest templates that align with your goals.

Step 2: Choose a Template

You'll be presented with a selection of templates tailored to different use cases, such as:

- **Project Tracker**
- **Marketing Campaign Planner**
- **To-Do List**
- **Content Calendar**

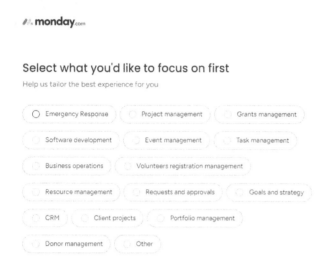

Choose a template to kickstart your workspace, or skip this step to create a board from scratch later.

Setting Up Your Profile

Customizing your profile is an essential step to making Monday.com feel like your own workspace. Here's how to do it:

Step 1: Access Your Profile Settings

- After logging in, click on your avatar (profile picture) in the top-right corner of the dashboard.

- Select **"My Profile"** from the dropdown menu.

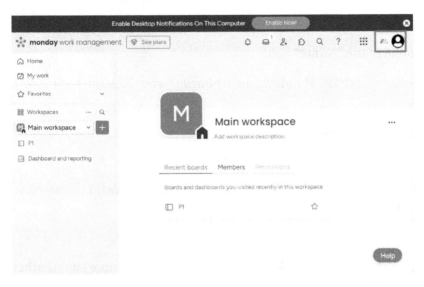

Step 2: Upload a Profile Picture

A profile picture helps your team members identify you quickly. To upload one:

- Click on the profile picture placeholder.

- Select an image from your computer or device.

- Crop and adjust the image as needed.

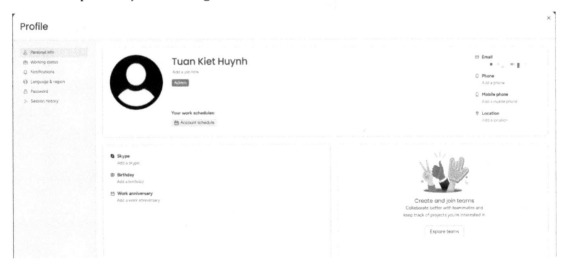

If you prefer not to upload a picture, you can choose an avatar or keep the default initials.

Step 3: Add Your Full Name

- Enter your full name in the **"Name"** field.

- This will be displayed across Monday.com whenever you interact with items, boards, or updates.

Step 4: Update Your Contact Information

- Add your email address and phone number (optional).

- These details are useful for receiving notifications or enabling team members to contact you directly.

Step 5: Set Your Job Title

- Adding your job title (e.g., Marketing Manager, Team Lead, Developer) helps other team members understand your role.

Step 6: Choose a Color Theme

- Monday.com allows you to customize the platform's appearance with light or dark mode.

- Navigate to **Settings** > **Theme** and select your preferred option.

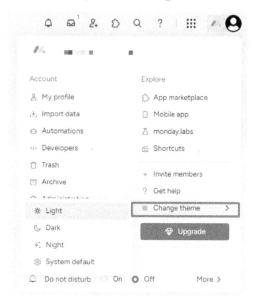

Personalizing Your Notifications and Preferences

Customizing notifications ensures you stay updated without feeling overwhelmed.

Step 1: Adjust Notification Settings

- Go to **"Notifications"** under your profile settings.

- Choose how you'd like to receive updates:

  - **Email Notifications**

  - **Push Notifications** (on mobile devices)

  - **In-App Notifications**

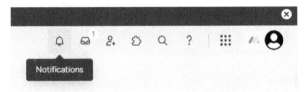

Step 2: Set Your Working status

- Define your working hours to control when you receive notifications.

- Go to **Settings** > **Working status** and set your time zone and availability.

Tips for a Successful Profile Setup

- **Use a Clear Profile Picture:** Helps team members recognize you easily.

- **Keep Contact Details Up-to-Date:** Ensures seamless communication.

- **Enable Only Relevant Notifications:** Avoid notification fatigue by selecting critical updates only.

- **Regularly Review Profile Settings:** As your role or team evolves, update your profile to reflect these changes.

By following these steps, you'll have your Monday.com account set up and ready for efficient collaboration. Once your profile is complete, you can move on to exploring the platform's interface and creating your first workspace.

1.2 Navigating the Monday.com Interface

1.2.1 Main Dashboard Overview

The main dashboard in Monday.com serves as the central hub for navigating your workflows, projects, and tasks. It is designed to provide you with an organized view of all your workspaces, boards, and tasks, offering quick access to the tools you need for better project management. This section will walk you through the main dashboard's layout, its essential components, and how to use it effectively to boost productivity.

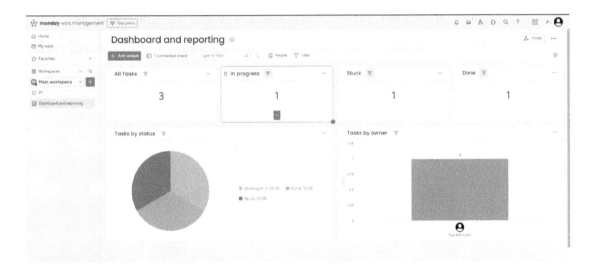

What Is the Main Dashboard?

The dashboard is the first thing you see when logging into Monday.com. It acts as a bird's-eye view of your workspace, enabling you to monitor project progress, access boards, and gain insights into your team's activities. Understanding how to navigate and use the dashboard will help you stay organized and make the most out of Monday.com.

Key Features of the Main Dashboard

1. The Left Sidebar

The left sidebar is the primary navigation tool within the main dashboard. It allows you to move seamlessly between boards, workspaces, and tools. Key elements include:

- **Workspace Menu:** This dropdown shows all the workspaces you are part of. Clicking on a workspace will display its associated boards and activities.

- **Search Bar:** Quickly locate specific items, boards, or workspaces using the search function. You can search by keyword, tags, or team member names.

- **Favorites:** This section lets you bookmark boards or dashboards you frequently use, providing instant access.

- **Inbox:** View all updates and messages across your workspaces in one place. This is especially useful for keeping track of ongoing conversations and mentions.

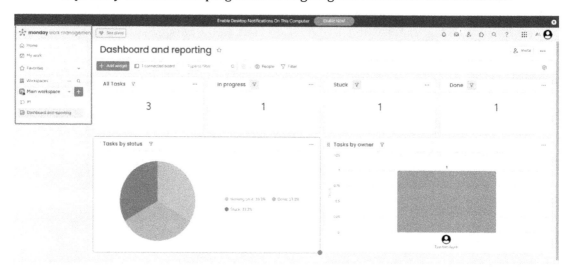

2. The Main Workspace Area

The center of the dashboard is where the magic happens. It displays all the boards, tasks, and widgets you've added. Here are some common components:

- **Boards List:** All boards within the selected workspace appear here. You can click on a board to open and start managing tasks.

- **Quick Add Button:** This button allows you to quickly add new boards, dashboards, or automations without navigating to separate menus.

- **Widgets:** If you've set up a dashboard, widgets will appear here. Widgets can display progress bars, charts, calendars, and task overviews.

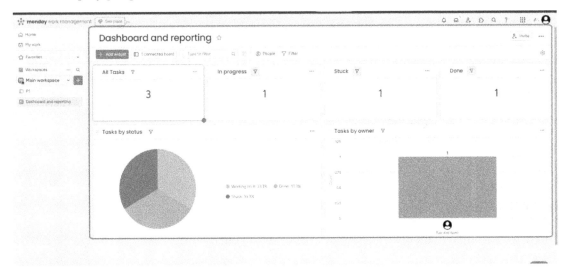

3. The Top Navigation Bar

At the very top of the dashboard, you'll find a navigation bar with key tools and settings:

- **Profile Icon:** Access your account settings, notification preferences, and subscription details here.

- **Notifications Bell:** View recent updates, comments, and system notifications.

- **Quick Search:** Use the global search to locate anything across all boards and workspaces.

- **Help and Support:** Access Monday.com's help center, tutorials, and customer support.

4. Customizing the Main Dashboard

Customizing the dashboard allows you to tailor it to your workflow and preferences. Here's how:

- **Adding Widgets:** To add widgets to your dashboard, click on the "Add Widget" button. Choose from options like timelines, workload views, and custom charts.

- **Reorganizing Boards:** Drag and drop boards in the sidebar to rearrange them for easier access.

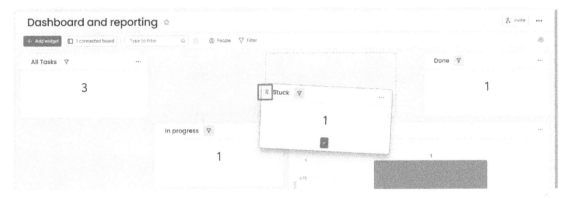

- **Personalizing Themes:** Go to your profile settings to change the dashboard's theme and color scheme.

Navigating Boards from the Dashboard

Opening Boards

From the dashboard, click on any board in the sidebar or main workspace area to open it. Boards are the foundation of Monday.com, containing all tasks, columns, and updates related to specific projects or workflows.

Switching Between Boards

You can switch between boards quickly using the left sidebar or by searching for the board name in the search bar. This makes it easy to jump between multiple projects without losing track.

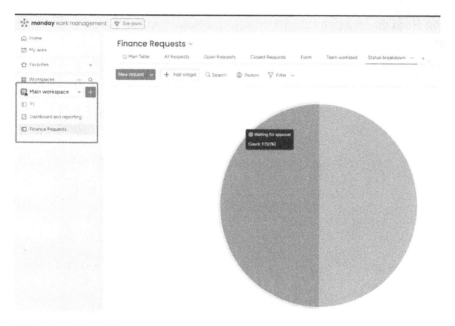

Filtering Boards

The dashboard allows you to apply filters to quickly find boards or tasks that meet specific criteria. For example, you can filter boards by owner, due date, or status to narrow your focus.

Using the Inbox and Notifications Effectively

Inbox

The inbox consolidates all communication across your boards. This includes updates, comments, and mentions. You can filter messages by project, sender, or date, ensuring you never miss important updates.

Notifications

The notifications bell at the top of the dashboard provides real-time alerts for activity in your workspaces. You'll receive notifications for:

- New comments or mentions.

- Updates to tasks you're assigned to.

- Status changes on tracked items.

To avoid notification overload, customize your preferences by clicking on your profile icon and adjusting the settings.

Tips for Maximizing Dashboard Efficiency

1. **Organize Your Sidebar:** Arrange your most-used workspaces and boards at the top of the sidebar for quick access.

2. **Use Favorites:** Favorite the boards or dashboards you frequently visit. They will appear in the "Favorites" section of the sidebar, saving you time.

3. **Leverage Widgets:** Use widgets to visualize data directly on your dashboard. For instance, use a workload widget to see which team members are overbooked or a chart widget to track project progress.

4. **Regularly Update Boards:** Keep boards up-to-date to ensure your dashboard reflects the most accurate information. Update task statuses, due dates, and assignees regularly.

5. **Set Clear Notifications:** Decide which updates are essential for your work and disable unnecessary notifications to avoid distractions.

Common Dashboard Mistakes to Avoid

1. **Overcrowding the Sidebar:** Adding too many boards or workspaces can make the sidebar cluttered and difficult to navigate. Archive or delete old boards to keep it clean.

2. **Ignoring Notifications:** Failing to check or manage notifications can result in missed deadlines or overlooked updates.

3. **Underutilizing Widgets:** Widgets are powerful tools that provide valuable insights at a glance. Make sure to use them effectively by selecting the ones that align with your workflow.

Conclusion

The main dashboard in Monday.com is a powerful tool that keeps your work organized and accessible. By mastering its layout and features, you can improve your workflow, enhance team collaboration, and stay on top of all your projects. Take the time to explore its customization options, use widgets for data visualization, and optimize your notifications for a smoother experience.

1.2.2 Key Features of the Navigation Bar

The navigation bar in Monday.com serves as the central hub for accessing all the key features and tools you need to manage your projects and workflows. Whether you're managing tasks, collaborating with your team, or analyzing data, the navigation bar is your gateway to an efficient workflow. This section will break down the navigation bar into its core components and provide step-by-step instructions for using each feature effectively.

Overview of the Navigation Bar

The navigation bar is located on the left side of the Monday.com interface. It consists of several key sections that help you quickly access your workspaces, boards, dashboards, notifications, and more. The navigation bar is designed to be intuitive, making it easy for both new and experienced users to navigate Monday.com efficiently.

Here's a breakdown of the primary features of the navigation bar:

1. **Search Everything**

2. **Inbox**

3. **Notifications**

4. **My Work**

5. **Workspaces**

6. **Boards**

7. **Dashboards**

8. **Apps Marketplace**

9. **Help and Support**

10. **Account Settings and Profile Management**

Now, let's dive into each of these features in detail.

---

1. Search Everything

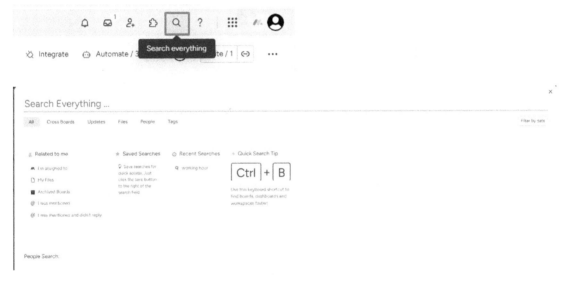

The **Search Everything** tool is your shortcut to finding anything within your Monday.com account. This feature allows you to locate items, updates, boards, or even specific conversations across all your workspaces.

How to Use Search Everything:

1. Click on the **magnifying glass icon** located at the top of the navigation bar.

2. Type in a keyword related to the item or board you're looking for.

3. Use the filters (e.g., "Boards," "Updates," "People") to narrow down your search results.

4. Click on the relevant result to jump directly to that item or board.

Pro Tips:

- Use exact phrases in quotation marks (e.g., "Marketing Campaign") for more accurate results.

- Regularly tag items and updates with clear, descriptive names to make them easier to search.

2. Inbox

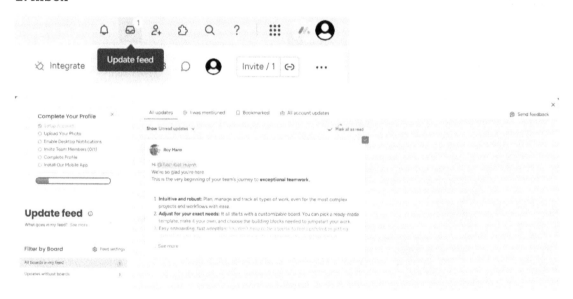

The **Inbox** feature is where all your team communications and updates are consolidated. It ensures that you never miss an important comment or update related to your tasks.

How to Use the Inbox:

1. Click on the **envelope icon** in the navigation bar.

2. View all recent updates in chronological order.

3. Use filters such as "Unread Updates" or "Mentions" to prioritize your review.

4. Click on an update to jump directly to the item or board it pertains to.

Best Practices for the Inbox:

- Check your inbox daily to stay updated on team communications.

- Use the **Mark as Read** option to keep your inbox organized.

- Respond to updates directly from the inbox to save time.

3. Notifications

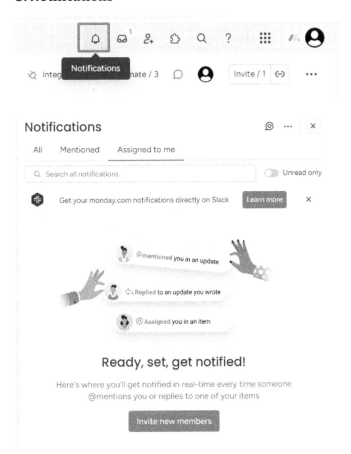

The **Notifications** section alerts you to key activities within your boards, such as when someone assigns you a task, changes the status of an item, or mentions you in a comment.

How to Use Notifications:

1. Click on the **bell icon** in the navigation bar.

2. Review all recent notifications.

3. Use filters like "Unread" or "Mentions" to focus on the most important updates.

4. Click on a notification to view the related item, task, or update.

Pro Tips for Managing Notifications:

- Adjust your notification settings to avoid unnecessary alerts.

- Enable push notifications on your mobile app to stay informed when you're on the go.

- Use the "Mark All as Read" option to declutter your notification feed after reviewing.

4. My Work

The **My Work** section is a personal dashboard that consolidates all tasks and items assigned to you across different boards and workspaces.

How to Use My Work:

1. Click on the **person icon** in the navigation bar.

2. View all tasks assigned to you, organized by due date.

3. Use filters to display tasks by status (e.g., "In Progress," "Overdue").

4. Click on a task to jump directly to its associated board or item.

Best Practices for My Work:

- Regularly review your tasks to prioritize deadlines effectively.

- Update task statuses directly from the My Work section.

- Use the "Due Soon" filter to focus on urgent tasks.

5. Workspaces

Workspaces are the foundation of Monday.com's organizational structure. The navigation bar provides easy access to all your workspaces.

How to Use Workspaces:

1. Scroll through the list of workspaces in the navigation bar.

2. Click on a workspace to view all the boards and projects within it.

3. Use the workspace menu to create new boards, invite members, or adjust workspace settings.

Pro Tips for Managing Workspaces:

- Organize your workspaces by department or project to keep things streamlined.

- Use clear and descriptive workspace names for easy identification.

- Regularly review and archive unused workspaces to maintain a clean interface.

6. Boards

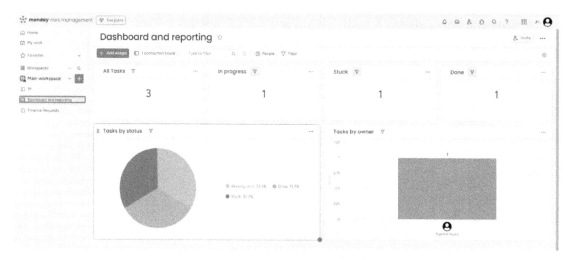

The **Boards** section lists all the boards within a workspace, allowing you to navigate directly to a specific board.

How to Use Boards in the Navigation Bar:

1. Click on a workspace to expand its list of boards.

2. Select a board to open it and view its tasks and items.

3. Use the search bar at the top of the navigation bar to quickly find a specific board.

7. Dashboards

Dashboards offer visual representations of your data, helping you analyze and monitor progress across your projects.

How to Access Dashboards:

1. Click on the **Dashboards** icon in the navigation bar.

2. Select an existing dashboard or create a new one.

3. Customize your dashboard with widgets to display charts, progress bars, and task summaries.

8. Apps Marketplace

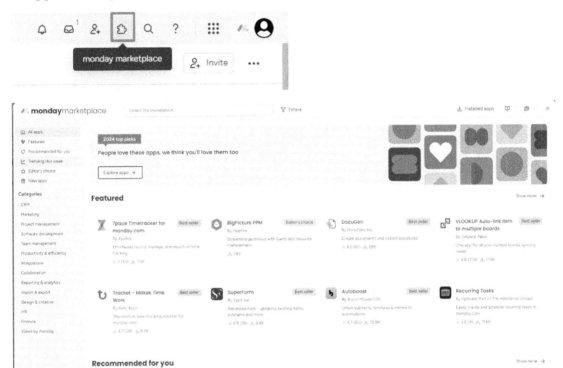

The Apps Marketplace is where you can find integrations and tools to enhance Monday.com's functionality.

How to Access the Marketplace:

1. Click on the **Apps Marketplace** icon.

2. Browse through available apps such as Zoom, Slack, or Google Drive.

3. Install apps and configure their settings to suit your workflow.

9. Help and Support

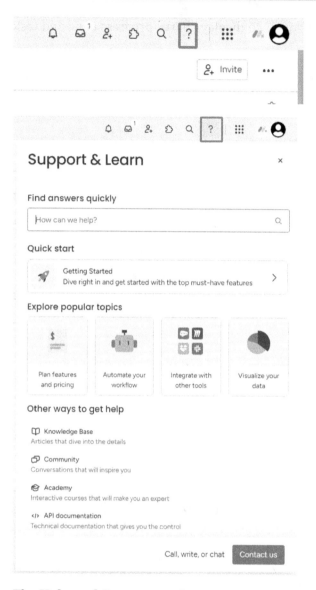

The **Help and Support** section connects you to resources such as tutorials, FAQs, and live chat.

How to Use Help and Support:

1. Click on the **question mark icon** in the navigation bar.

2. Access the Help Center for tutorials and guides.

3.   Contact customer support for troubleshooting or questions.

10. Account Settings and Profile Management

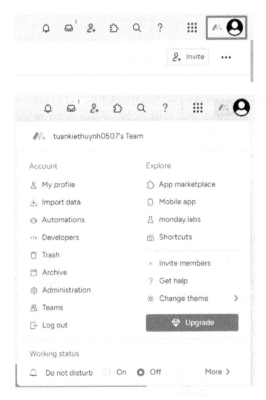

This section allows you to customize your profile and manage account settings.

How to Access Account Settings:

1.   Click on your profile picture at the bottom of the navigation bar.

2.   Update your profile details, such as your name and photo.

3.   Adjust settings like time zones, notifications, and billing preferences.

By understanding and leveraging the features of the navigation bar, you can navigate Monday.com with ease, streamline your workflow, and stay on top of your projects.

Whether you're searching for items, managing tasks, or collaborating with your team, the navigation bar is your key to better organization.

1.2.3 Understanding Boards and Workspaces

Monday.com is built around two fundamental concepts: **Boards** and **Workspaces**. These are the backbone of the platform, enabling users to organize, collaborate, and manage tasks effectively. Understanding how Boards and Workspaces function and interact is crucial for leveraging the full power of Monday.com. In this section, we will delve deep into what Boards and Workspaces are, their unique features, and how to use them to streamline your workflow.

What Are Workspaces?

A **Workspace** in Monday.com acts as a container that holds related Boards, files, and team activities. Think of it as a digital office where all resources and team collaboration for a specific department, project, or purpose are housed. For example, you could have separate Workspaces for **Marketing**, **Product Development**, **HR**, and **Sales**.

Here are the key features of Workspaces:

1. **Organization at Scale**: Workspaces allow you to group Boards, files, and tools in a way that makes them easy to navigate and manage, especially in large teams or organizations with multiple projects running simultaneously.

2. **Customization**: Each Workspace can be customized to fit the unique needs of your team. For example, you might set specific themes, member permissions, or notification preferences tailored to that Workspace.

3. **Collaboration and Focus**: Workspaces are ideal for keeping team members focused. Only members invited to a Workspace can access its Boards and content, which prevents distractions from irrelevant tasks or projects.

4. **Privacy and Permissions**: Workspaces can be set as **private** (accessible only to invited members) or **open** (accessible to all users in your organization). This ensures that sensitive data is protected while still promoting transparency where necessary.

How to Create and Use Workspaces Effectively

To create a new Workspace:

1. Navigate to the left-hand sidebar on your dashboard.

2. Click the **"+ Add Workspace"** button.

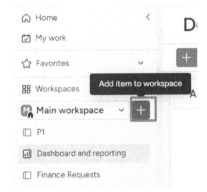

3. Name your Workspace and set its visibility (private or open).

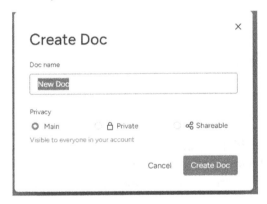

4. Invite relevant team members by entering their email addresses or selecting them from your team list.

5. Customize the Workspace settings, including color themes and icons, to make it visually distinct.

Once your Workspace is set up, it's time to populate it with Boards.

What Are Boards?

A **Board** is where the magic happens in Monday.com. It is a table-like structure that organizes and displays tasks, data, and workflows. Each Board is fully customizable, making it suitable for various purposes, from project management to event planning.

Boards are made up of **columns**, **rows** (referred to as "items"), and **groups**. Here's a breakdown of these elements:

*   **Groups:**
    Groups are color-coded sections within a Board that help categorize items. For example, in a project management Board, you might use groups like "To Do," "In Progress," and "Completed."

- **Columns:**
  Columns define the type of information you want to track for each item. For example, you can have columns for task owners, due dates, priorities, and more.

- **Items:**
  Items are the individual rows within a group that represent tasks, projects, or data points. For example, each item could represent a specific task, such as "Design Homepage Mockup."

Types of Boards in Monday.com

There are three main types of Boards in Monday.com:

1. **Main Boards**

   o These Boards are visible to everyone in the Workspace by default.

   o They are ideal for general projects or workflows that multiple team members need to access.

2. **Private Boards**

   o Private Boards are only accessible to the creator and the members they specifically invite.

   o These Boards are perfect for sensitive projects or when working on initial drafts before sharing with a wider team.

3. **Shareable Boards**

   o Shareable Boards can be shared with people outside your organization, such as clients or freelancers.

   o They are great for collaborative projects involving external stakeholders.

How to Create a New Board

Creating a new Board is simple and highly customizable. Here's how:

1. Navigate to the **Workspace** where you want the Board to reside.

2. Click the **"+ Add"** button at the top of the Workspace view.

3. Select **"Board"** from the dropdown menu.

4. Name your Board and choose the type (Main, Private, or Shareable).

5. Choose whether to start with a blank Board, use a template, or import data (e.g., from Excel).

The Relationship Between Boards and Workspaces

While Workspaces are the broader containers, Boards serve as the specific projects or workflows within them. Here's an analogy:

- A **Workspace** is like a filing cabinet for a specific department or project category.

- A **Board** is like a folder within that filing cabinet, containing the individual tasks, data, and information related to a specific project or workflow.

This structure allows you to separate and organize your projects while still maintaining an overarching view of team activities.

Customizing Boards for Better Organization

Customization is where Monday.com truly shines. Boards can be tailored to suit any workflow or project. Here's how to maximize their potential:

1. **Column Types**: Monday.com offers a variety of column types, such as:

   o **Text Columns:** Add notes or descriptions.

   o **Status Columns:** Track task progress (e.g., "Not Started," "In Progress," "Done").

   o **Date Columns:** Set deadlines or milestones.

   o **People Columns:** Assign tasks to team members.

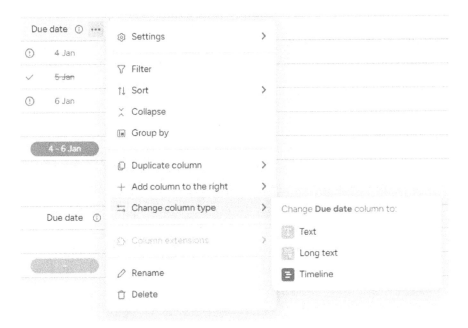

2. **Grouping Items**: Use Groups to categorize your tasks. For example, in a product development Board, you could create Groups like "Phase 1: Planning," "Phase 2: Development," and "Phase 3: Testing."

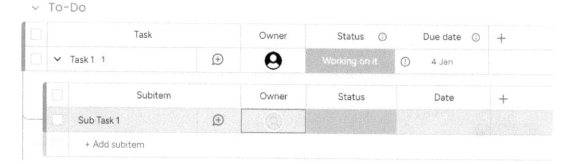

3. **Color-Coding**: Assign colors to Groups or Status columns to make Boards visually clear and easy to scan.

4. **Templates**: Monday.com offers a wide range of templates, such as marketing calendars, CRM pipelines, and event planning Boards. Templates save time and provide pre-designed structures to start with.

Using Boards for Collaboration

Boards in Monday.com are more than just static tables—they are dynamic collaboration tools. Here are some key features:

1. **Task Assignments**: Assign team members to specific tasks or items using the People column. This ensures accountability and transparency.

2. **Updates Section**: Each item has an Updates section where team members can leave comments, share progress, or attach files. This serves as a built-in communication tool, reducing the need for external emails.

3. **File Sharing**: Attach files directly to items or comments for seamless collaboration. For example, designers can upload mockups, or marketers can attach campaign drafts.

4. **Real-Time Editing**: Multiple users can edit a Board simultaneously, ensuring everyone is working with the latest data.

Best Practices for Organizing Boards and Workspaces

1. **Define a Clear Naming Convention**: Name Workspaces and Boards descriptively. For example:

   o   Workspace: "Marketing Team"

   o   Board: "Q1 Campaign Planning"

2. **Limit Board Complexity**: Avoid clutter by only including necessary columns and Groups. Too much information can overwhelm team members.

3. **Archive Old Boards**: Once a project is complete, archive its Board to keep your Workspace clean and focused on active tasks.

4. **Train Your Team**: Ensure all team members understand how to use Boards and Workspaces effectively. Regular training sessions can boost productivity.

Conclusion

Understanding Boards and Workspaces is essential to mastering Monday.com. By organizing your projects into intuitive Workspaces and leveraging the flexibility of Boards, you can streamline workflows, enhance collaboration, and achieve better results. Whether you're managing a small team or coordinating large-scale projects, the combination of Boards and Workspaces provides the foundation for success.

The next section will explore **"1.3 Setting Up Your First Workspace"**, where you'll learn how to create and customize a Workspace to suit your specific needs.

1.3 Setting Up Your First Workspace

1.3.1 Creating a New Workspace

Monday.com is designed to provide flexibility and simplicity for organizing your workflows. Setting up a new workspace is the foundational step toward leveraging Monday.com's full potential. In this section, we'll walk you through the process of creating a new workspace, explaining the features and options available at each step. By the end of this guide, you'll have a functional workspace tailored to your needs.

What is a Workspace in Monday.com?

A workspace in Monday.com acts as a digital container that houses all your boards, dashboards, and workflows. It allows you to group related projects and tasks, making it easier for teams or individuals to stay organized. Think of it as the "home" for your specific projects, departments, or even clients.

For example:

- **Marketing Workspace:** Includes boards for campaigns, social media schedules, and analytics.

- **Human Resources Workspace:** Tracks recruitment, onboarding, and employee records.

- **Personal Productivity Workspace:** Manages daily tasks, personal goals, and reminders.

Step-by-Step Guide to Creating a New Workspace

Step 1: Access the Workspace Menu

1. Log in to your Monday.com account.

2. On the left-hand side of the interface, locate the **Workspace Selector** at the top of the navigation panel.

3. Click the dropdown menu and select the option **+ Add Workspace**.

Add new workspace ×

N

Workspace name

New Workspace

Privacy

○ Open   Closed

Every team member in the account can join

Cancel   Add workspace

Step 2: Choose a Workspace Name

1. In the pop-up window, you'll be prompted to name your new workspace.

2. Choose a name that reflects the purpose or scope of this workspace. For example:

    o "Product Development Team"

    o "Client Management"

    o "Event Planning"

3. Keep the name concise but descriptive enough for team members to understand its purpose at a glance.

Step 3: Select the Workspace Type

Monday.com offers three types of workspaces:

1. **Main Workspace:** Visible to all team members. Ideal for company-wide projects or information that should be accessible to everyone.

2. **Private Workspace:** Accessible only to selected members. Use this for sensitive or confidential projects.

3. **Shareable Workspace:** Designed for collaboration with external users, such as clients or freelancers.

Select the type that aligns with your project's requirements and click **Next** to proceed.

Customizing Your Workspace During Setup

Step 4: Adding a Workspace Icon (Optional)

To make your workspace easily recognizable, you can upload an icon or choose an emoji to represent it. This is especially helpful when managing multiple workspaces. For example:

- 🎨 for a creative team

- 📈 for sales and analytics

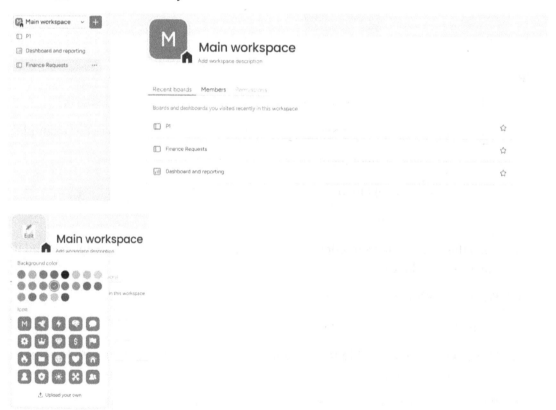

To add an icon:

1. Click the **Icon** field during setup.

2. Upload a custom image or select an emoji from the built-in library.

Step 5: Setting a Workspace Description

While optional, adding a description to your workspace is useful for clarifying its purpose, especially when onboarding new members.

- Example: *"This workspace is for managing product launches, including design, testing, and marketing campaigns."*

Step 6: Choosing a Workspace Template

Monday.com provides pre-made templates to help you get started faster. These templates are tailored to specific industries or functions, such as:

- **Project Management**

- **Content Calendar**

- **CRM (Customer Relationship Management)**

To use a template:

1. Click **Choose a Template** during setup.

2. Browse the library and select one that matches your needs.

3. Customize the template later to fit your workflow.

If you prefer to start from scratch, simply select **Blank Workspace** and build your structure manually.

Setting Permissions and Adding Team Members

Step 7: Configuring Permissions

Before finalizing your workspace setup, it's important to define who can access it and what they can do.

1. **Admins:** Have full control over the workspace, including the ability to invite new members, delete boards, and adjust settings.

2. **Members:** Can view and interact with boards but have limited access to administrative controls.

3. **Viewers:** Can only view boards and items without making changes.

To configure permissions:

1. Click the **Permissions** tab during setup.

2. Assign roles to team members based on their responsibilities.

Step 8: Inviting Team Members

Collaboration is at the heart of Monday.com. Once your workspace is ready, invite team members to join.

1. Click **Invite Members** at the top of your workspace.

2. Enter their email addresses and select their roles (Admin, Member, or Viewer).

3. Include a personalized message to explain the purpose of the workspace and their role within it.

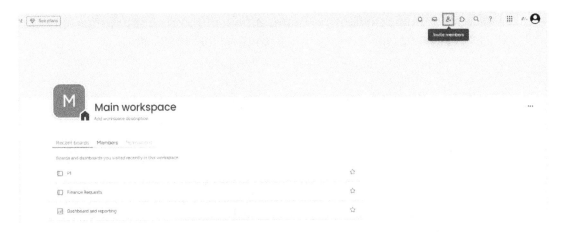

Example message:

"Hi Team! I've created a new workspace for our upcoming product launch. Please join and explore the boards to familiarize yourself with the tasks and timeline."

Tips for Organizing Your New Workspace

Tip 1: Group Boards by Function or Project

To keep your workspace organized, create separate boards for distinct functions or projects. For example:

- In a Marketing Workspace, you might have boards for **Campaigns**, **Content Creation**, and **Analytics**.

- In a HR Workspace, create boards for **Recruitment**, **Employee Onboarding**, and **Payroll Management**.

Tip 2: Use Color-Coded Columns

Add color-coded columns to make important details stand out. For example:

- Green for completed tasks

- Yellow for tasks in progress

- Red for tasks at risk

Tip 3: Leverage Workspace Templates

If you plan to create multiple similar workspaces, save time by creating a custom template. Once a workspace is set up, you can save it as a template for future use.

Common Challenges When Creating a Workspace and How to Overcome Them

1. **Challenge:** Overcomplicating the workspace structure.
   Solution: Start simple. Begin with basic boards and add complexity as your team becomes familiar with the platform.

2. **Challenge:** Team members not engaging with the workspace.
   Solution: Host a short onboarding session to demonstrate how the workspace supports their daily tasks.

3. **Challenge:** Difficulty deciding between a main, private, or shareable workspace.
   Solution: Consider who needs access. Use private workspaces for confidential projects and shareable ones for external collaboration.

Conclusion

Creating your first workspace in Monday.com is an exciting step toward better organization and productivity. By following the detailed instructions above, you can establish a workspace that not only meets your current needs but is also scalable for future growth.

In the next section, we'll dive deeper into inviting team members and customizing workspace settings to ensure seamless collaboration and workflow optimization.

1.3.2 Inviting Team Members

Inviting team members to your workspace is a crucial step in making the most out of Monday.com. This process ensures collaboration, streamlines communication, and keeps everyone on the same page for all your projects. Here's a step-by-step guide on how to invite team members effectively, customize their permissions, and foster collaboration.

Why Inviting Team Members Matters

Before diving into the details of inviting team members, it's essential to understand why this step is vital:

- **Centralized Communication**: Monday.com acts as a hub where all conversations, updates, and files are stored in one place, eliminating the need for scattered emails and messages.

- **Shared Responsibility**: By involving your team, you can distribute tasks, set clear responsibilities, and track progress seamlessly.

- **Transparency**: Team members gain visibility into ongoing projects, deadlines, and individual contributions.

- **Improved Collaboration**: By working together in a shared space, your team can collaborate in real-time, reducing bottlenecks and miscommunication.

Step 1: Identifying the Right Team Members

Before inviting users to your workspace, identify who needs access. Think about:

- **Key Stakeholders**: Managers or team leaders who need to oversee the project's progress.

- **Contributors**: Individuals directly responsible for completing specific tasks.

- **Collaborators**: External team members, freelancers, or clients who might need limited access to specific boards.

It's a good idea to keep your initial team small and grow it as your project evolves. Overloading your workspace with unnecessary users can create clutter and confusion.

Step 2: Inviting Team Members to Your Workspace

2.1 Sending Invitations

To invite team members:

1. **Go to Your Workspace Settings**

   o On the Monday.com dashboard, click on your workspace name in the left-hand navigation bar.

- o Select **"Invite Members"** from the dropdown menu.

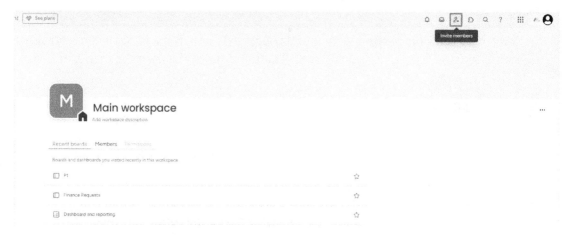

2. **Enter Email Addresses**

- o A pop-up window will appear. Here, you can input the email addresses of the people you want to invite.

- o If you're inviting multiple people, separate their email addresses with commas.

3. **Add a Personal Message (Optional)**

- o Include a short note explaining why they're being invited and what they should expect from Monday.com. For example:

"Hi Team,
I've invited you to our Monday.com workspace to help us collaborate better. This platform will be our central hub for tracking tasks and projects. Let me know if you have questions!"

4. **Send the Invitation**

    o   Click the **"Send Invite"** button. The recipients will receive an email with a link to join your workspace.

2.2 Accepting Invitations

Once you've sent the invitation, team members need to:

1.   Open the email they received from Monday.com.

2.   Click the **"Accept Invitation"** button.

3.   Create their account or log in if they already have one.

4.   Once logged in, they'll automatically be added to your workspace.

Step 3: Setting Permissions and Roles

3.1 Understanding Permissions

Monday.com offers several roles and permission levels to ensure that users have the right access based on their responsibilities:

*   **Admin**: Full access to all boards, settings, and workspace configurations. Ideal for team leaders or project managers.

*   **Member**: Can access and edit boards they are invited to. Suitable for team members actively working on tasks.

*   **Viewer**: Read-only access. Perfect for stakeholders or clients who need updates but don't actively contribute.

3.2 Assigning Roles

To assign roles during the invitation process:

1.   After entering email addresses in the invitation window, look for the **"Role"** dropdown menu.

2.   Select the appropriate role for each invitee.

    o   Example: Assign "Admin" to the project manager and "Viewer" to the client.

3. Confirm the roles before sending the invitation.

Step 4: Adding Guests and External Users

In some cases, you may want to collaborate with external parties, such as freelancers or clients, without giving them access to your entire workspace. This is where **Guests** come in.

4.1 What are Guests?

Guests are external users who have access only to specific boards. They do not see the entire workspace, ensuring security and privacy for your team.

4.2 How to Invite Guests

1. Open the board you want to share with the guest.

2. Click the **"Invite"** button at the top right corner of the board.

3. Enter the guest's email address.

4. Choose their permissions (e.g., read-only or editing access).

5. Send the invitation.

Step 5: Troubleshooting Common Issues

Occasionally, you may face challenges when inviting team members. Here are some common problems and solutions:

5.1 Invitee Didn't Receive the Email

- Check if the email address is correct.

- Ask the recipient to check their spam/junk folder.

- Resend the invitation by going to **Workspace Settings > Pending Invitations** and clicking **"Resend"**.

5.2 User Already Has a Monday.com Account

If the invitee is already using Monday.com with a different workspace, they'll still receive the invitation but will need to switch between workspaces. Make sure they know how to do this:

- Click the workspace icon in the top left corner.

- Select the desired workspace from the dropdown menu.

5.3 Permission Confusion

Ensure you've set the correct roles. If a user can't access a board, double-check their permissions in the board's settings.

Step 6: Onboarding Your Team Members

After successfully inviting your team, the next step is ensuring they understand how to use Monday.com effectively. Consider these onboarding practices:

6.1 Hosting a Workspace Tour

- Walk new members through your workspace, highlighting key boards, workflows, and expectations.

- Demonstrate how to update tasks, leave comments, and use @mentions.

6.2 Sharing Tutorials and Resources

- Share links to Monday.com's help center and video tutorials.

- Create a quick-start guide tailored to your team's workflows.

6.3 Assigning Test Tasks

- Create a sample board with dummy tasks for team members to practice editing, updating statuses, and adding comments.

Conclusion

Inviting team members is more than just sending an email—it's about building a collaborative environment where everyone feels empowered to contribute. By carefully selecting the right people, setting permissions, and providing proper onboarding, you can set the foundation for a successful and organized workspace on Monday.com.

1.3.3 Customizing Workspace Settings

Customizing your workspace settings in Monday.com is a crucial step toward creating a tailored environment that meets your team's unique needs. Whether you're managing a personal project, collaborating with a small team, or overseeing a complex organizational workflow, the customization options provided by Monday.com ensure that your workspace aligns with your objectives. This section explores how to optimize your workspace by customizing settings, layouts, permissions, and notifications.

Understanding Workspace Settings

Before diving into the customization process, it's important to understand what a workspace is in Monday.com. A workspace is essentially a container that organizes your boards, dashboards, and files into a unified structure. By customizing your workspace settings, you can create a productive, visually appealing, and functional environment for your team.

Key features you can customize include:

- **Workspace Name and Description**
- **Workspace Permissions and Privacy**
- **Appearance and Layout**
- **Notification Preferences**
- **Default Automations and Templates**

Step 1: Naming and Describing Your Workspace

The first step in customization is ensuring your workspace has a clear and descriptive name. This is especially important when managing multiple workspaces, as it helps team members quickly identify which workspace to use.

1. Updating the Workspace Name

1. Navigate to the **Workspace Settings** by clicking the three dots (...) next to the workspace name on the left-hand menu.

2. Select **Workspace Settings** from the dropdown menu.

3. In the **Workspace Name** field, enter a name that reflects the purpose or project associated with the workspace.

   o Example: For a marketing team, you might name it "Marketing Campaigns 2025."

4. Save your changes.

2. Adding a Workspace Description

A description provides context about the workspace's purpose, making it easier for team members to understand its function at a glance.

1. In the **Settings** panel, locate the **Workspace Description** field.

2. Write a brief, yet informative description.

   o Example: "This workspace is for planning, executing, and tracking all marketing campaigns for 2025. It includes campaign boards, timelines, and analytics dashboards."

3. Save the description, and it will be visible to all members.

Step 2: Managing Workspace Permissions and Privacy

Permissions are vital for controlling access to sensitive information and ensuring only authorized individuals can make changes. Monday.com offers flexible options to customize privacy and permissions.

1. Setting Workspace Privacy

There are three privacy settings in Monday.com:

- **Open**: Anyone in the organization can access the workspace.
- **Closed**: Only invited members can view and access the workspace.
- **Private**: Restricted to specific individuals or teams with explicit invitations.

To adjust privacy settings:

1. Go to **Workspace Settings > Privacy Options**.
2. Select the desired privacy level.
   - Example: For HR-related workspaces, use the "Private" setting to protect sensitive employee data.

2. Assigning Roles and Permissions

Roles in Monday.com determine what actions members can take within a workspace. These roles include:

- **Admin**: Full control over the workspace, including adding/removing members and adjusting settings.
- **Member**: Can edit and interact with boards but cannot change workspace-level settings.
- **Viewer**: Can only view boards and data without making any changes.

To assign roles:

1. Open the **Members** tab in **Workspace Settings**.
2. Click on a member's name and select their role from the dropdown menu.
3. Save changes.

Administration

Learn more

- General
- Customization
- Users
- Security
- Connections
- Billing
- Usage Stats
- Tidy Up
- Content Directory
- Apps
- Permissions
- Cross Account Copier

Permissions

💎 **Advanced permissions are part of the Enterprise plan**
Contact us to see how advanced permissions can keep your account secure and your work running smoothly.

Contact us   Request a trial

Default account roles

Admin

Member

Viewer

Guest

Custom account roles

Customized roles based on the default roles Learn more

+ New role

Admin permissions

Discover more about each permission. Learn more

Account ⌃

- ☑ Invite users from non-authorized domains
- ☑ Invite guests
- ☑ Upload files in boards and docs ⌄
- ☑ Delete files
- ☑ Create workspaces ⌄
- ☑ @Mention/Subscribe everyone in account
- ☑ Generate API tokens
- ☑ Create automations/integrations
- ☑ Create integrations ⌄

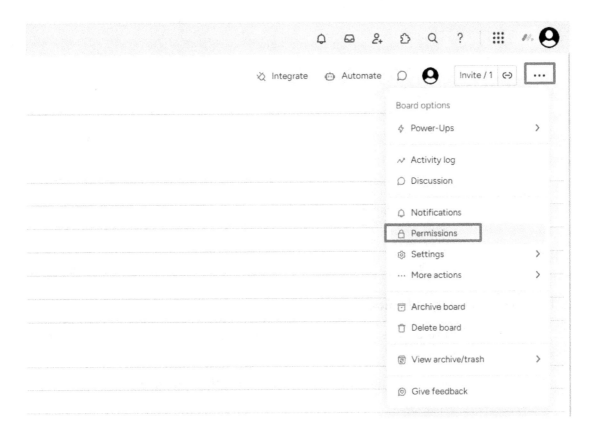

Step 3: Customizing the Workspace Appearance and Layout

A visually appealing workspace boosts productivity and encourages team engagement. Monday.com allows you to adjust colors, themes, and layouts to suit your preferences.

1. Changing the Workspace Theme

Themes allow you to match the workspace's appearance with your team's branding or personal preferences.

1. In **Workspace Settings**, navigate to the **Theme and Appearance** section.

2. Select from options such as light mode, dark mode, or custom color schemes.

3. Preview the theme and apply it.

2. Organizing Boards and Folders

An organized structure ensures team members can quickly locate the information they need.

1. Drag and drop boards into relevant folders within the workspace.

2. Use naming conventions for folders, such as "Q1 Reports" or "Onboarding Materials."

3. Add icons or colors to folders for easier identification.

Step 4: Setting Notification Preferences

Notifications keep your team updated on progress and changes within the workspace. However, excessive notifications can lead to information overload.

1. Adjusting Notification Settings

1. Open **Workspace Settings** > **Notifications**.

2. Customize which events trigger notifications, such as:

   o Item updates

   o Status changes

   o Deadline reminders

3. Encourage team members to adjust their personal notification settings in their profiles for a tailored experience.

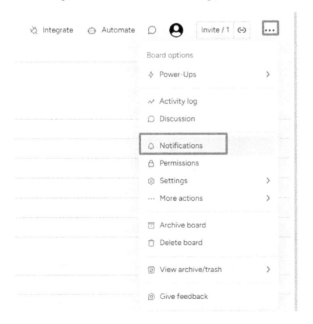

2. Using Notification Automations

Automations can send notifications to specific individuals or groups based on predefined triggers. For example:

- Notify the project manager when a task's status changes to "Stuck."

- Send a reminder to team members two days before a deadline.

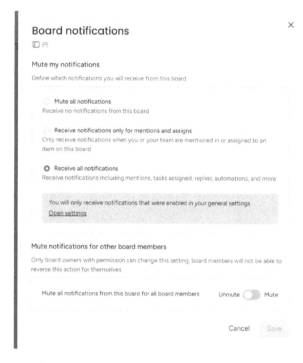

Step 5: Using Default Templates and Automations

Templates and automations can significantly enhance your workspace's functionality by reducing manual tasks.

1. Applying Default Board Templates

1. Go to the **Templates** library in your workspace.

2. Choose from templates like project management, sales pipelines, or employee onboarding.

3. Customize the template to suit your needs by renaming columns, adding automations, or modifying statuses.

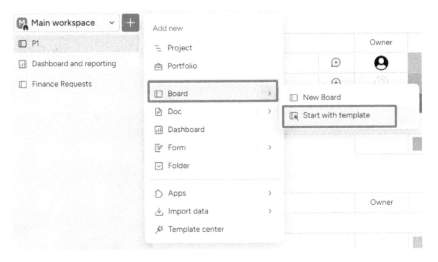

2. Creating Workspace-Level Automations

1. In **Workspace Settings**, navigate to **Automations**.

2. Select an automation recipe, such as:

   o "When a task is marked as complete, notify the team leader."

   o "When a new item is created, assign it to [Person X]."

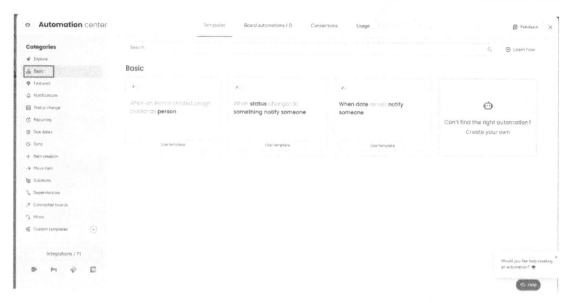

3. Test the automation to ensure it functions as intended.

Step 6: Testing and Optimizing Your Workspace

Customizing your workspace is an iterative process. Regularly gather feedback from team members to identify areas for improvement.

1. Conducting Workspace Audits

1. Schedule periodic reviews of the workspace's structure and settings.

2. Identify unused boards, outdated automations, or redundant columns.

2. Gathering Team Feedback

1. Use Monday.com's **Forms** feature to collect anonymous feedback.

2. Ask specific questions like:

   o "Are the current automations helpful?"

   o "What could improve your experience in this workspace?"

3. Implementing Improvements

Based on feedback, make adjustments to your workspace's layout, permissions, or workflows.

Conclusion

Customizing your workspace settings in Monday.com is a powerful way to create a collaborative, efficient, and organized environment. By leveraging the platform's extensive customization options, you can ensure that your workspace aligns with your team's goals and enhances productivity. Remember, customization is an ongoing process—regularly revisit your settings to adapt to evolving team needs.

CHAPTER II
Boards and Basic Functionality

2.1 Understanding Boards in Monday.com

2.1.1 What are Boards?

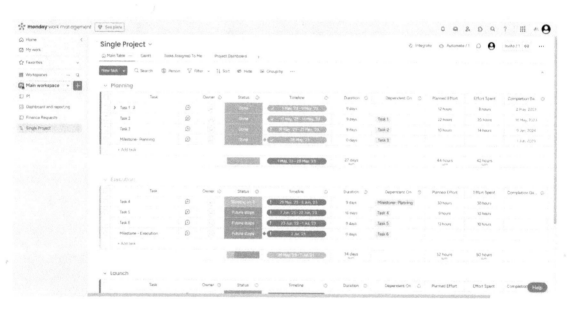

Boards are the foundation of Monday.com, serving as the primary structure where all tasks, projects, and workflows are organized and visualized. In simple terms, a **board** is a virtual workspace where you can manage everything from a single task to complex multi-departmental projects. Understanding what boards are and how they function is crucial to unlocking the full potential of Monday.com for better organization.

This section will explain the concept of boards in detail, their purpose, and how they can be used effectively.

1. The Concept of Boards in Monday.com

Think of boards in Monday.com as digital tables or spreadsheets, but with far more customization, automation, and collaboration capabilities. Each board consists of rows (called items) and columns, which store information related to your tasks, projects, or data. Boards are highly versatile and can be tailored to fit virtually any workflow.

Boards can represent:

- A single project or task list (e.g., "Marketing Campaign Q1").

- A team's daily or weekly workflow (e.g., "Design Team Workflow").

- A database or repository (e.g., "Client Contacts" or "Vendor List").

- A high-level view of strategic goals (e.g., "Company Roadmap 2025").

Every board in Monday.com is structured to promote transparency, collaboration, and efficiency, ensuring that all team members are on the same page.

2. The Purpose of Boards

The primary purpose of boards is to **organize and centralize information**. Whether you're an individual managing your to-do list or a large organization coordinating a complex project, boards act as the central hub where everything related to your work is stored and managed.

Key purposes of boards include:

1. **Task Tracking**: Boards let you track tasks from start to finish, ensuring no details slip through the cracks.

2. **Data Organization**: Organize various types of data (e.g., deadlines, budgets, or client information) in one place.

3. **Team Collaboration**: Boards provide visibility for all team members, allowing everyone to collaborate on shared goals.

4. **Workflow Automation**: Automate repetitive tasks and notifications to save time and reduce errors.

5. **Visualizing Progress**: Use different views (e.g., Timeline, Calendar, Kanban) to monitor progress and deadlines easily.

By providing this central platform, boards reduce the need for scattered tools like email threads, physical notebooks, or separate spreadsheets, bringing everything into one cohesive environment.

3. Board Structure Overview

To fully understand what a board is, it's important to break down its structure. Boards in Monday.com consist of the following core elements:

1. **Items (Rows)**

   o Items are the individual rows on a board.

   o Each item represents a specific task, project, or entity you are tracking. For instance, an item might be "Write Blog Post" in a content creation board or "Client A" in a sales pipeline board.

   o Items can contain detailed information such as assignees, due dates, and file attachments.

2. **Groups**

   o Groups are clusters of items that allow for logical organization within a board.

   o For example, in a project management board, groups might be used to represent task phases like "To Do," "In Progress," and "Completed."

   o Groups provide a clear visual distinction and help prioritize tasks.

3. **Columns**

   o Columns store additional data about each item, such as task owner, deadline, status, or priority.

   o Monday.com offers various column types, including:

- **Text**: For free-form notes or labels.

- **Status**: For tracking task progress (e.g., "Done," "In Progress").

- **Date**: For scheduling deadlines.

- **People**: To assign team members to specific tasks.

o Columns can be customized based on the board's purpose, offering unlimited flexibility.

4. **Views**

o Boards can be visualized in different formats, such as Kanban boards, timelines, calendars, and Gantt charts.

o Views make it easier to interpret complex data and adapt boards to different workflows.

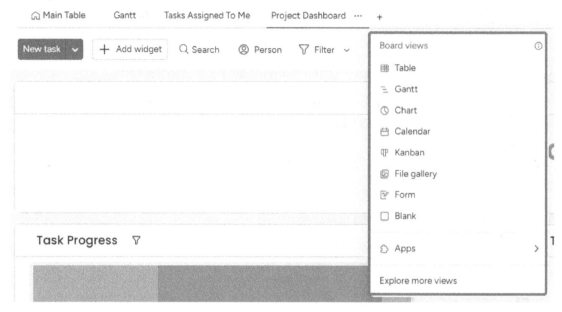

4. Types of Boards in Monday.com

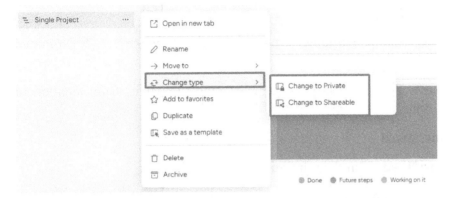

There are three main types of boards in Monday.com, each designed for a specific purpose:

1. **Main Boards**

   o Visible to all team members in your organization by default.

   o Ideal for company-wide projects, general workflows, or shared resources.

2. **Private Boards**

   o Only accessible to the creator and invited users.

   o Useful for sensitive or confidential projects, such as budgeting or HR initiatives.

3. **Shareable Boards**

   o Designed for collaboration with external stakeholders, such as freelancers or clients.

   o Allows users outside your organization to access specific projects while keeping internal data secure.

Choosing the right type of board ensures the proper level of collaboration and privacy for your workflow.

5. Practical Examples of Boards

To better understand boards, let's explore a few practical examples:

1. **Marketing Campaign Board**

    o   Groups: "Ideas," "In Progress," "Published."

    o   Columns: "Campaign Name," "Owner," "Status," "Launch Date," "Estimated Budget."

    o   Use case: Track the progress of marketing campaigns from ideation to execution.

2. **Sales Pipeline Board**

    o   Groups: "Leads," "In Negotiation," "Closed Deals."

    o   Columns: "Client Name," "Contact Info," "Deal Value," "Stage," "Next Steps."

    o   Use case: Manage sales opportunities and track revenue growth.

3. **Personal To-Do Board**

    o   Groups: "Today," "This Week," "Later."

    o   Columns: "Task," "Deadline," "Priority," "Completion Status."

    o   Use case: Organize and prioritize personal tasks and deadlines.

These examples highlight the versatility of boards and how they can adapt to virtually any need.

6. Benefits of Using Boards

Boards are one of Monday.com's most powerful features because they:

1. **Promote Clarity**: Everyone on the team knows what tasks are assigned, their status, and who is responsible.

2. **Increase Efficiency**: Customization and automation reduce the time spent on manual tracking.

3. **Enhance Collaboration**: Boards serve as a single source of truth, ensuring all team members are aligned.

4. **Support Scalability**: Whether managing personal tasks or company-wide projects, boards grow with your needs.

7. Tips for Using Boards Effectively

1. **Start Simple**: Begin with a basic structure and expand as needed. Overcomplicating boards can overwhelm users.

2. **Customize Columns**: Tailor columns to your workflow for maximum relevance.

3. **Leverage Automation**: Use automation recipes to handle repetitive tasks like status updates or deadline reminders.

4. **Regularly Clean Up**: Archive old items and groups to keep boards clean and easy to navigate.

5. **Encourage Team Adoption**: Provide training or guides for your team to fully utilize boards.

By understanding what boards are, their structure, and how they can be customized, you are laying a solid foundation for mastering Monday.com. Boards are not just task lists—they are dynamic tools for collaboration, organization, and productivity. The next section will explore how to create and customize your boards step-by-step.

2.1.2 Types of Boards: Private, Shareable, and Main

Boards are the backbone of Monday.com, where all your tasks, projects, and workflows are organized and managed. To maximize your use of Monday.com, it's essential to understand the three types of boards: **Private Boards**, **Shareable Boards**, and **Main Boards**. Each serves a distinct purpose, offering different levels of access, visibility, and collaboration. This section provides a detailed overview of these board types, their features, use cases, and tips for choosing the right type for your needs.

Private Boards

Definition:

Private boards are designed for confidential work. These boards are only visible to their creators and the specific team members they invite. They are ideal for projects that involve sensitive information or tasks that require limited access.

Key Features of Private Boards:

- **Restricted Access:** Only invited users can view and interact with the board.

- **Full Control:** The board creator determines who gets access and what level of permissions they have (e.g., viewer, editor, admin).

- **Safe Space for Experimentation:** Because these boards are private, they're perfect for brainstorming, testing workflows, or preparing projects before sharing them with a larger team.

Use Cases for Private Boards:

1. **HR and Recruitment:** Use a private board to manage confidential hiring processes, including candidate details, interview schedules, and feedback.

2. **Strategic Planning:** Plan company goals, budgets, or sensitive projects without exposing them to the entire team.

3. **Personal To-Do List:** Create a private space to manage your own tasks, prioritize work, and track progress without distractions.

How to Create a Private Board:

1. From your Monday.com workspace, click on the "+ Add" button in the left-hand menu.

2. Select "New Board" and choose "Private" from the board type options.

3. Name your board, customize its settings, and start adding content.

Tips for Using Private Boards Effectively:

- Add only the necessary team members to maintain confidentiality.

- Use private boards as a preparation space before making your project public.

- Regularly review and clean up private boards to keep them relevant and organized.

Shareable Boards

Definition:
Shareable boards allow you to collaborate with people outside your organization, such as clients, freelancers, or external vendors. These boards provide controlled access, making them ideal for partnerships and joint projects.

Key Features of Shareable Boards:

- **Flexible Access for External Users:** You can invite users outside your organization to work on the board without granting them access to your entire Monday.com account.

- **Customizable Permissions:** Decide who can view, edit, or manage the board's content.

- **Transparency:** Keeps everyone aligned by sharing relevant information while maintaining control over sensitive details.

Use Cases for Shareable Boards:

1. **Client Collaboration:** Share project timelines, deliverables, and updates with clients while keeping internal discussions private.

2. **Freelancer Coordination:** Assign tasks, set deadlines, and monitor progress with external contractors.

3. **Event Planning:** Collaborate with vendors and sponsors on event details such as budgets, schedules, and logistics.

How to Create a Shareable Board:

1. Click on "+ Add" in the left-hand menu and choose "New Board."

2. Select "Shareable" from the board type options.

3. Customize the board name and settings, then invite external collaborators by entering their email addresses.

Tips for Using Shareable Boards Effectively:

- Use column permissions to limit access to sensitive information.

- Regularly update the board to keep external collaborators informed.

- Set clear expectations for external users, such as deadlines and communication protocols.

Main Boards

Definition:
Main boards are the default type of board in Monday.com and are visible to everyone in your organization. They are designed for team-wide collaboration, transparency, and centralized project management.

Key Features of Main Boards:

- **Organization-Wide Visibility:** Any member of your organization can view and contribute to main boards.

- **Team Collaboration:** Ideal for projects that require input from multiple departments or team members.

- **Centralized Information:** Acts as a hub for team-wide updates, progress tracking, and resource sharing.

Use Cases for Main Boards:

1. **Company-Wide Announcements:** Share important updates, such as meeting schedules, organizational changes, or policy updates.

2. **Team Projects:** Manage collaborative projects where input from all team members is valuable.

3. **Resource Management:** Track shared assets, such as equipment, budgets, or time allocations.

How to Create a Main Board:

1. In the workspace, click on "+ Add" and select "New Board."

2. Choose "Main" as the board type.

3. Set up the board name, columns, and initial items to get started.

Tips for Using Main Boards Effectively:

- Use filters to focus on specific data when working with large teams.

- Assign tasks clearly to avoid confusion and ensure accountability.

- Regularly archive or delete outdated boards to maintain clarity.

Choosing the Right Board Type

Selecting the right board type is critical to ensuring your workflow remains efficient and secure. Here are some factors to consider when choosing between private, shareable, and main boards:

Factor	Private Board	Shareable Board	Main Board
Access Control	Limited to invited users only	Includes external collaborators	Visible to all team members
Confidentiality	High	Moderate	Low
Best For	Sensitive or personal projects	External partnerships or joint tasks	Team-wide collaboration
Examples	HR, budgets, personal tasks	Client work, events, vendor projects	Announcements, shared resources

Quick Tips:

- Use **Private Boards** for sensitive projects or brainstorming.

- Choose **Shareable Boards** when working with external users.

- Opt for **Main Boards** to foster transparency and collaboration across your team.

Common Mistakes to Avoid

1. **Sharing Sensitive Data on Main Boards:** Avoid posting confidential information on main boards where everyone can see it. Use private boards instead.

2. **Overloading Shareable Boards with Internal Details:** Keep external collaborators focused on relevant tasks by filtering out internal discussions.

3. **Lack of Clear Permissions:** Clearly define who can edit or view the content of private or shareable boards to prevent mistakes.

By understanding the differences between private, shareable, and main boards, you can choose the right type for each project and maximize your team's efficiency. Mastering these board types will help you maintain better organization, improve collaboration, and ensure the security of your data within Monday.com.

2.2 Creating and Customizing Boards

2.2.1 How to Create a New Board

Creating a new board in Monday.com is the foundation for managing and organizing your work effectively. Boards are the heart of Monday.com and act as the primary workspace where tasks, projects, and data are tracked and visualized. In this section, we'll explore every detail, step-by-step, on how to create a board, customize it to your needs, and set it up for success.

Step 1: Understanding the Purpose of a Board

Before creating a board, it's essential to understand what you need it for. Boards can be used for a wide variety of purposes, including:

- **Project Management:** Tracking project timelines, deliverables, and team responsibilities.

- **Task Management:** Listing daily, weekly, or monthly tasks and assigning them to team members.

- **CRM:** Managing customer relationships, sales pipelines, or client communications.

- **Personal Goals:** Tracking habits, personal goals, or personal productivity.

Start by identifying the primary goal of the board. Ask yourself:

- What type of information will this board hold?

- Who will access and update this board?

- How will the information flow (e.g., tasks moving through stages like "To Do," "In Progress," and "Done")?

Having a clear purpose will make the creation process smoother and ensure the board meets your needs.

Step 2: Accessing the Board Creation Tool

Once you've determined the purpose, you're ready to create your board. Follow these steps to access the board creation tool:

1. **Login to Monday.com:**

   o Open your Monday.com account in a web browser or mobile app.

   o Navigate to the workspace where you want to create the board.

2. **Locate the '+ Add' Button:**

   o On the left-hand sidebar, find the **"+ Add"** button next to "Boards" or "Workspaces." Click on it.

   o A dropdown menu will appear with options such as "New Board," "Import Data," or "Template Center."

3. **Select "New Board" Option:**

   o Click on the "New Board" option to create a board from scratch.

   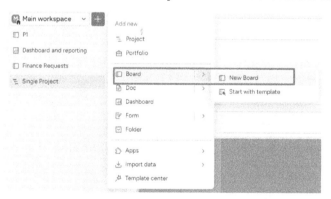

Step 3: Naming Your Board

Once you've selected the "New Board" option, the system will prompt you to name your board. Naming your board effectively is crucial for clarity and ease of use.

1. **Choose a Descriptive Name:**

   o   The board name should reflect its purpose. For example:

      ▪   **"Marketing Campaigns"** for tracking marketing projects.

      ▪   **"Team Tasks - Q1"** for tracking team responsibilities in the first quarter.

2. **Keep It Short and Clear:**

   o   Avoid overly long names. Keep it concise but meaningful.

Click **"Create"** after entering the name. The board will now appear in your selected workspace.

Step 4: Choosing Board Type

After naming your board, you will be prompted to choose a board type. There are three main types in Monday.com:

1. **Main Boards:**

   o   Accessible to all team members in the workspace.

   o   Ideal for general projects or tasks that everyone needs to see.

2. **Private Boards:**

   o Only visible to the creator and those they invite.

   o Perfect for confidential projects, personal task tracking, or sensitive information.

3. **Shareable Boards:**

   o Accessible to team members and external stakeholders (e.g., clients or freelancers).

   o Useful for projects requiring collaboration with people outside your organization.

Choose the board type that best suits your needs. If you're unsure, start with a Main Board, as you can always change the type later.

Step 5: Selecting a Template or Starting from Scratch

Monday.com offers two options for creating boards:

1. **Using Templates:**

   o Templates are pre-designed boards tailored for specific use cases (e.g., Project Management, CRM, Event Planning).

   o To use a template:

      ▪ Click on the **"Template Center"** when prompted.

      ▪ Browse through categories or search for a specific template.

      ▪ Preview the template and click **"Use Template"** to apply it to your new board.

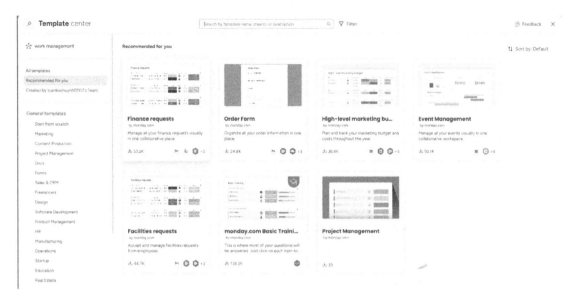

2. **Starting from Scratch:**

- ○ If you prefer complete control, select **"Blank Board."**
- ○ This option allows you to design your board exactly as you envision it.

Step 6: Setting Up Columns

Columns are the building blocks of your board. They hold the data and provide structure. After creating your board, you'll see an empty layout with the option to add columns. Here's how:

1. **Click on "+ Add Column"**

- ○ On the right-hand side of the board, click **"+ Add Column."**

2. **Choose the Right Column Type:**

   o   Monday.com offers various column types, including:

   ▪   **Text Column:** For notes, descriptions, or details.

   ▪   **Person Column:** To assign tasks to team members.

   ▪   **Date Column:** To set due dates or deadlines.

   ▪   **Status Column:** To track progress (e.g., "To Do," "In Progress," "Done").

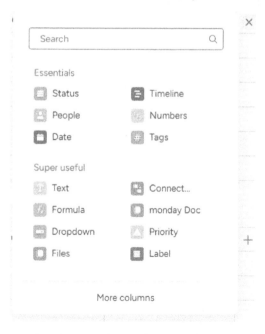

3. **Customize Column Titles:**

- o   Rename columns to suit your needs. For example:

  - **Task Name**

  - **Owner**

  - **Deadline**

Step 7: Adding Groups

Groups help you organize items into categories. For instance:

- In a project management board, groups might be **"Week 1," "Week 2,"** and **"Week 3."**

- In a CRM board, groups could represent sales stages like **"Leads," "Negotiations,"** and **"Closed Deals."**

1. **Click on "+ Add Group"**

   - o   At the top of the board, click the **"+ Add Group"** button.

2. **Name the Group:**

   - o   Enter a name that describes the category.

Step 8: Saving and Sharing the Board

Once your board structure is ready, don't forget to save and share it with your team.

1. **Save Your Changes:**

    o Monday.com saves automatically, but review your setup to ensure everything is in place.

2. **Invite Team Members:**

    o Use the **"Invite"** button to add collaborators. Assign roles to ensure proper access levels.

Pro Tips for Board Creation

- **Start Simple:** Begin with a basic layout and add complexity as needed.

- **Leverage Templates:** Templates save time and provide inspiration for board design.

- **Color-Code Groups:** Use color coding to make groups visually distinct.

- **Test Your Workflow:** Add a few sample items to test the board's usability.

By following these steps, you'll have a functional, well-structured board ready to organize your projects, tasks, or goals. This structured approach ensures clarity, collaboration, and efficiency from the start.

2.2.2 Adding Columns: Types and Functions

When creating a board in Monday.com, columns are essential for structuring your data and tasks. They allow you to track, organize, and display specific information relevant to your workflow. This section will guide you step-by-step on how to add, configure, and make the most out of columns in Monday.com.

---

1. What Are Columns in Monday.com?

Columns are the building blocks of any board. Each column represents a specific type of information you want to track or display for the items on your board. For example:

- **Tasks** can have columns for due dates, status updates, and assigned team members.

- **Projects** might include budget columns, milestones, and progress percentages.

Columns allow you to visualize your data and customize your board to suit your workflow. Depending on your board's purpose, the choice of columns will vary.

2. Types of Columns in Monday.com

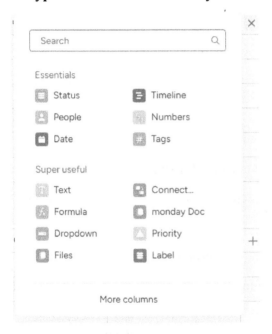

Monday.com offers a wide variety of column types. Here's an overview of the most commonly used columns and their functions:

1. **Text Column**

    o   **Function:** Allows you to input free text.

    o   **Use Case:** Track names, descriptions, or notes for each item.

- **Example:** Add a "Task Name" or "Notes" column to describe the tasks or projects in detail.

2. **Status Column**

   - **Function:** Enables you to track the progress or condition of an item with customizable labels (e.g., "In Progress," "Done," "Stuck").

   - **Use Case:** Monitor task progress or project milestones.

   - **Example:** Use labels like "To-Do," "In Progress," and "Completed" for tasks in a project.

3. **Date Column**

   - **Function:** Displays specific dates.

   - **Use Case:** Use it for deadlines, milestones, or event dates.

   - **Example:** Add a "Due Date" column to track task completion deadlines.

4. **People Column**

   - **Function:** Assigns tasks to team members.

   - **Use Case:** Helps you see who is responsible for specific tasks or items.

   - **Example:** Assign a task to a team member like "John Doe" or "Jane Smith."

5. **Dropdown Column**

   - **Function:** Offers a dropdown menu with predefined options.

   - **Use Case:** Create consistency by allowing users to choose from predefined options.

   - **Example:** Use for categories like "Department" or "Priority" (e.g., Low, Medium, High).

6. **Timeline Column**

   - **Function:** Tracks a date range.

   - **Use Case:** Plan project phases or event schedules.

   - **Example:** Visualize timelines for tasks spanning multiple days.

7. **Checkbox Column**

   o **Function:** Adds a checkbox to mark items as complete.

   o **Use Case:** Simple task tracking or quality assurance checklists.

   o **Example:** Use for binary decisions like "Approved" or "Reviewed."

8. **Numbers Column**

   o **Function:** Tracks numeric values like quantities, percentages, or budgets.

   o **Use Case:** Monitor budgets, hours worked, or progress percentages.

   o **Example:** Add columns for "Budget ($)" or "Progress (%)".

9. **Link Column**

   o **Function:** Attaches external links to an item.

   o **Use Case:** Provide additional resources or references.

   o **Example:** Link to project documents, websites, or task resources.

10. **Formula Column**

    o **Function:** Performs calculations using values from other columns.

    o **Use Case:** Automate calculations such as totals, differences, or percentages.

    o **Example:** Calculate "Total Hours Worked" using start and end times.

11. **Tags Column**

    o **Function:** Adds customizable tags for better organization and filtering.

    o **Use Case:** Group and filter tasks by tags like "Urgent," "Client A," or "Design."

    o **Example:** Quickly find all tasks related to a specific project by searching for its tag.

12. **Files Column**

    o **Function:** Attach files directly to items.

    o **Use Case:** Centralize resources like contracts, designs, or reports.

- o **Example:** Attach PDFs or images related to a task or deliverable.

---

3. How to Add Columns to a Board

Adding columns in Monday.com is straightforward and customizable:

1. **Locate the "Add Column" Button**

   - o Open the board where you want to add a column.

   - o Click the **"+" button** on the right side of your board's column headers.

2. **Choose a Column Type**

   - o A dropdown menu will appear showing all available column types.

   - o Select the column type you need (e.g., Status, Date, People).

3. **Name Your Column**

   - o After selecting the column type, name it based on its purpose.

   - o For example, if you choose a Status column, you can name it "Task Status" or "Progress."

4. **Customize the Column Settings**

   - o Depending on the column type, you can configure additional settings. For example:

      - ▪ **Status Column:** Define labels such as "In Progress" or "Completed."

      - ▪ **Dropdown Column:** Add options like "Low," "Medium," and "High Priority."

5. **Save and Arrange the Column**

   - o Once added, you can drag and drop the column to rearrange its position.

---

4. Tips for Using Columns Effectively

To make the most of your columns, consider these best practices:

1. **Plan Your Columns Before Creating a Board**

   o   Identify the key data you need to track. Avoid adding unnecessary columns that might clutter your board.

2. **Use Consistent Naming Conventions**

   o   Consistent column names across boards make it easier for team members to understand and navigate.

3. **Leverage Status Columns for Progress Tracking**

   o   Add clear and actionable labels in the Status column. Color-code them for better visibility (e.g., green for "Completed," red for "Stuck").

4. **Use Dropdowns to Standardize Data**

   o   Dropdown columns ensure data consistency, especially when team members input recurring information like "Priority" or "Department."

5. **Automate Updates Using Columns**

   o   Pair columns with automation to streamline workflows. For example, trigger an email notification when a Status column is updated to "Completed."

6. **Combine Columns for Advanced Tracking**

   o   Use multiple columns together to track detailed information. For instance:

      ▪   A Status column for task progress.

      ▪   A People column to assign responsibility.

      ▪   A Date column for task deadlines.

7. **Regularly Clean Up and Optimize Columns**

   o   Periodically review and remove unused or redundant columns. This keeps your board organized and efficient.

---

5. Common Mistakes to Avoid

1. **Overloading Your Board with Too Many Columns**

      o   Stick to essential columns to avoid overwhelming your team.

2. **Unclear or Redundant Column Names**

      o   Ambiguous column names can confuse team members. Always name columns descriptively.

3. **Inconsistent Labeling in Status Columns**

      o   Ensure all team members use consistent labels. Mislabeling can cause reporting errors.

By following these detailed steps and tips, you'll be able to effectively add and customize columns in Monday.com. Columns are a powerful tool to structure your data, enhance visibility, and create an organized workflow tailored to your team's needs.

2.2.3 Renaming and Organizing Columns

When using Monday.com, **renaming and organizing columns** effectively is key to creating boards that are both functional and visually appealing. Columns are the backbone of your boards, representing specific data fields like statuses, deadlines, assignees, and more. Proper column organization not only enhances clarity but also helps your team collaborate efficiently. This section will guide you step by step on how to rename and organize columns to optimize your workflows.

1. Why Renaming Columns is Important

Renaming columns helps to:

- **Make the board more intuitive:** Clear, descriptive column names ensure everyone understands the purpose of each column.

- **Reflect your workflow:** Tailoring column names to fit your process adds context to the tasks you're managing.

- **Avoid confusion:** Default column names like "Status" or "Date" might not always represent their actual use. Customizing them removes ambiguity.

For example, instead of keeping a generic column named "Status," you might rename it to "Project Phase" to indicate which stage a task is in.

2. How to Rename Columns

Renaming a column in Monday.com is a straightforward process. Follow these steps:

1. **Locate the Column Header:** On your board, find the column you want to rename. The name will appear at the top of the column.

2. **Click on the Column Name:**

   o Hover over the column name, and a pencil icon will appear.

   o Click the pencil icon or simply double-click the column name.

3. **Edit the Name:**

   o Type the new name into the text box.

   o Make sure the name is descriptive but concise (e.g., "Task Priority" instead of just "Priority").

4. **Save the Changes:**

   o Press the "Enter" key or click outside the text box to save the new name.

Pro Tips for Renaming Columns:

- Use **consistent naming conventions** across your boards, such as capitalizing the first letter of each word or avoiding unnecessary abbreviations.

- Keep names short but informative. For example, "Assigned Team Member" is better than "Person Handling the Task."

- Consider adding emojis to column names to make them visually distinct. For instance, "💼 Task Owner" or "☐ Task Status."

3. Organizing Columns: The Basics

Once you've renamed your columns, the next step is to organize them. The way you arrange your columns can greatly influence how easy it is to navigate and interpret the board. Here's how to organize columns effectively:

3.1 Rearranging Columns

1. **Click and Drag:**

   o Hover over the column header until your cursor changes to a hand icon.

   o Click and hold the column header, then drag it to the desired position.

2. **Release to Drop:**

   o Drop the column in the new position by releasing the mouse button.

   o Monday.com allows you to reorder columns freely, so experiment with arrangements that work best for your workflow.

3.2 Prioritizing Key Columns

- Place the most important columns (e.g., "Task Name," "Status," and "Deadline") near the left side of the board, as these are typically the first fields users review.

- Less frequently used columns, such as "Notes" or "Attachments," can be placed further to the right.

3.3 Grouping Related Columns

If you have multiple columns that relate to a single aspect of your workflow, arrange them together for better clarity. For example:

- Group all timeline-related columns (e.g., "Start Date," "End Date," "Duration") side by side.

- Place all assignment-related columns (e.g., "Assigned To," "Department," "Priority Level") in the same section.

4. Advanced Techniques for Column Organization

4.1 Using Column Freezing

If your board has many columns, freezing specific ones can help you keep important information visible while scrolling.

- **How to Freeze Columns:**

   o Scroll to the far-right side of your board.

- o   Right-click on a column header and select "Freeze this Column."
- o   The frozen column will remain visible on the left side of the board as you scroll horizontally.

This feature is especially useful for boards with a large number of columns, ensuring that critical fields like "Task Name" or "Status" are always visible.

4.2 Duplicating Columns for Similar Workflows

Sometimes, you might need a column with the same structure but for a different purpose. Instead of creating a new one from scratch:

1.   Hover over the column header.

2.   Click on the three-dot menu (ellipsis).

3.   Select "Duplicate Column."

You can then rename the duplicated column to fit its new purpose.

4.3 Hiding Unused Columns

If certain columns are not immediately relevant, consider hiding them to declutter the board.

- •   Click on the three-dot menu in the top right corner of the board.
- •   Select "Hide/Show Columns."
- •   Uncheck the columns you want to hide.

Hiding columns doesn't delete them—they remain accessible if you need them later.

---

5. Best Practices for Renaming and Organizing Columns

1.   **Align Columns with Your Workflow:**

- o   Think about the logical order in which tasks are completed or reviewed. Arrange columns accordingly.

2.   **Audit Your Board Regularly:**

- o   Over time, boards can become cluttered with unnecessary columns. Periodically review and remove or hide unused ones.

3. **Standardize Across Teams:**

   o If multiple teams are using Monday.com, ensure a consistent structure across boards to make collaboration easier.

4. **Use Colors and Tags for Visual Cues:**

   o Use column backgrounds or icons to make important fields stand out.

5. **Test and Adjust:**

   o Don't hesitate to experiment with column placement and naming until you find a structure that works best for your team.

6. Common Issues and How to Solve Them

- **Problem: Columns are hard to read on mobile devices.**

  o **Solution:** Minimize the number of columns and prioritize critical ones for better mobile accessibility.

- **Problem: Team members are confused by column names.**

  o **Solution:** Rename columns to be more descriptive and add tooltips or notes where necessary.

- **Problem: Columns are frequently being rearranged by mistake.**

  o **Solution:** Use Monday.com's permission settings to limit who can edit board structures.

By mastering column renaming and organization, you'll create cleaner, more intuitive boards that align perfectly with your workflows. These practices will not only save time but also enhance team productivity, ensuring everyone stays on the same page.

2.3 Adding and Managing Items

2.3.1 Adding Items to a Board

In Monday.com, "Items" are the building blocks of your boards. Each item represents a task, project, or any unit of work that you want to track. Adding items to a board is an essential step in organizing your workflows and making your Monday.com boards actionable. This section provides a step-by-step guide to help you understand how to add items to your boards effectively and how to customize them for better organization.

Step 1: Accessing the Board

Before you can add items, you need to access the board where you want to work. Follow these steps to navigate to your desired board:

1. Open your Monday.com workspace.

2. Locate the board you wish to work on in the left-hand sidebar.

3. Click on the board name to open it.

If you haven't created a board yet, go back to **Section 2.2.1: How to Create a New Board** for a quick guide.

Step 2: Understanding the Board Layout

Once you're on the board, you'll see it is divided into groups and columns:

- **Groups**: These are color-coded sections that help categorize your items (e.g., "To-Do," "In Progress," "Completed").

- **Columns**: These represent the specific details or attributes of each item (e.g., Due Date, Status, Priority, Assigned To).

Adding an item means creating a new row under one of these groups.

Step 3: Adding a New Item

Adding a new item to your board is straightforward. Follow these steps:

1. Navigate to the group where you want to add the item.

2. Look for the **"+ Add"** button at the bottom of the group.

3. Click on the **"+ Add"** button.

4. A new row will appear. This is your new item.

Step 4: Naming Your Item

The first column on any board is typically the "Item Name" column. Use this field to enter the name or title of your item. This could be a task, a project name, or any label that represents the work unit. For example:

- If you're managing a marketing campaign, your item could be titled "Create Social Media Content."

- If you're organizing a product launch, an item might be named "Finalize Product Packaging."

Keep the names concise yet descriptive so your team can quickly understand what each item represents.

Step 5: Filling in Column Data

After naming your item, you can begin populating the other columns with relevant data. Here are some common types of columns and how to use them:

1. **Status Column**:

- o Use the dropdown menu to set the current status of the item (e.g., "Not Started," "In Progress," or "Completed").
- o You can customize these statuses to match your workflow.

2. **Date Column**:
   - o Click the calendar icon to assign a due date or start date for the item.
   - o This helps your team stay on track and meet deadlines.

3. **People Column**:
   - o Assign team members to the item by clicking on the column and selecting their name.
   - o This ensures everyone knows who is responsible for completing the task.

4. **Priority Column**:
   - o Use this column to set the priority level of the task (e.g., "High," "Medium," "Low").
   - o This helps your team focus on the most critical tasks first.

5. **Text Column**:
   - o Add any additional notes or descriptions to provide context for the item.
   - o For example, you might write "Draft blog post and get it reviewed by the design team."

Step 6: Rearranging and Grouping Items

Once you've added items, you can organize them further:

1. **Reordering Items**:
   - o Drag and drop items to reorder them within a group.
   - o This is especially useful for prioritizing tasks.

2. **Moving Items Between Groups**:

      o   Drag an item from one group to another to reflect its current status. For example, move an item from "To-Do" to "In Progress."

3. **Duplicating Items**:

      o   Right-click on an item and select "Duplicate" if you need a copy of it.

      o   This is helpful for recurring tasks or creating templates for similar tasks.

Step 7: Using Quick Add for Faster Input

For situations where you need to add multiple items quickly, Monday.com offers a **Quick Add** feature:

1. Click the "+ Add" button at the top of the board (or within a group).

2. Type the item name, press **Enter**, and immediately type the next item.

3. Repeat this process until all your items are added.

This is an efficient way to input a large number of tasks in one go.

Step 8: Customizing Items with Subitems

For complex tasks that require multiple steps, you can break them down using **Subitems**:

1. Click on the **"+"** icon next to an item to add a subitem.

2. Enter the details for each subitem (e.g., individual steps, deadlines, or assignments).

3. Use subitems to track progress on smaller tasks while keeping the main item organized.

Step 9: Importing Items from External Sources

If you already have a list of tasks in another format, Monday.com allows you to import them directly into your board:

1. Click on the **"Import"** button in the top-right corner of the board.

2. Select the source of your data (e.g., Excel, Google Sheets, or Trello).

3. Map the imported columns to your Monday.com board columns.

4. Review and finalize the import to populate your board with items.

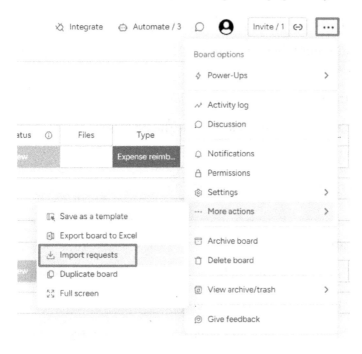

Best Practices for Adding Items

- **Be Specific**: Use clear and concise item names to avoid confusion.

- **Use Templates**: If you frequently add similar items, save time by using board templates with predefined columns and settings.

- **Keep it Organized**: Regularly review your items to ensure they are in the correct groups and have up-to-date details.

- **Engage Your Team**: Encourage team members to add their tasks directly to the board to ensure transparency and accountability.

Common Mistakes to Avoid

1. **Overloading Items with Too Much Information**: Instead, use the "Notes" or "Updates" section to add additional context.

2. **Not Assigning Responsibility**: Always use the "People" column to assign tasks to specific individuals.

3. **Ignoring Deadlines**: Ensure that every task has a due date to maintain accountability.

4. **Using Generic Names**: Avoid vague titles like "Task 1" or "Project A" that don't convey meaningful information.

By following these steps and tips, you can effectively add and manage items in Monday.com, creating a clear and organized workflow for yourself and your team. Properly structured items serve as the foundation for a successful Monday.com board, enabling smooth collaboration and efficient task management.

2.3.2 Editing, Duplicating, and Deleting Items

In Monday.com, effectively managing items on your boards is a cornerstone of keeping your workflows organized and up-to-date. Editing, duplicating, and deleting items are fundamental actions you'll perform to ensure your boards stay relevant and structured. Let's break down each of these tasks step by step to help you master these essential functions.

Editing Items

Editing items in Monday.com allows you to update details, make corrections, and adjust information as your tasks evolve. Here's how to edit items and use the editing features to their full potential:

Step 1: Locate the Item to Edit

1. Navigate to the board where the item you want to edit is located.

2. Use the search bar at the top of the board if you have many items and need to find it quickly.

3. Click on the item's name or the specific column you want to edit.

Step 2: Edit the Item's Name or Text

1. Hover over the item's name or text field (depending on your column type).

2. Click on the text to enter edit mode.

3. Make your changes directly in the text field.

4. Press **Enter** or click outside the field to save your changes.

Step 3: Update Column-Specific Details

Each column type offers unique editing options. Here are some examples:

- **Status Columns**: Click the dropdown menu in the column to select a new status, such as "In Progress" or "Completed."

- **Date Columns**: Click the date field to open a calendar and choose a new date.

- **Numbers Columns**: Update numerical values directly by clicking and typing.

- **Dropdown Columns**: Click to open the list of options and select the appropriate value.

Step 4: Use Bulk Editing (Optional)

If you need to make similar changes to multiple items:

1. Select multiple items by clicking the checkbox to the left of each row.

2. Click the **Edit Column** button that appears at the top of the board.

3. Apply the desired changes to all selected items simultaneously.

Editing Best Practices

- Regularly review your board to ensure all item details are accurate and up-to-date.

- Add relevant details to each item to give your team clarity about the task.

- Avoid leaving columns blank unless absolutely necessary, as this can lead to confusion.

Duplicating Items

Duplicating items is a useful feature for tasks or projects that follow similar patterns or templates. Instead of starting from scratch, you can copy an existing item and customize it as needed. This is especially helpful for recurring tasks or standard operating procedures.

Step 1: Access the Item's Options Menu

1. Locate the item you want to duplicate on the board.

2. Hover over the item to reveal the options menu (usually represented by three vertical dots).

3. Click on the **Options Menu** to open the dropdown.

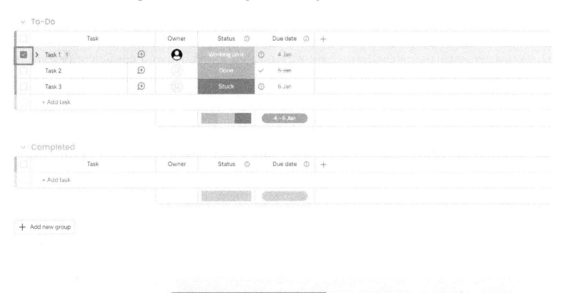

Step 2: Duplicate the Item

1. From the options menu, select **Duplicate**.

2. Choose whether to duplicate just the item or the item and its updates (comments and activity history).

Step 3: Customize the Duplicated Item

1. The duplicated item will appear directly below the original, marked as "Copy of [Item Name]."

2. Click on the duplicated item to make any necessary adjustments, such as changing the item name, status, or other details.

Advanced Duplication Options

- **Duplicate with Subitems**: If the original item contains subitems, you can choose to duplicate those as well. This ensures that all subtasks remain linked to the new item.

- **Duplicate Across Boards**: If you need the same item on another board, use the "Move to Board" feature after duplicating it.

Best Practices for Duplicating Items

- Use clear naming conventions for duplicated items to avoid confusion (e.g., "Task Name - January").

- Regularly review duplicated items to ensure they are customized for their new purpose.

- Avoid duplicating too many items without organizing them, as this can clutter your board.

Deleting Items

At times, you may need to remove outdated or irrelevant items to keep your board clean and focused. Deleting items in Monday.com is straightforward but comes with important considerations to ensure you don't lose critical information.

Step 1: Open the Options Menu

1. Locate the item you want to delete on the board.

2. Hover over the item to reveal the options menu (three vertical dots).

3. Click on the **Options Menu** to open the dropdown.

Step 2: Delete the Item

1. Select **Delete** from the dropdown menu.

2. Confirm your action in the popup dialog box.

Step 3: Recover Deleted Items (If Needed)

Monday.com offers a feature to recover deleted items within a certain timeframe:

1. Navigate to the **Recycle Bin** by clicking your profile picture in the lower-left corner and selecting **Recycle Bin** from the menu.

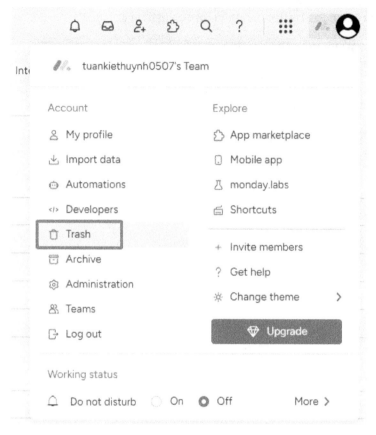

2. Locate the deleted item in the list.

3. Click **Restore** to return the item to its original board.

Deleting Multiple Items

If you need to delete several items at once:

1. Select multiple items by clicking the checkboxes next to their rows.

2. Click the **Delete** button at the top of the board.

3. Confirm the deletion in the popup dialog box.

Permanent Deletion

If you're sure an item is no longer needed, you can permanently delete it from the Recycle Bin. Be cautious, as this action cannot be undone.

Practical Tips for Managing Items

1. **Plan Before Editing or Deleting**: Ensure you have a clear understanding of the item's purpose before making changes or removing it.

2. **Communicate with Your Team**: If an item affects other team members, notify them before making significant edits or deletions.

3. **Back Up Critical Information**: Use Monday.com's export feature to download data before deleting important items.

Conclusion

Mastering the skills of editing, duplicating, and deleting items in Monday.com will empower you to manage your boards more effectively. These actions, while simple, are the backbone of maintaining organized and efficient workflows. By following the steps and best practices outlined in this section, you'll ensure your boards remain clean, relevant, and aligned with your team's goals. Whether you're updating task details, reusing templates, or removing outdated tasks, these tools will help you optimize your use of Monday.com.

2.3.3 Grouping Items for Better Organization

When working on complex projects or managing multiple tasks in Monday.com, grouping items effectively is essential for maintaining clarity, improving efficiency, and ensuring that your team stays on track. In this section, we'll explore how to group items in Monday.com, why grouping is important, and best practices for organizing your boards in a way that maximizes productivity.

What Are Groups in Monday.com?

Groups in Monday.com are a way to organize items within a board into distinct sections. Think of groups as folders or categories that allow you to separate tasks, projects, or information based on specific criteria such as status, priority, team members, or deadlines. Each group serves as a container for related items, helping you structure your board visually and logically.

For example, in a project management board, you might create groups like:

- **"To Do"** for pending tasks.

- **"In Progress"** for tasks currently being worked on.

- **"Completed"** for tasks that are finished.

Alternatively, if you're tracking sales leads, you could use groups like:

- **"New Leads"** for prospects you've just added.

- **"Contacted"** for leads you've reached out to.

- **"Negotiating"** for leads in the discussion phase.

- **"Closed Deals"** for successful sales.

How to Create and Manage Groups in Monday.com

1. Creating a New Group

To create a new group:

1. Open the board where you want to add a group.

2. Click on the **"Add Group"** button at the bottom of your board (or in the left sidebar, depending on your layout).

3. Enter a name for your group. This name should be clear and descriptive to help your team immediately understand the purpose of the group.

For instance, if you're working on a content calendar, your group names might include:

- "Drafts"

- "Under Review"

- "Published"

Once your group is created, it will appear on your board as a new section, with space to add items underneath it.

2. Moving Items Between Groups

Sometimes, you'll need to reorganize tasks by moving items between groups. To do this:

- **Drag and Drop**: Click and hold an item, then drag it to the desired group. Release the mouse to drop it in place.

- **Bulk Move**: To move multiple items at once, select the checkboxes next to each item, click on the **"Move to"** option in the toolbar, and choose the target group.

Moving items between groups is particularly useful for workflows that involve status updates, such as moving a task from "To Do" to "In Progress."

3. Renaming Groups

If you need to rename a group to better reflect its purpose:

- Hover over the group's name.

- Click the pencil icon that appears.

- Enter the new name and press **Enter** to save.

This is helpful when project requirements or workflows change, and group names need to be adjusted to stay relevant.

4. Deleting Groups

If a group is no longer needed:

- Click the three-dot menu (ellipsis) next to the group name.

- Select **"Delete Group."**

- Confirm the deletion.

Note: Deleting a group will also delete all items within it, so ensure you no longer need the items or have moved them elsewhere before proceeding.

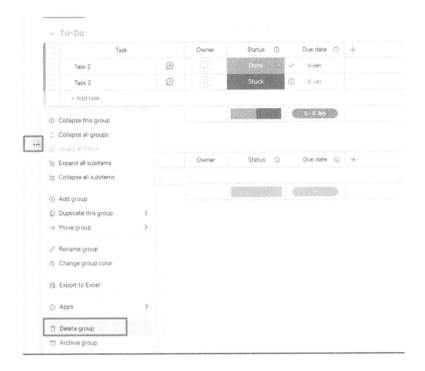

Best Practices for Grouping Items

1. Use Logical Categories

Group items based on meaningful categories relevant to your workflow. This could include:

- **Phases of a Project**: Group tasks into "Planning," "Execution," and "Review" phases.

- **Timeframes**: Use groups like "Week 1," "Week 2," and "Week 3" for time-sensitive tasks.

- **Departments**: Separate tasks for "Marketing," "Sales," and "Development" teams.

Logical grouping helps team members locate items quickly and understand the broader structure of the project.

2. Keep Groups Consistent Across Boards

If you're using multiple boards, maintain consistent group names and structures to avoid confusion. For example, if your project boards all have groups for "To Do," "In Progress," and "Completed," team members will find it easier to navigate and update tasks.

3. Limit the Number of Groups

While it might be tempting to create many groups for detailed categorization, having too many can make your board overwhelming. Stick to a manageable number of groups that cover your key categories.

4. Regularly Review and Update Groups

As projects progress, your groups may need to evolve. Schedule periodic reviews to ensure your groups still align with your workflow. Remove outdated groups or merge groups if necessary.

Advanced Features for Grouping Items

1. Conditional Automations with Groups

Monday.com allows you to set up automations that interact with groups. For instance:

- Automatically move items to the "Completed" group when their status changes to "Done."

- Send notifications when a task is added to the "Urgent" group.

To set up an automation:

1. Click on **"Automations"** at the top of your board.

2. Select a pre-made automation recipe or create a custom one.

3. Configure the conditions and actions based on your groups.

2. Filtering by Group

To focus on specific parts of your board, use the filter feature to view items within a particular group. This is especially useful for large boards where scrolling through all groups might be time-consuming.

- Click the **"Filter"** button at the top of your board.

- Select the desired group to narrow down your view.

3. Duplicating Groups

If you need to replicate a group for a similar project or workflow:

- Click the three-dot menu next to the group's name.

- Select **"Duplicate Group."**

- Choose whether to duplicate the group with or without its items.

Duplicating groups can save time when setting up recurring workflows or templates.

Common Challenges and How to Address Them

1. Overcrowded Groups

If a group contains too many items, it may become difficult to navigate. Consider splitting the group into smaller subcategories or using additional boards to manage the workload.

2. Misplaced Items

Items occasionally end up in the wrong group, causing confusion. To avoid this:

- Train team members on the importance of placing items in the correct group.

- Use automations to move items to the appropriate group based on predefined criteria.

3. Group Overlap

If your group criteria are too broad, items might fit into multiple groups. To resolve this, refine your group definitions and clarify their purposes.

Examples of Grouping Strategies in Different Use Cases

1. Event Planning Board

- **Group 1: "Pre-Event Tasks"**

- **Group 2: "Event Day Activities"**

- **Group 3: "Post-Event Follow-Ups"**

2. Product Development Board

- Group 1: "Backlog"
- Group 2: "Current Sprint"
- Group 3: "Completed Features"

3. Recruitment Board

- Group 1: "New Applicants"
- Group 2: "Interviews Scheduled"
- Group 3: "Offers Sent"

Conclusion

Grouping items in Monday.com is a fundamental strategy for staying organized and ensuring your team works efficiently. By creating meaningful groups, using advanced features like automations, and following best practices, you can transform a cluttered board into a streamlined workflow. Regularly evaluate and refine your grouping strategy to adapt to changing project needs, and you'll unlock the full potential of Monday.com for better organization.

CHAPTER III
Collaborating with Your Team

3.1 Inviting Team Members to Boards

3.1.1 Adding New Users

Adding team members to boards in Monday.com is one of the most critical steps in fostering collaboration and ensuring that all stakeholders have access to the information and tasks they need. This process allows you to seamlessly integrate your team into your workflow, enabling them to contribute, update, and track progress in real-time. Below is a comprehensive guide to adding new users to your boards, along with best practices and tips for effective team management.

1. Understanding the Basics of User Roles in Monday.com

Before adding new users to your boards, it's important to understand the types of roles available in Monday.com. This knowledge ensures that you assign the appropriate level of access based on the responsibilities of each user.

- **Admin Users:** Admins have full control over the workspace. They can invite new members, manage permissions, and access all boards within the workspace. This role is ideal for managers, project leads, or team coordinators.

- **Members:** Members have access to the boards they are invited to and can contribute by creating, editing, and managing tasks. This role suits team members actively working on tasks.

- **Guests:** Guests are external users who can only access specific shareable boards. This is ideal for clients, freelancers, or collaborators outside your organization.

- **Viewers:** Viewers have read-only access to boards. They can view updates and progress but cannot make any changes.

---

2. Step-by-Step Guide to Adding New Users

Here is a detailed walkthrough for adding new users to your boards:

Step 1: Navigate to Your Board

1. Open Monday.com and log in to your account.

2. Select the board where you want to invite team members.

   o   You can access your boards from the main dashboard or workspace menu.

Step 2: Click the "Invite" Button

1. On the top-right corner of the board, locate the **"Invite"** button.

2. Click the button to open the invitation menu.

Step 3: Enter Email Addresses

1. In the invitation menu, you'll see a field to input email addresses.

2. Enter the email addresses of the individuals you want to invite.

   o   You can add multiple email addresses at once by separating them with commas.

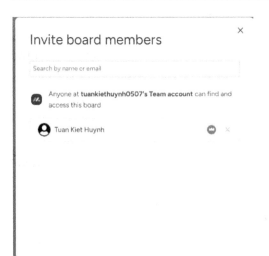

Step 4: Assign Roles

1. Choose the appropriate role for each user (Admin, Member, Guest, or Viewer).

   o   For internal team members, use the **Member** role.

   o   For external collaborators, select the **Guest** role.

2. Review the permissions associated with each role to ensure proper access.

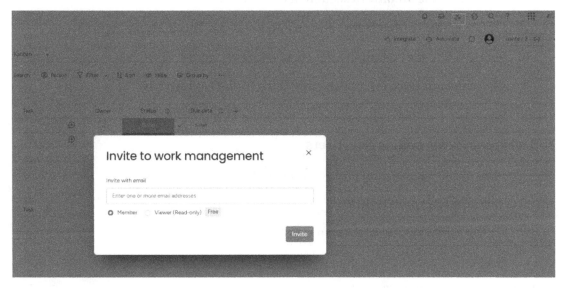

Step 5: Send Invitations

1. Click the **"Send Invitation"** button.

2. Monday.com will send an invitation email to each recipient with a link to join the board.

Step 6: Confirm Invitation Status

1. After sending invitations, you can check the invitation status.

    o Go to **Board Members** in the settings menu to see who has accepted their invitations.

2. If necessary, resend invitations to individuals who haven't joined yet.

3. Bulk Inviting Users

If you're adding a large group of users, Monday.com offers a bulk invitation feature to save time.

Using the Bulk Invite Feature

1. Open the workspace where you want to add multiple users.

2. Navigate to the **Members** section in the workspace menu.

3. Click the **"Invite Members"** button and select the **"Bulk Invite"** option.

4. Upload a CSV file containing the email addresses of the users you want to invite.

5. Assign default roles for all users and click **"Send Invitations."**

4. Best Practices for Adding New Users

To ensure a smooth onboarding process, follow these best practices:

Clarify Roles and Responsibilities

- Clearly communicate each team member's role within the board.

- Assign permissions that align with their tasks to avoid confusion or errors.

Onboard New Users with Training

- Provide an overview of how Monday.com works, especially if users are unfamiliar with the platform.

- Offer training sessions or share resources such as video tutorials or help articles.

Limit Guest Access

- Be cautious when inviting external collaborators. Use the **Guest** role and restrict their access to only the boards they need.

Regularly Review Permissions

- Periodically review user permissions to ensure they align with current project needs.

- Remove users who no longer need access to the board to maintain security and reduce clutter.

5. Troubleshooting Common Issues

Here are some common issues you may encounter while adding new users and how to resolve them:

Issue 1: Invitations Not Received

- **Solution:** Ask the invitee to check their spam folder for the invitation email. If they still can't find it, resend the invitation from the **Board Members** section.

Issue 2: User Unable to Join the Board

- **Solution:** Ensure the email address is entered correctly. Confirm that the recipient has created a Monday.com account.

Issue 3: Incorrect Role Assigned

- **Solution:** Go to the **Board Members** section and update the user's role. You can change their role from Member to Guest, Admin, or Viewer as needed.

Issue 4: Exceeding User Limits

- **Solution:** Check your subscription plan to see if it supports additional users. If necessary, upgrade your plan to accommodate more team members.

6. Benefits of Adding Users Strategically

Adding users effectively ensures better collaboration and productivity. Here are some of the benefits:

- **Improved Communication:** Team members can easily share updates, files, and comments directly on the board.

- **Centralized Information:** All stakeholders have access to the same data, reducing miscommunication and redundancy.

- **Accountability:** Assigning items to specific users ensures that everyone knows their responsibilities.

- **Real-Time Collaboration:** Multiple team members can work on the same board simultaneously, tracking progress and updates in real-time.

7. Conclusion

Adding new users to boards in Monday.com is a straightforward but powerful feature that sets the foundation for effective teamwork. By following the steps outlined in this guide, you can ensure that all team members are seamlessly integrated into your workflow. Remember to assign roles thoughtfully, provide adequate onboarding, and periodically review user permissions to maintain an organized and efficient workspace.

3.1.2 Setting Permissions and Roles

Setting permissions and roles is a critical aspect of managing your team effectively on Monday.com. It ensures that team members have the appropriate level of access to boards, data, and tools while maintaining security and privacy for sensitive information. This section provides a comprehensive guide on how to set permissions and roles in Monday.com, covering everything from understanding the types of roles available to best practices for managing permissions.

What Are Permissions and Roles in Monday.com?

Permissions and roles in Monday.com determine what team members can see and do within a workspace, board, or item. Properly setting permissions helps:

- Protect sensitive data by restricting access to authorized users.

- Avoid accidental changes to critical workflows or data.

- Clearly define responsibilities within your team.

Monday.com offers a flexible system for assigning roles and permissions, making it suitable for both small teams and large organizations.

Types of Roles in Monday.com

Monday.com categorizes roles into the following main types:

1. **Admin**:

    o Full access to all boards, workspaces, and account settings.

    o Can manage users, billing, and account-level integrations.

    o Ideal for team leaders, IT admins, or project managers who oversee multiple teams.

2. **Member**:

    o Can access shared boards and workspaces, contribute to tasks, and collaborate with others.

    o Permissions vary depending on the board or workspace settings.

    o Suitable for most team members who need to actively participate in workflows.

3. **Viewer**:

    o Read-only access to boards.

    o Cannot make changes, add items, or update statuses.

    o Perfect for stakeholders or clients who only need visibility into progress.

4. **Guest**:

- o   Limited access to shareable boards.

- o   Cannot view private boards or account-level settings.

- o   Ideal for external collaborators, such as contractors or clients.

How to Set Permissions and Roles in Monday.com

Step 1: Accessing the Permissions Settings

To set permissions, follow these steps:

1.   Open the board or workspace where you want to set permissions.

2.   Click the **"Share"** button or the **"Board Settings"** menu (three dots in the top-right corner).

3.   Navigate to the **"Permissions"** tab to manage roles and access levels.

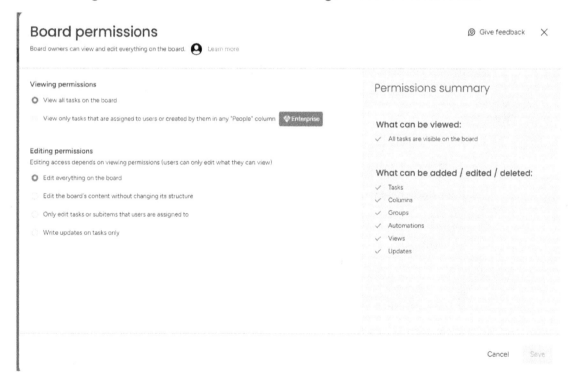

Step 2: Assigning Roles

You can assign roles when inviting new users or by editing the roles of existing members.

For New Users:

1. Click the **"Invite"** button on the board or workspace.

2. Enter the email addresses of the people you want to invite.

3. Select their role (Admin, Member, Viewer, or Guest) from the dropdown menu.

4. Customize their permissions if necessary.

5. Click **"Send Invitation"**.

For Existing Users:

1. Open the board or workspace settings.

2. Find the user list under the **"Members"** section.

3. Locate the user whose role you want to change.

4. Click the dropdown menu next to their name and select their new role.

Step 3: Configuring Permissions on Boards

Monday.com allows you to configure board-specific permissions for finer control.

1. **Private Boards**:

   o Only invited users can access the board.

   o Perfect for sensitive projects or confidential data.

2. **Shareable Boards**:

   o Accessible to both internal members and external guests.

   o Ideal for projects involving clients or external collaborators.

3. **Main Boards**:

   o Visible to all team members in the workspace.

   o Best for general updates or team-wide projects.

To adjust permissions:

- Open the board settings.

- Under the **"Permissions"** tab, set who can:

    o Edit content (items, statuses, and columns).

    o Invite new users.

    o Change board settings.

Best Practices for Setting Permissions and Roles

1. **Adopt the Principle of Least Privilege**:

    o Assign the minimum level of access required for each user to perform their role.

    o For example, assign Viewer roles to clients and Member roles to team members.

2. **Regularly Review Permissions**:

    o Periodically check user roles and permissions to ensure they align with your team's needs.

    o Remove access for users who no longer need it.

3. **Use Private Boards for Sensitive Data**:

    o Restrict access to critical projects by using private boards and limiting invitations.

4. **Leverage Viewer Roles for Oversight**:

    o Use Viewer roles to give stakeholders visibility without risking accidental edits.

5. **Set Clear Ownership**:

    o Assign Admin roles sparingly to avoid conflicts or unintended changes to settings.

    o Designate one or two people as board or workspace owners to maintain control.

Common Scenarios for Permissions Management

1. **Onboarding New Team Members**:
   - When adding new hires, assign them Member roles and give access only to relevant boards.
   - Create a "Welcome" board to provide resources and onboarding materials.

2. **Collaborating with External Partners**:
   - Use Guest roles to limit access to specific shareable boards.
   - Avoid giving Admin or Member roles to external collaborators.

3. **Managing Large Teams**:
   - Break down teams into smaller groups with their own private boards.
   - Use Main Boards for team-wide announcements and updates.

4. **Restricting Critical Boards**:
   - For financial or legal boards, set permissions so only Admins can edit data.
   - Use automation to notify team members about changes instead of granting full access.

Troubleshooting Permissions Issues

1. **User Cannot Access a Board**:
   - Check if the user is added to the board or workspace.
   - Verify their role and adjust if necessary.

2. **User Cannot Make Changes**:
   - Ensure the board permissions allow them to edit content.
   - Verify they are not assigned a Viewer role.

3. **External Guest Cannot See Items**:

    o   Confirm the board is shareable and the guest has been properly invited.

Conclusion

Setting permissions and roles effectively in Monday.com is essential for secure and efficient collaboration. By understanding the different roles available and configuring permissions based on your team's needs, you can ensure that everyone has the appropriate level of access. Always review and update permissions regularly to maintain control over your workflows and prevent unauthorized access.

3.2 Communication Tools in Monday.com

3.2.1 Comments and Updates on Items

Effective communication is the backbone of any successful team collaboration, and Monday.com provides a variety of tools to keep team members informed, engaged, and aligned. One of the most powerful features in Monday.com is the ability to leave **comments and updates** on individual items. This feature acts as a central communication hub for each task or project, ensuring that all relevant information is easily accessible. In this section, we'll explore the **Comments and Updates** functionality in detail, including how to use it, best practices, and its benefits for team collaboration.

What Are Comments and Updates?

In Monday.com, every item (or task) has an **Updates Section** where team members can add comments, ask questions, and share information. This feature functions as a **real-time discussion thread** attached directly to the task, eliminating the need for scattered email threads or external chat tools.

Key highlights of the Comments and Updates feature:

- **Centralized Communication**: All discussions about an item stay in one place, making it easy to refer back to previous conversations.

- **Real-Time Notifications**: Team members are notified immediately when someone posts a comment or update, keeping everyone in the loop.

- **Rich Media Support**: Updates can include text, images, files, and even embedded links for enhanced communication.

How to Add Comments and Updates

Adding a comment or update to an item is simple and intuitive:

1. **Accessing the Updates Section**:
   - Navigate to the item you want to comment on.

o Click on the **speech bubble icon** or the "Updates" tab in the item view. This will open the Updates Section for that specific item.

2. **Writing a Comment**:

o Type your message into the text box provided. Use the formatting toolbar to bold important text, add bullet points, or insert links.

o Press **Enter** to post your comment or click the **Post** button.

3. **Adding Files or Media**:

o To attach a file, click the **attachment icon** (usually a paperclip symbol) and upload your file.

o You can also drag and drop files directly into the Updates Section.

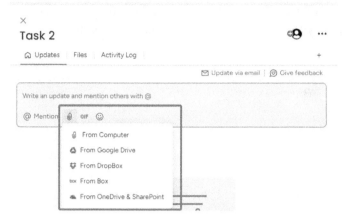

4. **Using Emojis**:

   o Add emojis to your comment by clicking on the **smiley face icon** or typing a colon : followed by the emoji name (e.g., :smile:). Emojis can help convey tone and make communication more engaging.

5. **Tagging Team Members**:

o   Use the **@mention feature** to tag specific team members (e.g., @John). This ensures the tagged person receives a notification and knows the comment is directed at them.

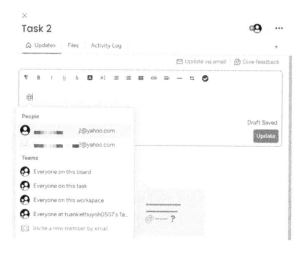

Best Practices for Comments and Updates

To maximize the effectiveness of the Comments and Updates feature, consider the following best practices:

1. Be Clear and Concise

- Avoid lengthy messages that may overwhelm the recipient. Use short, clear sentences to communicate your thoughts.

- If the update is complex, consider breaking it into sections or using bullet points for better readability.

2. Use Tags to Engage the Right People

- Always tag the relevant team members who need to see or act on your comment.

- Avoid tagging too many people unnecessarily, as this may lead to confusion or notification fatigue.

3. Keep Conversations Focused on the Item

- Use the Updates Section only for discussions directly related to the item. For broader conversations, consider using team-level communication tools like Monday.com's dashboards or email.

4. Respond Promptly

- Aim to respond to updates in a timely manner to keep tasks moving forward. Delayed responses can slow down project progress.

5. Avoid Overcommunication

- While it's important to keep everyone informed, avoid excessive updates that may clutter the Updates Section. Instead, consolidate information into fewer, more comprehensive posts.

Advanced Features in the Updates Section

1. Pinning Important Updates

Monday.com allows you to pin specific updates to the top of the Updates Section. This feature ensures that critical information (e.g., task instructions or key decisions) is always visible.

How to Pin an Update:

- Locate the update you want to pin.

- Click the **three-dot menu** next to the update and select **"Pin to Top"**.

2. Adding Replies to Specific Comments

If someone has posted a comment, you can reply directly to it, creating a nested conversation. This helps keep discussions organized and ensures that responses are clearly linked to the original comment.

How to Reply:

- Hover over the comment you want to reply to.

- Click the **"Reply"** button that appears below the comment.

- Type your response and press **Enter** to post it.

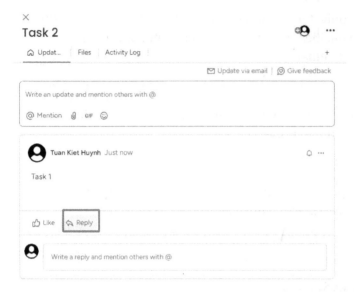

3. Editing or Deleting Comments

Made a mistake in your comment? You can edit or delete it to ensure accuracy.

How to Edit or Delete a Comment:

- Hover over your comment and click the **three-dot menu**.

- Choose **"Edit"** to modify the comment or **"Delete"** to remove it.

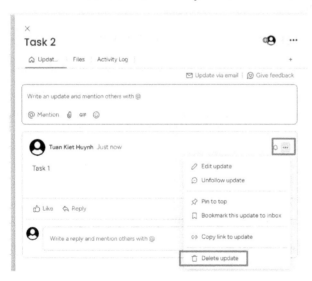

4. Search Functionality

The Updates Section includes a search feature that allows you to find specific comments quickly. This is especially useful for large teams with lengthy discussions.

How to Search Updates:

- Open the Updates Section and look for the **search bar**.

- Enter keywords or phrases to locate the relevant comment or update.

Benefits of Using Comments and Updates

1. Enhanced Transparency

- All team members have access to the same information, reducing miscommunication and misunderstandings.

2. Improved Accountability

- With @mentions and timestamped updates, it's easy to track who is responsible for specific actions or decisions.

3. Time-Saving

- The centralized Updates Section eliminates the need for back-and-forth emails or searching for information in multiple places.

4. Better Context for Decision-Making

- Updates provide a historical record of all discussions related to a task, enabling better decision-making based on past conversations.

Real-Life Examples of Using Comments and Updates

Example 1: Clarifying Task Instructions

Scenario: A team member is unsure about the details of a task.
Solution: Another team member posts an update clarifying the instructions and attaches relevant documents.

Example 2: Requesting Status Updates

Scenario: A manager needs an update on a delayed task.
Solution: The manager comments on the task, tagging the responsible person using @mention.

Example 3: Sharing Feedback

Scenario: A designer submits a draft of a new logo.
Solution: The team provides feedback in the Updates Section, attaching annotated versions of the design for reference.

Conclusion

The Comments and Updates feature in Monday.com is a powerful tool for fostering effective communication and collaboration. By centralizing all task-related discussions in one place, it eliminates the need for external communication channels and ensures that everyone stays aligned. By following best practices and leveraging advanced features, teams can maximize the value of this functionality, improving both productivity and efficiency.

3.2.2 Using @Mentions Effectively

Communication is the backbone of collaboration, and Monday.com's **@mentions** feature is a powerful tool to streamline team communication. This feature allows you to directly notify specific team members, groups, or entire boards about updates, tasks, or issues that require attention. In this section, we'll dive deep into how to use @mentions effectively to improve team engagement, ensure accountability, and enhance overall efficiency.

What Are @Mentions in Monday.com?

@Mentions are a built-in communication tool in Monday.com that allows users to tag individuals, teams, or groups in item updates, comments, and discussions. When someone is mentioned, they receive a notification that draws their attention to the specific item or comment where they've been tagged. This eliminates the need for lengthy emails or back-and-forth messages across other platforms, centralizing communication within Monday.com.

Why Use @Mentions?

- **Direct Communication:** Notify the right person or team about a specific task or issue.

- **Improved Accountability:** Tagging ensures that tasks and responsibilities are assigned clearly.

- **Time-Saving:** Cut down on unnecessary meetings or email chains by directly addressing team members.

- **Centralized Context:** Keep all communications tied to a specific item or project in one place.

How to Use @Mentions

1. Tagging Individuals

To tag an individual team member in Monday.com:

1. Navigate to the **Updates section** of any item or board.

2. In the text box, type the **@ symbol** followed by the person's name (e.g., @John Doe).

3. Select the user from the dropdown list that appears.

4. Finish your message and hit **Post**.

Once tagged, the individual will receive a notification in their inbox. They can click the notification to jump directly to the update, ensuring they see the relevant context immediately.

Example Use Case:

- When a task is delayed, you can tag the person responsible: *"@Sarah, can you provide an update on the status of the client proposal?"*

2. Tagging Teams or Groups

If you want to notify an entire team or group instead of an individual:

1. Ensure that your team or group is already set up in Monday.com.

2. In the text box, type the **@ symbol** followed by the team's name (e.g., @Marketing Team).

3. Select the team from the dropdown.

4. Post your update.

Everyone in the team will receive the notification, ensuring that critical information reaches all relevant members.

Example Use Case:

- To inform the marketing team about an update: *"@Marketing Team, please review the campaign assets and provide feedback by Friday."*

3. Tagging Everyone on a Board

If your message or update is relevant to all team members associated with a specific board:

1. Type **@everyone** in the text box.

2. Post your update.

This tags every person with access to the board, making it ideal for announcements or important updates.

Example Use Case:

- To notify all board members of a deadline extension: *"@everyone, the project deadline has been extended to next Wednesday. Please adjust your tasks accordingly."*

Best Practices for Using @Mentions

While @mentions are highly effective, they can be overused or misused, leading to notification fatigue. Follow these best practices to ensure optimal results:

1. Be Specific with Your Mentions

- Tag only those who need to be involved in the conversation or task. Avoid using @everyone unnecessarily, as it can overwhelm team members with irrelevant notifications.

2. Provide Context

- When tagging someone, always include enough information for them to understand the purpose of the mention. For example, instead of just saying, *"@John, please check this,"* provide details: *"@John, can you review the attached report for accuracy before the client meeting?"*

3. Combine @Mentions with Deadlines

- Use @mentions to assign clear deadlines along with tasks. For instance: *"@Emily, please finalize the design draft by EOD Friday."*

4. Follow Up When Necessary

- If someone doesn't respond to an @mention within a reasonable time frame, follow up with a polite reminder. Monday.com's notification settings ensure they see the initial message, but follow-ups can reinforce urgency if needed.

Advanced Tips for Using @Mentions

1. Use @Mentions in Automations

Monday.com allows you to incorporate @mentions into automation recipes. For example:

- Create an automation that sends an update with an @mention when a task status changes to "Stuck."
  Automation Example: "When status changes to Stuck, notify @Manager."

2. Leverage the Inbox Feature

The **Inbox** in Monday.com consolidates all @mentions and notifications in one place. Encourage team members to regularly check their inbox to avoid missing critical updates.

3. Combine @Mentions with File Attachments

When tagging someone, attach relevant files to the update to provide all necessary resources. This saves time and ensures the recipient has everything they need.

Example:
"@Alex, please review the attached presentation and suggest edits."

Common Challenges and Solutions

1. Overuse of @Mentions

Challenge: Excessive tagging can lead to notification fatigue.
Solution: Use @mentions judiciously and ensure the message is relevant to the tagged individual.

2. Missed Notifications

Challenge: Team members might overlook notifications in busy periods.
Solution: Encourage team members to enable email or mobile push notifications for critical updates.

3. Confusion in Large Teams

Challenge: In large teams, tagging the wrong person can happen.
Solution: Double-check the dropdown list when tagging to ensure you select the correct individual or team.

Real-Life Scenarios for Effective @Mentions

1. **Task Handoffs:**
   "@David, I've completed the research phase. Can you take over the analysis?"

2. **Requesting Feedback:**
   "@Laura, can you review this draft and share your thoughts?"

3. **Updating Stakeholders:**
   "@Management Team, the project is 80% complete, and we're on track for the deadline."

4. **Resolving Issues:**
   "@IT Support, there seems to be a bug in the system affecting our board. Can you check?"

Conclusion

@Mentions in Monday.com are more than just a notification tool; they're an integral part of building a collaborative and organized team environment. By mastering this feature, you can improve communication, ensure accountability, and keep all team members aligned on shared goals.

In the next section, we'll explore **File Sharing and Attachments**, diving into how to securely share and manage files within Monday.com for seamless collaboration.

3.2.3 File Sharing and Attachments

Efficient communication and seamless collaboration are vital to any team's success. In Monday.com, the ability to share files and attach documents directly to items, updates, and boards simplifies the process of keeping everyone informed and on the same page. This section will guide you through how to use file-sharing and attachment features effectively to enhance teamwork and streamline project management.

Understanding the Importance of File Sharing in Monday.com

File sharing in Monday.com ensures that critical documents, resources, and references are easily accessible to team members without requiring external tools or platforms. Whether it's a project plan, a marketing asset, or a contract draft, files can be attached directly to relevant items, making them easily searchable and readily available whenever needed.

Key Features of File Sharing and Attachments in Monday.com

- **Centralized Document Management:** Store all your files in one location directly tied to the task, project, or team.

- **Version Control:** Keep updated files without the confusion of managing multiple versions.

- **Collaboration:** Allow team members to comment on, discuss, and collaborate around shared files in real-time.

- **Seamless Integration:** Connect external file storage solutions like Google Drive, Dropbox, or OneDrive to manage and attach files.

How to Attach Files in Monday.com

Step 1: Adding Files to an Item

Attaching a file to an item ensures the relevant document is tied to a specific task or deliverable.

1. Open the **board** and locate the **item** you want to attach a file to.

2. Click on the item to open its **item details** pane.

3. In the "Updates" section, locate the paperclip icon labeled **Attach Files**.

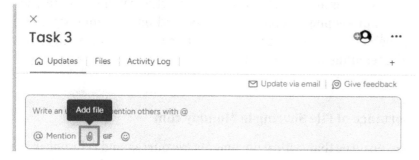

4. Choose one of the following file attachment methods:

   o **Upload from Your Computer:** Select a file directly from your device.

   o **Add from Cloud Services:** Connect your Google Drive, Dropbox, or OneDrive accounts to upload files from these services.

   o **Link to a URL:** Add a link to an online document or file for quick access.

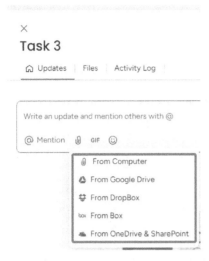

5. Once attached, the file will appear in the "Files" section of the item for all team members to view and download.

Step 2: Adding Files to Updates

Updates are an excellent way to communicate progress, add context, or provide instructions alongside attachments.

1. Open the item you're working on.

2. Navigate to the **Updates** tab.

3. Write your update or comment in the text box, and click the **Attach Files** option below the box.

4. Select the file to upload and hit **Post Update**.

Step 3: Adding Files to a Board

If a file applies to the entire board rather than a specific item, it can be added to the board itself.

1. Navigate to the board where you want to add the file.

2. Click on the **Board Description** section at the top of the board.

3. Use the attachment button to upload a file or link it from a cloud storage service.

4. The file will now be accessible to anyone who views the board.

Managing Attachments

Viewing and Downloading Files

- To view a file, simply click on its name in the **Files** section of an item or update.

- To download, hover over the file name, and click the **Download** button that appears.

Organizing Files

Files can be organized within the **Files View**, which consolidates all attachments on a board into a single, searchable location:

1. Add the **Files View** by clicking the **+ Add View** button at the top of the board.

2. Select "Files" from the view options.

3. Browse, filter, and manage all files associated with the board.

Replacing and Updating Files

If you need to update a file:

1. Delete the outdated version from the "Files" section of the relevant item.

2. Upload the new version as described in the steps above.

Collaborating on Shared Files

Adding Comments to Files

Files attached to updates can be discussed through the **comment feature** in Monday.com.

1. Open the update containing the attached file.

2. Use the **Comment** section to ask questions, provide feedback, or discuss details about the file.

Using @Mentions in File Discussions

Tagging team members ensures they're notified about file-related discussions. For example:

- "Hey @John, can you confirm the data in this Excel file is correct?"

Real-Time Collaboration via Cloud Integrations

For files stored on Google Drive, OneDrive, or Dropbox, team members can collaborate in real-time without leaving Monday.com. Simply link the file, and changes made in the cloud service will reflect immediately.

Best Practices for File Sharing in Monday.com

1. **Label Files Clearly:** Use consistent naming conventions to ensure files are easy to find (e.g., "Marketing_Plan_Q1_2025.pdf").

2. **Restrict File Access Wisely:** Set permissions to prevent sensitive files from being accessed by unauthorized team members.

3. **Use Updates for Context:** Always provide a brief explanation when attaching files so team members understand their purpose.

4. **Organize Regularly:** Use the Files View to periodically review and clean up outdated or unnecessary attachments.

5. **Take Advantage of Integrations:** Utilize cloud storage platforms to keep files synced and accessible.

Common Issues and Troubleshooting

1. **Problem: File Won't Upload**

   o   Ensure the file size doesn't exceed the maximum limit.

   o   Check your internet connection and retry.

   o   Use a supported file format (e.g., PDF, JPG, DOCX).

2. **Problem: Unable to Access Cloud Files**

   o   Verify that your cloud account is properly integrated.

   o   Check permissions on the cloud file itself.

3. **Problem: File Attachments Not Displaying**

- o Refresh the browser or app.

- o Ensure you have the necessary permissions to view files on the board.

Conclusion

File sharing and attachments in Monday.com are powerful tools that simplify teamwork by keeping all documents organized, accessible, and connected to the tasks they support. By mastering these features, your team can reduce miscommunication, eliminate versioning chaos, and ensure everyone has access to the information they need when they need it. Take full advantage of Monday.com's file-sharing capabilities to boost productivity and achieve better results.

3.3 Notifications and Alerts

3.3.1 Setting Notification Preferences

Notifications are an essential aspect of using Monday.com effectively. They ensure that team members stay informed about updates, changes, and tasks without overwhelming their inboxes. In this section, we'll guide you step-by-step on how to set up and customize notification preferences to suit your workflow and keep your team productive.

1. Understanding Monday.com Notifications

Before customizing your notification settings, it's important to understand the types of notifications that Monday.com offers:

- **Bell Notifications**: These are in-app notifications that appear under the bell icon on the Monday.com interface. They alert users to changes or updates related to boards, items, and comments.

- **Email Notifications**: These are notifications sent directly to your email inbox for major updates, mentions, or reminders.

- **Mobile Push Notifications**: If you have the Monday.com app installed on your phone, you can receive real-time updates via push notifications.

Each type of notification serves a specific purpose, and you can choose how and when to receive them based on your needs.

2. Accessing Notification Settings

To customize your notification preferences, follow these steps:

1. **Log In to Your Account**: Open Monday.com in your web browser or mobile app and log in to your account.

2. **Go to Your Profile**: Click on your profile picture or initials located in the bottom-left corner of the interface.

3. **Open Settings**: From the dropdown menu, select **"My Profile"**, then click on the **"Notifications"** tab.

4. **Explore Notification Options**: You'll see different categories for notifications, such as **bell notifications**, **email notifications**, and **mobile push notifications**.

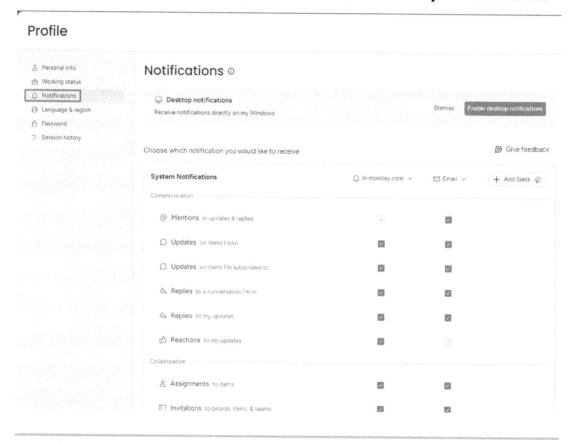

3. Customizing Bell Notifications

Bell notifications are helpful for real-time updates when you are actively using Monday.com. Here's how you can customize them:

- **Enable or Disable Specific Notifications**:
  Under the bell notifications settings, you can enable or disable updates for:

  o New comments or updates on items you're subscribed to.

  o Changes in the status of items assigned to you.

o   Mentions of your name in comments or updates.

- **Adjust Notification Timing**:
  If you find the notifications overwhelming, you can limit them to specific times. For example, you may only want to receive updates during work hours.

- **Set Board-Specific Notifications**:
  You can customize notifications for individual boards by navigating to the board's settings:

0.   Open the board you want to adjust.

1.   Click on the three-dot menu in the upper-right corner.

2.   Select **"Board Notifications"** and choose which events you want to be notified about.

4. Customizing Email Notifications

Email notifications are perfect for staying informed when you're not actively using Monday.com. To customize your email preferences:

- **Daily Digest Emails**:
  Monday.com can send a daily summary of activity across your boards. This option is ideal if you don't want to be inundated with individual email updates throughout the day.

- **Instant Email Updates**:
  Enable this option to receive immediate updates for:

  o   New assignments.

  o   Status changes on tasks you're following.

  o   Direct mentions in comments.

- **Unsubscribing from Specific Boards**:
  If you're receiving too many emails from a specific board, you can unsubscribe from its email notifications by:

0.   Navigating to the board.

1.   Clicking the three-dot menu in the top-right corner.

2.   Selecting **"Unsubscribe from Emails"**.

---

5. Setting Mobile Push Notifications

For on-the-go updates, push notifications via the Monday.com mobile app are invaluable. To customize these:

- **Enable Push Notifications**:
    - Open the Monday.com app on your phone.
    - Go to **Settings** and tap **"Notifications"**.
    - Toggle on push notifications for updates you want to receive.

- **Choose Notification Types**:
  You can select specific types of updates to receive, such as:
    - Task assignments.
    - Comments or mentions.
    - Deadlines approaching.

- **Set Do Not Disturb Times**:
  To prevent interruptions outside work hours, set a "Do Not Disturb" schedule within the app.

---

6. Fine-Tuning Notification Preferences for Teams

If you're managing a team, it's crucial to ensure everyone's notification settings align with your workflow. Here are some best practices:

- **Encourage Use of Mentions**: Train your team to use @mentions strategically to reduce unnecessary notifications. For example, only mention teammates when their immediate input or action is required.

- **Set Default Notifications for New Members**: As a board owner, you can establish default notification settings for new members joining your boards. This ensures consistency across the team.

- **Regularly Review Notification Settings**: Periodically review your team's notification preferences to ensure they are receiving critical updates without being overwhelmed.

7. Managing Notification Overload

While notifications are helpful, too many can lead to "notification fatigue." Here's how to avoid it:

- **Limit Subscriptions**: Only subscribe to boards, items, or groups that are directly relevant to your work.

- **Use Automations to Reduce Manual Notifications**: Set up automations to handle routine updates, such as notifying a team when a task's status changes.

- **Rely on Dashboards for Overviews**: Instead of receiving notifications for every small change, use dashboards to get a comprehensive view of your team's progress.

8. Testing and Adjusting Your Settings

Once you've customized your notification preferences, spend a week testing them out. Observe whether you're staying informed without feeling overwhelmed. Adjust your settings as necessary.

Conclusion

Customizing your notification preferences in Monday.com is a simple yet powerful way to stay organized and focused. By understanding the types of notifications available and tailoring them to your workflow, you can ensure that you and your team remain informed about critical updates without unnecessary distractions. Regularly reviewing and fine-tuning these settings will help you maintain an optimal balance between staying connected and minimizing interruptions.

3.3.2 Managing Alerts for Team Activity

Effective communication is a cornerstone of successful team collaboration. One of the most powerful features of Monday.com is its ability to notify team members in real-time about updates, changes, or requests within the platform. Alerts and notifications ensure that everyone stays on the same page, no matter how large or small the team may be.

Monday.com offers a robust notification system, providing users with a wide range of customizable alerts that can be tailored to meet specific needs and preferences. In this section, we will explore how to manage and customize alerts for team activity effectively, ensuring that you never miss important updates and stay informed about what's happening within your boards.

Why Notifications Matter in Monday.com

Before diving into how to manage alerts, let's first understand why they are essential for team collaboration. Notifications serve several important purposes, including:

- **Keeping Teams Informed:** In large teams or complex projects, it's easy for things to get lost in the shuffle. Notifications help everyone stay up to date on task statuses, comments, and changes.

- **Improving Response Times:** Alerts inform users when actions are required on their tasks, allowing for faster decision-making and more efficient workflows.

- **Reducing the Risk of Missed Deadlines:** By setting up timely reminders and alerts, you can ensure that tasks stay on track and deadlines are met.

- **Enhancing Accountability:** Notifications help ensure that team members are aware of their responsibilities and are accountable for actions they need to take.

Setting Up Team Activity Alerts

To manage alerts for team activity, the first step is ensuring that you have properly set up notifications in Monday.com. The platform offers multiple ways to control how and when you receive alerts. Here's how to begin:

Step 1: Accessing Notification Settings

In Monday.com, the notification settings are located in the profile settings. Follow these steps to access and modify them:

1. **Go to Your Profile:** Click on your avatar or profile picture in the bottom left corner of the Monday.com interface.

2. **Select 'Notification Settings':** From the drop-down menu, click on **'Notification Settings'**.

3. **Adjust Notification Preferences:** Here, you can control how and when you receive alerts. Monday.com offers options to receive notifications for the following:

   o   Updates on items you're following

   o   Changes in status, due dates, or other relevant fields

   o   Comments, mentions, or replies on tasks you're part of

   o   Board or workspace-wide activity

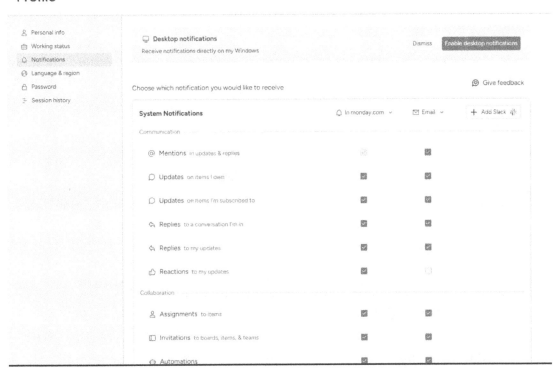

Step 2: Choosing How You Want to Be Notified

Monday.com offers various channels for notifications. These channels can be customized to suit your team's preferences:

1. **Email Notifications:** Receive an email notification for specific activities, such as task updates or status changes. This is useful for more formal communication.

2. **In-App Notifications:** Notifications that appear directly within the platform, often in the top right corner of the screen. This is great for real-time collaboration and keeping track of activity while using Monday.com.

3. **Mobile Push Notifications:** Ideal for team members who are always on the go. These alerts push to your mobile device, ensuring that team activity doesn't slip under the radar.

You can also choose how often you want to be notified, whether it's instant, daily, or weekly summaries.

Customizing Alerts for Specific Team Activity

To tailor alerts for team activity in a way that makes the most sense for your workflow, Monday.com offers fine-tuned customization. Here's how to manage specific team alerts for various activities:

1. Activity on Items You're Following

In Monday.com, you can follow specific items (tasks, projects, or boards) to receive alerts whenever something changes. To customize these alerts:

- **Following an Item:** When you follow an item, you'll get notifications about updates, comments, status changes, and more. To follow an item:

    1. Click on the item.

    2. Toggle the **'Follow'** button located at the top of the item details.

    3. Select whether you want notifications for all updates or only specific changes.

- **Customizing Updates:** Once you follow an item, go into your notification settings and select whether you want alerts for:

    o **Status Changes**

- **Due Date Updates**

- **Assignee Changes**

- **Column Changes** (e.g., budget updates, task priority changes)

These notifications are particularly useful in project management where you need to stay updated on key deliverables assigned to different team members.

2. Task Assignment and Reassignment Alerts

When a task is assigned or reassigned to you, you want to be notified immediately. This ensures that there's no ambiguity around ownership of tasks.

To customize task assignment alerts:

1. Go to **'Notification Settings'**.

2. Ensure **'Assigned to Me'** notifications are turned on.

3. Select whether you prefer immediate notifications via email or in-app alerts.

This is especially useful for managers who want to track task allocation and ensure that team members are always informed about their responsibilities.

3. Alerting for Board-Wide or Workspace-Wide Changes

Sometimes, board-level changes require notifications to keep everyone in the loop. For example, a manager might want to know if a deadline for a team project is approaching or if a major update is posted in the shared workspace.

- **Managing Board Notifications:**

    1. Access your board settings by clicking on the three-dot menu on the board's upper-right corner.

    2. Click on **'Notification Settings'**.

    3. Choose who should receive alerts for changes such as status updates, due date adjustments, or comments.

These notifications help keep the team aligned on major project milestones or new instructions from leadership.

Managing Notification Overload

While notifications are extremely valuable, it's easy to get overwhelmed by them, especially when you're working on large teams or multiple projects. Managing notification overload is a common challenge in Monday.com, but it's easy to address with the right settings.

1. Adjusting Frequency and Priority

You don't need to receive every notification for every change. You can prioritize certain types of alerts over others:

- **High-Priority Alerts:** Set up your profile to receive only critical alerts, such as task assignments, due dates, or comments requiring your immediate attention.

- **Daily or Weekly Summaries:** Opt for daily or weekly email summaries instead of real-time alerts for less urgent items.

- **Muted Items or Boards:** If a project is in a stable phase with minimal updates, consider muting notifications for less essential changes, such as minor updates or non-urgent comments.

2. Setting Silent Hours

To avoid disruption, you can set "silent hours" during which you won't receive notifications. This can be useful to respect personal time or after-hours work schedules. You can adjust this setting in the **'Notification Settings'** section.

3. Using the Do Not Disturb Mode

When you need to focus or participate in a meeting, use the **Do Not Disturb** mode. This feature temporarily pauses notifications for a set period of time.

Best Practices for Managing Alerts for Team Activity

To make sure your team is using Monday.com's notification system effectively, here are some best practices:

1. **Set Clear Guidelines for Notifications**: Ensure your team knows what types of notifications are essential. For instance, developers might need notifications for task status changes, while project managers might prioritize updates on deadlines.

2. **Encourage Consistent Use of Comments and @Mentions**: For clarity, encourage your team to use @mentions when tagging specific individuals in comments or updates. This ensures that team members only receive alerts when they are directly involved.

3. **Regularly Review Notification Settings**: As teams evolve, so do communication needs. Periodically review and adjust notification settings based on your current workflow and team dynamics.

4. **Use Dashboards to Track Team Activity**: For project managers, using Monday.com's dashboard view helps track team activity without needing to rely solely on email alerts. Dashboards give a comprehensive overview of the status of various tasks and projects.

5. **Training Team Members**: Make sure your team knows how to adjust their own notification settings to reduce the risk of missed information while preventing notification overload.

Conclusion

Managing alerts for team activity within Monday.com is a powerful tool to keep projects on track and ensure that communication remains effective and timely. By customizing your notification settings, you can ensure that you and your team receive the right alerts, without overwhelming anyone with unnecessary information. With a well-structured notification system, your team can stay focused, collaborate seamlessly, and make better decisions faster.

CHAPTER IV
Automations and Integrations

4.1 Introduction to Automations

4.1.1 What are Automations?

Automations are one of the most powerful features in Monday.com, designed to streamline workflows, reduce repetitive tasks, and enhance productivity by letting the platform handle routine processes for you. In this section, we'll explore what automations are, why they're essential, and how they can transform the way you and your team work.

Understanding Automations

At its core, an automation is a predefined rule or workflow that triggers a specific action when certain conditions are met. In Monday.com, automations allow users to program the platform to execute tasks automatically, saving time and reducing human error.

For example:

- When a task's status changes to "Done," automatically notify the manager.

- If a due date is approaching, send a reminder email to the task owner.

- When a new item is created, assign it to a specific team member.

These automations ensure that no critical steps are overlooked, and they keep your team aligned without the need for constant manual intervention.

The Key Components of an Automation

Automations in Monday.com are built using a simple logic that can be customized to fit your unique needs. Each automation consists of three primary components:

1. **Trigger**: The event that initiates the automation.
   Examples:

   - A status changes (e.g., "In Progress" to "Completed").

   - An item is created.

   - A due date arrives.

2. **Condition (Optional)**: A specific rule or filter that determines when the trigger should cause an action.
   Examples:

   - Only apply the automation to items in a specific group or column.

   - Only notify team members if the item priority is "High."

3. **Action**: What the automation does once the trigger and condition are met.
   Examples:

   - Send an email or notification.

   - Move an item to another group.

   - Change the status of a task.

Why Automations Are Essential

Automations are not just a convenience—they are a necessity for teams looking to scale their operations efficiently. Here are some of the primary benefits of using automations in Monday.com:

1. **Time-Saving**: By automating repetitive tasks like status updates, reminders, or assignments, your team can focus on higher-value activities instead of manual admin work.

2. **Error Reduction**: Human errors, like forgetting to send reminders or missing deadlines, can be avoided. Automations ensure consistency and accuracy in task management.

3. **Improved Collaboration**: Automations keep everyone informed. For example, notifying relevant team members when a task's status changes ensures smooth communication.

4. **Increased Productivity**: Teams can achieve more in less time by eliminating manual processes and allowing the platform to take care of routine tasks.

5. **Customization**: With Monday.com's flexible automation builder, workflows can be tailored to match the unique requirements of your team or project.

Common Use Cases for Automations

To better understand the power of automations, let's look at some common scenarios where automations are highly effective:

1. **Task Management**:

    o   Automatically assign tasks to team members when a new item is created.

    o   Move completed tasks to an "Archived" group to declutter your board.

2. **Deadlines and Reminders**:

    o   Send reminders to team members when a deadline is approaching.

    o   Notify stakeholders if a task is overdue.

3. **Project Progress**:

    o   Update the project status when all sub-tasks are marked as complete.

    o   Automatically create follow-up tasks once a milestone is reached.

4. **Cross-Team Collaboration**:

    o   Notify the sales team when the marketing team updates the status of a campaign.

    o   Automatically create a new item in a development board when a customer feedback item is submitted.

The Automation Center in Monday.com

Monday.com provides a user-friendly **Automation Center**, where you can explore, create, and manage automations for your boards.

Navigating the Automation Center:

1. Go to your board and click on the "Automations" button at the top of the screen.

2. In the Automation Center, you'll find a variety of pre-made templates categorized by use case, such as notifications, deadlines, and task updates.

3. Use the search bar to find a specific type of automation or browse through categories to discover new possibilities.

Types of Automations in Monday.com

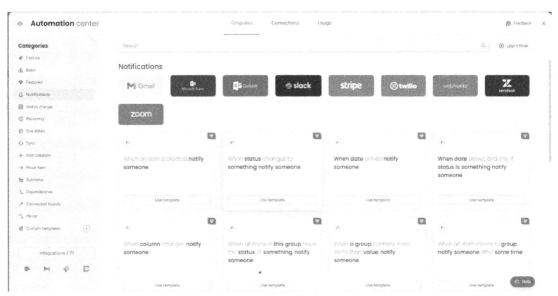

Monday.com offers a wide range of automation templates to suit different needs. Some popular categories include:

1. **Status Change Automations**:

   o When a status changes to a specific value, perform an action.
     Example: "When status changes to Done, move item to Completed group."

2. **Date-Based Automations**:

   o Trigger actions based on dates.
     Example: "When the due date arrives, send a reminder to the task owner."

3. **Item Creation Automations**:

- o Trigger actions when a new item is added to a board.
  Example: "When an item is created, assign it to John."

4. **Recurring Automations**:

- o Perform actions on a regular schedule.
  Example: "Every Monday, create a new weekly planning task."

5. **Custom Automations**:

- o Build complex workflows using custom triggers, conditions, and actions.

Building Your First Automation

To help you get started, let's walk through an example of creating a simple automation:

Scenario: You want to automatically notify a team member when a task's status changes to "Stuck."

1. **Go to the Automation Center**: Click on the "Automations" button on your board.

2. **Choose a Template**: Look for a template like "When status changes, notify someone."

3. **Customize the Automation**:

   - o Set the trigger: "When status changes to Stuck."

   - o Set the action: "Notify [team member's name] with the message: 'Task is stuck. Please review.'"

4. **Save and Activate**: Click "Save" to activate your automation.

Best Practices for Using Automations

1. **Start Simple**: Begin with basic automations before exploring more complex workflows.

2. **Test Your Automations**: Run a few test cases to ensure the automation behaves as expected.

3. **Keep Automations Organized**: Name your automations clearly so they are easy to identify and manage.

4. **Monitor and Optimize**: Regularly review your automations to ensure they are still relevant and efficient.

Conclusion

Automations are a game-changer in Monday.com, allowing teams to focus on meaningful work by handling repetitive tasks automatically. By understanding the basic structure of automations, exploring templates, and following best practices, you can unlock the full potential of Monday.com and create workflows that are both efficient and error-free.

In the next section, we'll dive deeper into **4.1.2 How to Set Up an Automation**, where we'll provide step-by-step instructions for creating custom automations tailored to your team's needs.

4.1.2 How to Set Up an Automation

Automations in Monday.com are a powerful way to simplify repetitive tasks, improve workflow efficiency, and ensure that nothing falls through the cracks. By setting up automations, you can minimize manual intervention and let Monday.com handle routine actions like sending reminders, changing statuses, or notifying team members when certain conditions are met. This section provides a detailed, step-by-step guide to setting up automations, from basic configurations to advanced customizations.

Step 1: Understanding Automation Basics

Before diving into the steps, let's break down the key components of an automation in Monday.com:

- **Trigger**: This is the event that starts the automation. For example, a trigger could be when a status changes, a date arrives, or an item is created.

- **Action**: This is the result of the trigger. For example, an action could be sending a notification, creating a new item, or updating a column.

- **Recipe**: Monday.com automations are built using "recipes," which are pre-defined templates that combine a trigger and an action.

Step 2: Accessing the Automations Center

1. Open the board where you want to set up an automation.

2. Click on the **"Automations"** button in the top-right corner of the board. This opens the Automations Center, where you can browse, customize, and manage automation recipes.

3. In the Automations Center, you'll see three main sections:

   o **Featured Automations**: Pre-selected popular automation recipes.

   o **Categories**: Recipes grouped by functionality (e.g., notifications, dates, dependencies).

   o **My Automations**: Automations you've already created for the board.

Step 3: Choosing an Automation Recipe

Monday.com provides a variety of automation recipes. To set up an automation:

1. Use the search bar in the Automations Center to find a recipe that matches your needs. For example, type "due date" or "status change."

2. Browse through the automation templates displayed in the search results.

3. Select a recipe by clicking on it.

Example: If you want to send a notification when a task's status changes to "Done," you would select the recipe:
"When status changes to something, notify someone."

Step 4: Customizing the Recipe

After selecting a recipe, you'll need to customize it to fit your workflow. This involves:

1. **Defining the Trigger**:

   o In the example above, click on the word "status" in the recipe to select the specific status column from your board.

   o Next, click on "something" to choose the specific status value, such as "Done."

2. **Configuring the Action**:

   o Click on "someone" to choose the person or team to notify. You can select a specific person, all board subscribers, or even dynamic assignments like "Person in the Assignee column."

   o Optionally, customize the notification text to include relevant details about the task. For example:

"Task [Item Name] has been marked as Done. Great job!"

3. **Adding Additional Parameters** (if applicable):

○ Some recipes allow for more complex configurations, like setting conditions or filtering which items the automation applies to.

When status changes to something   +   ☐

↓

Then move item to group   +   ☐

Create automation

Step 5: Testing Your Automation

Before relying on your automation, it's crucial to test it:

1. Perform the trigger action manually on your board. For example, change the status of a task to "Done."

2. Observe the resulting action to ensure it behaves as expected (e.g., a notification is sent).

3. If the automation doesn't work as intended, revisit the Automations Center to adjust the settings.

Step 6: Managing Automations

Once you've set up an automation, you can manage it in the Automations Center:

1. **Viewing All Automations**:

   ○ Click on the "My Automations" tab to see a list of all active automations on the board.

2. **Editing Automations**:

- Locate the automation you want to edit, click on the three-dot menu beside it, and select "Edit." Update the trigger or action as needed.

3. **Disabling Automations**:

- If you no longer need an automation, you can disable it temporarily without deleting it. This is useful for testing new workflows.

4. **Deleting Automations**:

- To permanently remove an automation, select "Delete" from the three-dot menu.

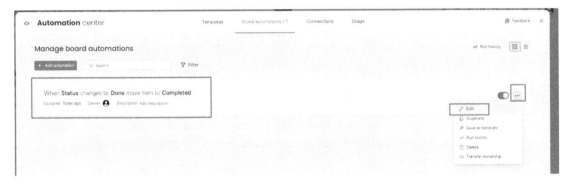

Examples of Common Automations

Here are a few examples of popular automation use cases to inspire you:

- **Recurring Task Automation**:
  Recipe: "Every time period, create an item."

  - Use this to automatically generate recurring tasks, such as weekly status reports or monthly budget reviews.

- **Due Date Reminders**:
  Recipe: "When date arrives, notify someone."

  - Set this up to remind team members about upcoming deadlines.

- **Task Handoff Notifications**:
  Recipe: "When status changes to something, assign someone."

- Ideal for workflows where tasks are handed off between team members, such as moving a design task from "In Progress" to "Review."

Advanced Tips for Automation Setup

1. **Combine Multiple Automations**:

   - Create complementary automations to handle complex workflows. For example, one automation can update a status, while another sends a notification based on that status change.

2. **Use Conditional Automations**:

   - Add conditions to your automations for more precise actions. For instance, notify a specific person only if the task priority is "High."

3. **Monitor Automation Performance**:

   - Check your board's activity log to track when automations are triggered. This helps identify potential issues or areas for improvement.

Best Practices for Automations

1. **Start Small**: Begin with basic automations and gradually incorporate more complex recipes as you become familiar with the system.

2. **Avoid Overlapping Automations**: Ensure that multiple automations don't conflict or trigger redundantly, which can lead to unnecessary actions.

3. **Regularly Review Automations**: Periodically revisit your automations to ensure they're still aligned with your current workflow.

By following these steps, you can set up and manage automations in Monday.com to enhance your team's productivity and streamline your workflows. With practice, automations will become an indispensable tool for better organization and efficiency.

4.2 Popular Automation Recipes

4.2.1 Due Date Reminders

Due date reminders are one of the most practical and widely used automation recipes in Monday.com. They help teams stay on track by ensuring deadlines are not missed and tasks are completed on time. Whether you're managing a team project, personal to-do lists, or a large-scale campaign, setting up automated due date reminders is a game-changer for productivity and accountability.

In this section, we'll explore the concept of due date reminders, their importance, and how to set them up in Monday.com. Additionally, we'll share tips for using them effectively and troubleshooting common issues.

What are Due Date Reminders?

A due date reminder is an automated notification triggered when a task's deadline is approaching or has passed. These reminders can be sent to individuals or groups and delivered through various channels, such as email, in-app notifications, or integrations like

Slack. Due date reminders help users prioritize their workload and avoid the last-minute rush.

Key benefits include:

- **Improved Time Management:** Ensures that all tasks are completed on time.

- **Increased Accountability:** Team members are reminded of their responsibilities.

- **Better Communication:** Reduces the need for manual follow-ups and status checks.

How to Set Up a Due Date Reminder in Monday.com

Setting up a due date reminder in Monday.com is simple and can be customized to meet your needs. Follow these steps:

Step 1: Identify the Tasks Requiring Reminders

Start by identifying the tasks, boards, or workflows where reminders are needed. For example, you might want reminders for:

- Upcoming deadlines for deliverables.

- Overdue tasks that require immediate attention.

- Recurring tasks, such as weekly reports or monthly reviews.

Ensure your board includes a "Due Date" column, as this column is essential for setting up due date automations.

Step 2: Access the Automation Center

1. Open the board where you want to set up the reminder.

2. Click on the **"Automations"** button located at the top right corner of the screen.

3. From the dropdown menu, select **"Create Custom Automation"** or browse pre-built recipes.

Step 3: Choose the Reminder Automation Recipe

In the automation center, you'll find a variety of automation recipes. For due date reminders, select one of the following options:

1. **"When date arrives, notify someone."**

   o This recipe sends a notification when the due date matches the current date.

2. **"When date arrives, move item to group."**

   o This recipe moves the task to a specific group, such as "Today" or "Overdue."

3. **"When date is X days away, notify someone."**

   o This recipe sends a notification a set number of days before the due date (e.g., 1 day, 3 days, or 7 days).

Step 4: Customize the Automation

Once you've chosen a recipe, customize it to suit your workflow:

1. **Specify the Trigger:** Define when the automation should activate. For example:

   o "When the due date is 2 days away..."

   o "When the due date passes..."

2. **Select the Action:** Choose what happens when the trigger condition is met. Common actions include:

   o Sending a notification to a specific person or team.

   o Moving the item to a different group (e.g., "Urgent" or "Overdue").

   o Updating the status column (e.g., changing status to "Delayed").

3. **Assign Recipients:** Identify who should receive the reminder. Options include:

   o The person assigned to the task.

   o A team lead or manager.

    o   A specific user or email address.

Step 5: Save and Activate the Automation

Once all details are configured, click **"Save"** to activate the automation. The system will now automatically send reminders based on the conditions you've set.

Best Practices for Using Due Date Reminders

To maximize the effectiveness of due date reminders, follow these best practices:

1. **Set Realistic Reminders:** Avoid overwhelming users with excessive notifications. For example, a reminder 2–3 days before the due date is often sufficient.

2. **Use Clear and Actionable Language:** Customize notification messages to include specific instructions or deadlines. For example:

   o   "Reminder: Task X is due in 2 days. Please review and update the status."

3. **Leverage Status Columns:** Combine reminders with status updates to provide additional context. For example, tasks marked as "In Progress" may not need the same reminders as tasks marked "Stuck."

4. **Assign Responsibility:** Ensure every task has an owner. Reminders are most effective when sent to the person responsible for the task.

5. **Review and Adjust Automations:** Regularly review your automation settings to ensure they align with your team's needs.

Examples of Effective Due Date Reminders

Here are a few examples of how due date reminders can be applied in different scenarios:

1. **Project Deadlines:**

   o   Reminder: "The project milestone 'Phase 1 Design' is due tomorrow. Ensure all tasks are completed."

2. **Recurring Reports:**

- o Reminder: "The monthly sales report is due in 3 days. Please update the data and submit for review."

3. **Client Deliverables:**

   - o Reminder: "The client presentation for 'ABC Corp' is due today. Finalize and upload the slides."

Troubleshooting Common Issues

1. **Reminders Not Sending:**

   - o Ensure the automation is active and correctly configured.

   - o Verify that the due date column is filled out for all relevant tasks.

2. **Duplicate Notifications:**

   - o Check for overlapping automations that may trigger multiple reminders.

   - o Consolidate similar automations to avoid confusion.

3. **Wrong Recipients:**

   - o Confirm that the automation is set to notify the correct user or team.

   - o Adjust settings if notifications are going to unintended recipients.

Why Use Due Date Reminders in Monday.com?

Due date reminders eliminate the need for manual follow-ups and allow teams to focus on meaningful work. By automating reminders, you can:

- Reduce stress caused by missed deadlines.

- Improve team accountability and communication.

- Enhance overall productivity and efficiency.

When used effectively, due date reminders empower teams to stay organized and on track, ensuring projects are completed successfully.

4.2.2 Status Change Triggers

Status change triggers are one of the most powerful automation tools in Monday.com. They allow you to set automated actions that occur when the status of an item changes. This feature eliminates manual follow-ups, streamlines workflows, and ensures that nothing falls through the cracks. In this section, we'll dive deep into what status change triggers are, how they work, and how you can use them to optimize your processes.

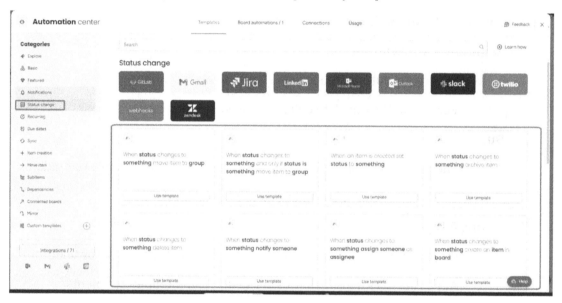

What Are Status Change Triggers?

A status change trigger is an automation rule that activates when the status of an item changes to a specific value. For example:

- If a task status changes from "In Progress" to "Completed," you can trigger an action such as notifying your team or archiving the task.

- If a task status changes to "Stuck," you can assign the item to a specific team member or send an email alert.

These triggers are especially useful in managing task progress, ensuring accountability, and maintaining efficiency in your workflows.

Why Use Status Change Triggers?

Here are some reasons why you should incorporate status change triggers into your workflows:

1. **Save Time**: By automating repetitive tasks, such as notifying team members or updating fields, you can save valuable time.

2. **Ensure Consistency**: Automations ensure that tasks are handled in a consistent manner, reducing errors caused by human oversight.

3. **Boost Accountability**: Status triggers can alert team members or managers when specific milestones are reached or when issues arise.

4. **Improve Workflow Visibility**: Automated actions help everyone on the team stay informed about the progress of tasks.

5. **Reduce Stress**: With automation handling routine actions, you can focus on more strategic and creative tasks.

How to Set Up a Status Change Trigger

Setting up a status change trigger in Monday.com is straightforward. Here's a step-by-step guide:

Step 1: Open the Automation Center

1. Navigate to the board where you want to set up the automation.

2. Click on the **"Automations"** button located in the top-right corner of the board.

3. Select **"Create Custom Automation"** to start building your automation.

Step 2: Define the Trigger

1. In the automation builder, choose **"When status changes"** as the trigger.

2. Specify the status column you want to monitor.

    o   For example, select the column labeled "Task Status."

3. Choose the status value that will activate the trigger.

o For example, select "Completed," "Stuck," or any custom status you've created.

Step 3: Define the Action

1. After defining the trigger, select the action you want to occur when the status changes.

2. Common actions include:

   o **Notify someone:** Send a notification to a specific person or team.

   o **Assign item:** Reassign the item to another team member.

   o **Move item:** Move the item to a different group or board.

   o **Update column:** Update the value in another column (e.g., set a due date).

   o **Send email:** Trigger an email to stakeholders or clients.

Step 4: Customize Additional Settings

1. Add conditions to make the automation more specific (optional).

   o For example, trigger the action only if the due date is within a certain range.

2. Add multiple actions if needed.

   o For example, notify a team member and update a column simultaneously.

Step 5: Save and Activate

1. Once you've configured the trigger and action, click **"Save"** to finalize the automation.

2. Ensure that the automation is toggled on.

Practical Examples of Status Change Triggers

1. Escalating Delays

If the status of a task changes to "Stuck," you can:

- Automatically notify the team leader.

- Update the priority column to "High."

- Send a Slack message to the project channel for immediate attention.

2. Tracking Completed Tasks

When a task status changes to "Completed," you can:

- Move the item to a "Completed Tasks" group for archiving.

- Notify the client or stakeholder via email.

- Record the completion date in a "Date Completed" column.

3. Assigning Follow-Up Actions

If a task status changes to "Ready for Review," you can:

- Assign the item to a reviewer.

- Set a due date for the review process.

- Notify the reviewer with a detailed message.

4. Triggering Cross-Board Actions

If the status changes to "Approved" on a marketing board, you can:

- Create a corresponding item on a production board.

- Notify the production team to begin work.

- Update the project timeline on the master board.

Best Practices for Using Status Change Triggers

1. **Keep Automations Simple**: Start with basic automations before adding complexity. Overloading a board with too many triggers can make it difficult to manage.

2. **Use Descriptive Status Names**: Ensure your status values are clear and meaningful (e.g., "Pending Approval" vs. "Waiting").

3. **Test Your Automations**: After setting up a trigger, test it with sample data to ensure it works as intended.

4. **Combine Triggers and Conditions**: Use conditions (e.g., due dates, priority levels) to make your automations more targeted and effective.

5. **Monitor Automation Logs**: Check the automation logs periodically to troubleshoot issues and optimize performance.

Advanced Tips for Status Change Triggers

1. **Chain Automations Together**: Use multiple automations to create complex workflows. For example, a status change to "In Progress" could trigger an email notification, which in turn sets a new due date.

2. **Leverage Custom Fields**: Combine status changes with custom columns like "Progress Percentage" or "Budget" to trigger highly specific actions.

3. **Integrate with Third-Party Tools**: Pair status change triggers with integrations like Slack, Gmail, or Microsoft Teams for seamless communication across platforms.

4. **Use Automations for Reporting**: Trigger actions that update reporting dashboards, such as moving completed tasks to a summary board.

By mastering status change triggers, you can take full advantage of Monday.com's automation capabilities to ensure smoother workflows, greater team accountability, and improved efficiency across your projects. Whether you're managing a small team or a large enterprise, these tools will help you stay organized and focused on your goals.

4.2.3 Recurring Task Automations

Recurring tasks are essential for teams and individuals who deal with repetitive workflows, routine activities, or scheduled deliverables. Monday.com's automation features allow users to set up recurring tasks seamlessly, ensuring nothing slips through the cracks. In this section, we will explore the concept of recurring task automations, their benefits, and step-by-step guidance on how to create them, followed by best practices and troubleshooting tips.

What Are Recurring Task Automations?

Recurring task automations are rules or triggers set up within Monday.com that automatically create or reset tasks on a specified schedule. For example, you can automate a weekly team meeting checklist, a monthly report preparation reminder, or even daily tasks like monitoring system updates.

These automations save time, reduce manual effort, and ensure consistency in task management. By automating recurring tasks, teams can focus more on execution and less on remembering to create repetitive tasks.

Why Use Recurring Task Automations?

The benefits of using recurring task automations are multifold:

1. **Improved Productivity:** Automating repetitive tasks eliminates the need for manual creation, freeing up time for more critical activities.

2. **Consistency and Accuracy:** Ensures that recurring tasks are always created on time without human error.

3. **Accountability:** Keeps team members aligned and aware of their responsibilities by setting clear deadlines for routine tasks.

4. **Better Time Management:** Helps teams focus on execution rather than administrative details.

5. **Reduced Cognitive Load:** Removes the need to remember every recurring task, allowing users to focus on strategic priorities.

How to Set Up Recurring Task Automations

Creating a recurring task automation in Monday.com is straightforward. Follow these detailed steps to set it up:

Step 1: Define the Purpose of the Automation

Before you begin, identify what task or workflow you want to automate. Examples include:

- Weekly performance reviews.

- Monthly billing or invoicing tasks.

- Daily social media content scheduling.

Step 2: Navigate to Automations

1. Open the board where you want to set up the recurring task.

2. Click the **Automations** button at the top of the board.

3. In the Automations Center, click **"+ Create Automation"** to start.

Step 3: Select a Pre-Built Recipe

1. Scroll through the list of pre-built automation recipes.

2. Look for the recipe labeled **"Every time period, create an item."**

   o This recipe is specifically designed for recurring tasks.

3. Click **Customize** to modify the recipe.

Step 4: Configure the Automation

1. **Define the Frequency:**

   o Select the time interval for the recurring task. Options include daily, weekly, monthly, or a custom schedule.

   o Example: For a weekly meeting checklist, set the frequency to "Every Monday at 9:00 AM."

2. **Name the Item:**

   o Specify the task name that will appear on the board.

   o Example: "Weekly Team Sync Agenda."

3. **Choose the Group:**

   o   Decide which group on the board the new task will appear in (e.g., "To Do," "In Progress," or "Completed").

4. **Assign Ownership:**

   o   Assign the task to a specific team member or group of members.

   o   Example: Assign the task to the team lead.

5. **Set Status or Other Attributes:**

   o   Predefine certain attributes like task status, due date, or priority level.

   o   Example: Set the task status as "Not Started."

Step 5: Activate the Automation

1. Review the automation details to ensure everything is accurate.

2. Click **Activate** to enable the recurring task automation.

3. Once activated, the automation will run according to the schedule you've defined.

Examples of Recurring Task Automations

Here are a few real-world examples to help you understand how recurring automations can be applied:

1. **Weekly Staff Meeting Agenda:**

   o   Automation: Every Monday at 9:00 AM, create an item called "Staff Meeting Agenda" in the "Meetings" group, assign it to the manager, and set the due date to the same day.

2. **Monthly Invoicing Reminder:**

   o   Automation: On the 1st of every month, create a task named "Prepare Invoices" in the "Finance" group and assign it to the finance team.

3. **Daily Website Updates Check:**

- ○ Automation: Every day at 8:00 AM, create a task named "Website Maintenance" in the "IT Tasks" group, assign it to the IT team lead, and set the priority to "High."

Best Practices for Recurring Task Automations

1. **Use Clear Naming Conventions:**

   - ○ Name your recurring tasks descriptively to avoid confusion. For example, "Weekly Marketing Report" instead of just "Report."

2. **Assign Tasks Strategically:**

   - ○ Ensure recurring tasks are assigned to the right person or team to avoid bottlenecks.

3. **Set Realistic Schedules:**

   - ○ Avoid overwhelming your team by overloading the board with too many recurring tasks. Space out tasks based on actual needs.

4. **Monitor and Adjust Automations:**

   - ○ Periodically review your recurring task automations to ensure they're still relevant and effective.

5. **Incorporate Dependencies if Needed:**

   - ○ Use subitems or dependency settings for tasks that rely on the completion of previous steps.

Troubleshooting Recurring Task Automations

Even with the best setup, you may encounter issues. Here's how to handle common problems:

1. **Automation Not Running as Scheduled:**

   - ○ Check the automation settings to ensure the correct time and frequency are set.

   - ○ Verify that your timezone is correctly configured in the account settings.

2. **Task Attributes Missing:**

   o Ensure all fields (e.g., task name, due date, status) are properly configured in the automation recipe.

3. **Overlapping or Duplicate Tasks:**

   o Review all active automations to avoid conflicts between multiple recipes.

4. **Automation Stopped Working:**

   o Check if the board automation limit has been reached (this depends on your Monday.com plan).

   o Deactivate and reactivate the automation to refresh it.

Conclusion

Recurring task automations in Monday.com are a game-changer for teams and individuals looking to streamline their workflows and enhance productivity. By automating repetitive tasks, you can save time, reduce manual errors, and focus on what truly matters—delivering results. Following the steps and best practices outlined in this section will ensure your recurring tasks run smoothly and consistently, empowering you to stay organized and efficient.

4.3 Integrating Monday.com with Other Tools

4.3.1 Overview of Available Integrations

Integrating Monday.com with other tools is one of the platform's most powerful features. It allows users to connect Monday.com with the apps and software they already use, creating a seamless workflow that enhances productivity, collaboration, and organization. In this section, we will provide a comprehensive overview of the available integrations, their use cases, and the benefits they bring to your workflows.

Why Integrations Matter

In today's interconnected work environment, it is rare for a team or individual to rely on just one tool to manage their tasks, projects, or data. Instead, most workflows involve multiple applications—ranging from communication platforms like Slack and Zoom to storage solutions like Google Drive and Dropbox, and even data management tools like Salesforce or Jira. By integrating these tools into Monday.com, users can:

- **Save Time**: Eliminate the need for manual updates or switching between apps.

- **Centralize Information**: Gather all important data and tasks in one place.

- **Reduce Errors**: Sync data automatically, minimizing manual entry errors.

- **Boost Collaboration**: Enable teams to work together using their preferred tools while keeping everyone aligned within Monday.com.

Categories of Integrations

Monday.com offers a wide range of integrations, grouped into several categories based on their purpose and functionality. Let's explore these categories in detail:

1. Communication and Collaboration Integrations

These integrations ensure that your team stays connected, aligned, and informed throughout your projects.

- **Slack**:

    o Use case: Receive real-time updates, send messages directly from Monday.com to Slack channels, and notify team members of changes to tasks or deadlines.

    o Benefits: Keeps conversations and task updates in sync, reducing the need to jump between platforms.

- **Microsoft Teams**:

    o Use case: Share updates from Monday.com boards in Teams chats or channels and receive notifications about tasks.

    o Benefits: Streamlines communication for remote teams.

- **Zoom**:

    o Use case: Schedule Zoom meetings directly from Monday.com and link relevant tasks or items to meeting details.

    o Benefits: Simplifies scheduling and ensures all necessary context is available during meetings.

2. File and Document Storage Integrations

These integrations allow you to manage and access your files directly from Monday.com.

- **Google Drive**:

    o Use case: Attach files from Google Drive to Monday.com tasks and create a centralized hub for project documentation.

    o Benefits: Ensures version control and easy access to shared documents.

- **Dropbox**:

    o Use case: Link Dropbox files to Monday.com boards and store relevant resources alongside project updates.

    o Benefits: Reduces the time spent searching for critical files.

- **OneDrive**:

- o Use case: Add files from OneDrive to Monday.com boards and share them with team members.

- o Benefits: Seamless integration for teams using Microsoft's ecosystem.

---

3. Calendar and Scheduling Integrations

Managing time effectively is critical for any project. These integrations help you sync deadlines, events, and schedules with Monday.com.

- **Google Calendar**:

  - o Use case: Sync Monday.com tasks with your Google Calendar to keep track of deadlines and events.

  - o Benefits: Ensures no deadlines are missed by providing real-time calendar updates.

- **Outlook Calendar**:

  - o Use case: Sync tasks and meetings from Monday.com to your Outlook Calendar.

  - o Benefits: Perfect for teams that use Microsoft Outlook for scheduling.

---

4. CRM and Sales Integrations

If your team works in sales or customer relationship management, these integrations can save you hours of work.

- **Salesforce**:

  - o Use case: Sync Monday.com boards with Salesforce accounts to manage leads and opportunities.

  - o Benefits: Improves collaboration between sales and operations teams.

- **HubSpot**:

  - o Use case: Automate workflows by connecting HubSpot CRM with Monday.com boards to track deals, contacts, and activities.

- o Benefits: Reduces data duplication and ensures all client information is up to date.

5. Development and IT Integrations

For tech teams managing software development or IT projects, Monday.com offers integrations with popular tools.

- **Jira**:
    - o Use case: Sync tasks between Monday.com and Jira for software development teams.
    - o Benefits: Keeps developers and project managers aligned on goals and timelines.
- **GitHub**:
    - o Use case: Link GitHub repositories to Monday.com boards to track changes and issues.
    - o Benefits: Bridges the gap between technical teams and non-technical stakeholders.

6. Marketing and Advertising Integrations

Marketing teams can use these integrations to streamline campaigns and track their performance.

- **Facebook Ads**:
    - o Use case: Track ad performance data from Facebook Ads directly in Monday.com.
    - o Benefits: Centralizes ad analytics for quick decision-making.
- **Mailchimp**:
    - o Use case: Manage email campaigns and track metrics within Monday.com.
    - o Benefits: Simplifies campaign management and reporting.

7. Automation Tools and APIs

Monday.com's integration capabilities extend even further with automation tools like Zapier and Integromat, as well as its API for custom integrations.

- **Zapier**:
  - o Use case: Connect Monday.com to thousands of apps without coding, automating workflows like sending emails or updating spreadsheets.
  - o Benefits: Endless possibilities for automation.

- **Integromat**:
  - o Use case: Build more complex, multi-step automations that integrate Monday.com with other apps.
  - o Benefits: Tailored solutions for unique workflows.

- **Monday.com API**:
  - o Use case: Build custom integrations tailored to your organization's needs.
  - o Benefits: Complete flexibility for tech-savvy teams.

How to Decide Which Integrations to Use

Choosing the right integrations depends on your team's workflow and goals. Here are a few tips:

- **Identify Bottlenecks**: Look for processes that could be streamlined by connecting tools.

- **Evaluate Your Tool Stack**: Consider the tools your team already uses and see if Monday.com offers an integration.

- **Start Small**: Begin with a few key integrations and expand as needed.

Final Thoughts on Integrations

Monday.com integrations are designed to make your workflows smoother, faster, and more efficient. By leveraging these tools, you can create a centralized hub for all your work, ensuring your team stays aligned and productive. Whether you're syncing calendars, managing sales pipelines, or connecting with collaboration tools, Monday.com's integration capabilities provide the flexibility to adapt to your needs.

4.3.2 Connecting Google Drive, Slack, and Zoom

Integrating Monday.com with external tools like **Google Drive**, **Slack**, and **Zoom** can supercharge your workflow, enabling seamless collaboration, efficient communication, and streamlined project management. Below is a step-by-step guide on how to connect each of these tools to Monday.com, along with tips to optimize their use.

Introduction to Integrations in Monday.com

Before diving into the specifics, it's important to understand why integrations are powerful. By connecting Monday.com with external apps, you can:

- Centralize communication and file sharing.

- Automate repetitive tasks between tools.

- Eliminate the need to switch back and forth between platforms.

- Improve productivity by keeping everyone aligned in one platform.

Monday.com uses an **integration recipe system** to enable connections with tools. Recipes are pre-built templates that define how two tools interact, e.g., "When a file is uploaded to Google Drive, create an item in Monday.com."

Now, let's explore how to integrate Monday.com with **Google Drive**, **Slack**, and **Zoom**.

Connecting Google Drive to Monday.com

Step 1: Why Integrate Google Drive with Monday.com?

Google Drive is a widely-used cloud storage service that lets you store, organize, and share files. By integrating it with Monday.com, you can:

- Attach files directly to tasks or items in Monday.com.

- Automate file-sharing workflows.

- Access and manage Google Drive files without leaving Monday.com.

Step 2: Setting Up the Integration

1. **Navigate to the Integration Center**

    o Go to the board where you want to enable the integration.

    o Click the **"Integrate"** button in the top right corner of the board.

    o In the Integration Center, search for **Google Drive** in the search bar.

2. **Choose a Recipe**

    o Select a recipe that matches your workflow needs. Examples include:

        ▪ "When a file is uploaded to a Google Drive folder, create an item in Monday.com."

        ▪ "Attach a file from Google Drive to an item in Monday.com."

    o Click **"Add to Board"** to configure the recipe.

3. **Connect Your Google Account**

    o You'll be prompted to log in to your Google account and grant permissions to Monday.com.

- o Make sure you allow Monday.com to access your Google Drive files and folders.

4. **Configure the Recipe**

- o Specify the details for the integration, such as:
  - The Google Drive folder to monitor.
  - The type of items to create in Monday.com.
- o Save the recipe, and it will start running automatically.

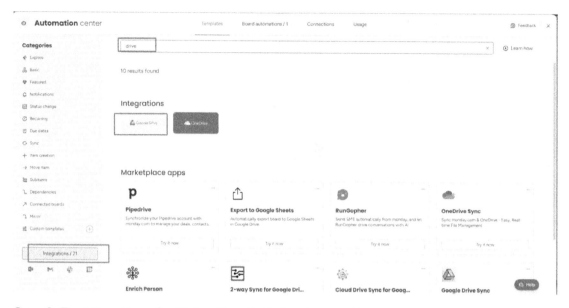

Step 3: Best Practices for Using Google Drive Integration

- **Centralize File Storage:** Attach relevant documents from Google Drive to specific tasks to avoid confusion.

- **Collaborate in Real-Time:** Link Google Docs, Sheets, or Slides so team members can collaborate directly from Monday.com.

- **Use Permissions Carefully:** Ensure the Google Drive folder you integrate has the appropriate sharing settings for your team.

Connecting Slack to Monday.com

Step 1: Why Integrate Slack with Monday.com?

Slack is a popular team messaging platform. Integrating it with Monday.com allows you to:

- Receive Monday.com updates in Slack channels.

- Send task updates or reminders directly to Slack.

- Turn Slack messages into Monday.com items for better task tracking.

Step 2: Setting Up the Integration

1. **Open the Integration Center**

   o On your chosen board, click **"Integrate"** and search for **Slack**.

2. **Select a Recipe**

   o Common Slack recipes include:

     ▪ "Send a message in Slack when a status changes in Monday.com."

     ▪ "Create an item in Monday.com from a Slack message."

   o Choose a recipe and click **"Add to Board"**.

3. **Connect Your Slack Workspace**

   o Log in to your Slack account and authorize Monday.com to access it.

   o Choose the Slack workspace and channel where messages should be sent or received.

4. **Customize the Recipe**

   o Define conditions for the integration, such as:

     ▪ Which status updates trigger Slack messages.

     ▪ What information to include in the Slack notification.

   o Save the recipe to activate the integration.

Step 3: Tips for Effective Slack Integration

- **Avoid Overloading Channels:** Use filters to ensure only critical updates are sent to Slack.

- **Pin Important Items:** Pin Monday.com links in Slack channels for quick access to key tasks.

- **Use Personal Notifications:** Send updates to specific team members via direct messages in Slack.

Connecting Zoom to Monday.com

Step 1: Why Integrate Zoom with Monday.com?

Zoom is a leading video conferencing tool. By integrating it with Monday.com, you can:

- Schedule Zoom meetings directly from Monday.com.

- Automatically create Zoom meeting links and attach them to tasks.

- Keep track of meeting details and participants in one place.

Step 2: Setting Up the Integration

1. **Access the Integration Center**

    o Go to your board, click **"Integrate"**, and search for **Zoom**.

2. **Select a Recipe**

    o Popular Zoom recipes include:

        ▪ "Create a Zoom meeting when a new item is added to Monday.com."

        ▪ "Add a Zoom link to an item when a meeting is scheduled."

    o Click **"Add to Board"** to start configuring the recipe.

3. **Connect Your Zoom Account**

    o Log in to your Zoom account and authorize Monday.com to access it.

    o Grant permissions for creating meetings and accessing your calendar.

4. **Configure the Recipe**

    o Specify the integration details, such as:

        ▪ Which board items should trigger Zoom meetings.

        ▪ The meeting title and duration.

    o Save the recipe, and Zoom links will automatically appear in Monday.com.

Step 3: Best Practices for Using Zoom Integration

- **Attach Meetings to Tasks:** Ensure every scheduled Zoom meeting is linked to its corresponding task or project in Monday.com.

- **Automate Recurring Meetings:** Set up recipes for weekly team meetings to save time.

- **Track Attendance:** Use Monday.com to track who attended the meeting and follow up on action items.

Final Tips for Managing Integrations

1. **Test Your Integrations Regularly**

   o Run a few test scenarios to ensure your integrations are working as expected.

2. **Keep It Simple**

   o Avoid overloading boards with too many integrations, which can cause confusion.

3. **Train Your Team**

   o Educate your team members on how to use the integrations effectively.

4. **Monitor Activity**

   o Use Monday.com's activity log to track how integrations are performing and troubleshoot any issues.

By connecting Google Drive, Slack, and Zoom to Monday.com, you can transform your workflows, enhance collaboration, and improve your team's overall productivity.

4.3.3 Managing Integration Settings

Integrating Monday.com with other tools and platforms can significantly enhance your workflow, streamline operations, and improve collaboration. However, managing integration settings effectively is essential to ensure that these tools function smoothly without any disruptions. This section will guide you step by step on how to manage integration settings in Monday.com, troubleshoot common issues, and optimize integrations for your specific needs.

---

1. Understanding Integration Settings

When you integrate external tools with Monday.com, each integration comes with a set of customizable settings. These settings determine how the two platforms communicate, the type of data that gets synced, and the triggers or actions that occur.

Here's what integration settings typically include:

- **Triggers and Actions**: Define what events in Monday.com or the connected tool will initiate the integration. For example, a change in task status could trigger a notification in Slack.

- **Sync Frequency**: Determine how often data syncs between Monday.com and the external tool (real-time, hourly, or daily).

- **Permission Management**: Control who can modify or access the integration settings.

- **Field Mapping**: Customize how data fields in Monday.com correspond to fields in the external tool.

2. Accessing Integration Settings

Managing integration settings in Monday.com is simple and user-friendly. Follow these steps:

1. **Navigate to the Integration Center**:

    - Open your board in Monday.com.

    - Click on the "Integrations" button (represented by a plug icon) in the top right corner of your board.

    - You'll see a list of active integrations and available options for new integrations.

2. **Select the Integration to Manage**:

    - Identify the integration you wish to manage from the list of active integrations.

    - Click on the gear icon or "Settings" button next to the integration name.

3.   **Modify Integration Settings**:

- o   You'll now access a detailed settings page where you can adjust triggers, actions, sync preferences, and permissions.

- o   Make changes as needed and click "Save" to apply the updates.

3. Customizing Integration Workflows

Customizing your integration workflows ensures that they align with your team's processes. Here are some ways to fine-tune integrations for optimal results:

3.1 Adjusting Triggers and Actions

Triggers and actions are the foundation of any integration. Here's how to customize them:

- **Set Relevant Triggers**: For example, if you're integrating Slack, choose triggers like "When a task's status changes to 'Completed.'"

- **Define Clear Actions**: Specify actions such as "Send a Slack message to notify the team" or "Add a Google Calendar event for the due date."

3.2 Mapping Fields Between Platforms

Field mapping ensures that the right data flows between Monday.com and the integrated tool.

- **Automatic Mapping**: Some integrations automatically map fields based on similar names or types.

- **Manual Adjustments**: Adjust the mappings if the fields do not align correctly. For example, map Monday.com's "Due Date" column to Google Calendar's "Event Date."

3.3 Scheduling Sync Frequencies

Decide how frequently data updates should occur:

- **Real-Time Sync**: Ideal for critical workflows where updates must happen instantly (e.g., CRM updates).

- **Scheduled Syncs**: Use hourly or daily syncs for less urgent data to reduce system load.

4. Managing Permissions for Integrations

Integration settings should be accessible only to authorized team members. Here's how to manage permissions:

- **Assign Admin Rights**: Limit access to integration settings to board admins or specific team members.

- **Set User Roles**: Define roles such as viewers, editors, and admins, ensuring that only authorized users can modify integrations.

- **Audit Activity Logs**: Regularly review activity logs to monitor changes to integration settings.

5. Troubleshooting Common Integration Issues

Despite its robustness, integrations may occasionally encounter issues. Here's how to troubleshoot:

5.1 Authentication Errors

- **Issue**: The integration stops working due to expired credentials.

- **Solution**: Re-authenticate the connection by logging into the external tool through Monday.com's integration settings.

5.2 Data Sync Failures

- **Issue**: Data fails to sync between Monday.com and the external tool.

- **Solution**:

    o Check the sync frequency settings.

    o Ensure that the fields are mapped correctly.

    o Verify that there are no API limits on the external tool.

5.3 Missing Permissions

- **Issue**: A team member cannot access integration settings or certain data.

- **Solution**: Review and update permissions in the integration settings to grant appropriate access.

6. Optimizing Integration Settings for Better Organization

To make the most of integrations, consider these best practices:

6.1 Use Templates for Repeated Workflows

- Create and save integration templates for workflows that occur frequently.

- For example, if you use Google Drive for document storage, create an automation that automatically links new tasks to a shared folder.

6.2 Consolidate Notifications

- Avoid overloading your team with notifications. For instance, instead of sending a Slack notification for every minor update, consolidate them into daily summaries.

6.3 Periodic Review of Integrations

- Schedule periodic reviews of integration settings to ensure they remain relevant to your team's evolving needs.

- Update triggers, actions, or mappings as processes change.

7. Advanced Tips for Managing Integrations

7.1 Using API for Custom Integrations

For advanced users or IT teams, Monday.com's API allows for custom integrations with unique workflows.

- **Example**: Sync Monday.com with a proprietary CRM tool or internal database.

- **Steps**: Use Monday.com's API documentation to set up endpoints, map fields, and test the connection.

7.2 Leveraging Third-Party Tools

Third-party tools like Zapier or Integromat can help bridge gaps between Monday.com and unsupported platforms.

- **Example**: Use Zapier to connect Monday.com with Asana or Trello.

8. Real-Life Examples of Effective Integration Management

- **Case 1: Marketing Team with Slack and Monday.com**
  A marketing team uses Monday.com for campaign planning. Integrating with Slack ensures real-time updates on campaign milestones. Notifications are grouped by campaign and delivered weekly to avoid overload.

- **Case 2: Project Management with Google Calendar**
  A project manager uses Monday.com to track deliverables and integrates with Google Calendar to ensure deadlines are visible. Syncs are scheduled daily, and calendar events are linked to specific tasks for easy reference.

- **Case 3: File Management with Google Drive**
  An HR team integrates Monday.com with Google Drive to manage recruitment documents. Automations are set up to upload interview schedules and candidate resumes directly to Drive.

9. Final Tips for Mastering Integration Management

- Regularly explore new integrations available in Monday.com's Integration Center.

- Use trial-and-error to refine your workflows until they're perfectly aligned with your needs.

- Train your team to understand and optimize integration settings to ensure smooth collaboration.

By managing integration settings effectively, you can maximize the value of Monday.com and create a seamless, organized workflow that boosts your team's productivity.

CHAPTER V
Views and Visualization Tools

5.1 Exploring Different Board Views

Monday.com offers a range of board views that help users visualize their tasks and workflows effectively. Among these, the **Kanban View** is one of the most popular and versatile options. It is particularly helpful for teams who prefer visual task management, enabling them to track progress, organize tasks, and optimize workflows efficiently.

5.1.1 Kanban View

The **Kanban View** in Monday.com transforms your board into a visual task management system that uses cards and columns to represent work items and their status. This view is ideal for tracking tasks across various stages in a project, from "To-Do" to "In Progress" and "Done." Below is a comprehensive guide to setting up, customizing, and maximizing the use of the Kanban View.

What is the Kanban View?

Kanban is a project management methodology originally developed in manufacturing to improve workflow efficiency. In Monday.com, the Kanban View allows you to represent tasks as cards, organized into columns that reflect different statuses or phases of a process. Each card provides a snapshot of a task, including details like its name, assignee, due date, and more.

This view helps users:

- **Visualize Workflows:** See all tasks and their current status at a glance.

- **Identify Bottlenecks:** Spot stages where tasks are piling up.

- **Enhance Collaboration:** Allow teams to easily update task progress.

How to Set Up the Kanban View in Monday.com

1. **Navigate to the Board You Want to Visualize**

    o Open the board that contains the tasks or items you want to display in the Kanban View.

2. **Switch to the Kanban View**

    o Click on the "+ Add View" button at the top of your board.

    o Select "Kanban" from the list of available views.

3. **Define the Status Column**

    o The Kanban View relies on a **Status Column** to group items into different categories (e.g., "To-Do," "In Progress," "Done").

    o Ensure your board has a Status Column. If not, add one by clicking on the "+ Add Column" button and selecting "Status."

4. **Customize Your Columns**

- o The Kanban View automatically generates columns based on the values in your Status Column.

- o Rename the status labels (e.g., "Backlog," "In Review") to fit your workflow.

- o Rearrange the columns by dragging and dropping them to match the desired order of your process.

5. **Add or Remove Cards**

- o Each item on your board appears as a card in the Kanban View.

- o To add a new card, switch back to the Table View, add a new item, and assign it a status.

Customizing the Kanban View

Monday.com allows you to tailor the Kanban View to suit your specific needs:

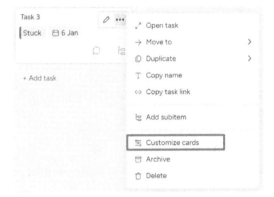

1. **Adjusting Card Content**

- o Click the three-dot menu in the Kanban View and select "Customize Cards."

- o Choose which fields to display on each card, such as the item name, assignee, due date, or priority.

2. **Color Coding**

- o Use color-coded labels in your Status Column to make tasks visually distinct.

- For example, "High Priority" tasks can have a red label, while "Low Priority" tasks can have a green label.

3. **Grouping by Additional Columns**

   - You can group your cards by fields other than status, such as "Assignee" or "Due Date."

   - This adds an additional layer of organization and makes it easier to focus on specific team members or deadlines.

4. **Collapsible Columns**

   - Hide columns that are not immediately relevant to declutter your view.

Best Practices for Using the Kanban View

1. **Keep Your Status Labels Simple**

   - Use clear and concise labels to avoid confusion (e.g., "Drafting," "Under Review," "Approved").

2. **Update Status Regularly**

   - Encourage team members to update the status of their tasks frequently to keep the board accurate and up-to-date.

3. **Limit Work in Progress (WIP)**

   - Set limits on the number of tasks in each column to prevent team members from being overwhelmed.

4. **Monitor Bottlenecks**

   - Regularly review columns to identify stages where tasks are piling up. Use this information to adjust resources or priorities.

5. **Use Automations to Simplify Updates**

   - Set up automations to move cards between columns automatically based on changes in status. For example:

     - "When a status changes to 'Done,' archive the item."

- "When a due date is reached and status is not 'Completed,' send a reminder."

Advantages of the Kanban View

1. **Improved Workflow Visibility**

   o The Kanban View provides a bird's-eye view of all tasks, helping teams identify progress and priorities at a glance.

2. **Enhanced Collaboration**

   o Teams can quickly update task statuses, share files, and comment on tasks directly within the cards.

3. **Streamlined Task Management**

   o Tasks move seamlessly between columns, making it easier to track their journey from start to finish.

4. **Customizable to Any Workflow**

   o Whether you're managing a software development sprint, marketing campaign, or personal to-do list, the Kanban View can adapt to your needs.

Real-Life Use Cases for the Kanban View

1. **Software Development Teams**

   o Track sprints and manage tasks like bug fixes, feature requests, and testing.

2. **Marketing Campaigns**

   o Visualize campaign stages such as planning, designing, launching, and analyzing.

3. **Recruitment Pipelines**

   o Manage candidate applications through stages like "Received," "Interviewing," and "Hired."

4. **Personal Task Management**

- o Use the Kanban View to organize your daily to-do list into "Pending," "In Progress," and "Completed."

Tips for Optimizing the Kanban View

1. **Combine with Other Views**

   - o Switch between the Kanban View and other views like Calendar or Timeline to gain different perspectives on your workflow.

2. **Use Tags for Additional Categorization**

   - o Add tags to tasks for quick filtering and grouping within the Kanban View.

3. **Analyze Progress with Dashboards**

   - o Pair the Kanban View with a Dashboard to track team performance and project metrics.

By mastering the Kanban View in Monday.com, you can bring clarity and efficiency to your workflows, empowering your team to work smarter and achieve more.

5.1.2 Timeline View

The **Timeline View** in Monday.com is a powerful visualization tool designed to help teams manage schedules, deadlines, and overlapping tasks effectively. It offers a Gantt-chart-like perspective, allowing users to see their project timelines and dependencies in one comprehensive view. Whether you're managing a product launch, planning an event, or tracking multiple projects, the Timeline View provides clarity on how tasks align over time. This section will guide you step by step in understanding, setting up, and using the Timeline View efficiently.

What is the Timeline View?

The **Timeline View** is a way to visualize data from your Monday.com boards, specifically focusing on tasks or projects with start and end dates. Unlike the default board view, which lists items in a tabular format, the Timeline View places tasks on a horizontal timeline. This layout makes it easy to:

- Identify task durations.

- Track overlapping responsibilities.

- Monitor project progress in real-time.

- Quickly spot and resolve scheduling conflicts.

Key Benefits of the Timeline View

1. **Comprehensive Scheduling**: View all tasks and deadlines in a single visual timeline.

2. **Improved Resource Management**: Understand how work is distributed among team members.

3. **Conflict Resolution**: Spot overlapping tasks and adjust schedules to avoid bottlenecks.

4. **Dynamic Adjustments**: Update timelines easily with drag-and-drop functionality.

5. **Progress Tracking**: Monitor the current status of ongoing tasks and ensure deadlines are met.

How to Set Up the Timeline View

Setting up the Timeline View is simple and can be done in just a few steps. Follow the guide below:

1. Add the Timeline View to Your Board

1.1. Open the board where you'd like to add the Timeline View.
1.2. Click the **"+"** icon next to the default views (located at the top of the board).
1.3. Select **"Gantt"** from the list of available views.
1.4. Name your view (e.g., "Project Timeline") and click **"Add View"**.

Pro Tip: You can set the Timeline View as your default view for the board by selecting the star icon next to its name.

2. Define Date Columns for the Timeline

The Timeline View requires data from the **Date** or **Timeline** columns to populate. If your board does not already have these columns, follow these steps:

2.1. **Add Date Columns**:

- Click the **"+"** icon at the far right of your board to add a new column.

- Select the **Date** or **Timeline** column type.

2.2. **Populate Start and End Dates**:

- Enter the start and end dates for each task or project item in your board.

- If you're unsure of the end date, you can leave it blank, but this may limit the timeline's accuracy.

2.3. **Link Date Columns to the Timeline View**:

- Once your Date or Timeline columns are filled, Monday.com will automatically pull this data into the Timeline View.

3. Adjust the Timeline Settings

After adding the Timeline View, you may need to customize its settings to suit your needs. Here's how:

3.1. **Group Tasks**:

- Use the grouping feature to organize tasks by team member, project, or status.

- For example, group tasks by **"Person"** to see what each team member is working on.

3.2. **Adjust Time Scale**:

- Zoom in or out to change the scale of the timeline (daily, weekly, or monthly view).

- Use the slider at the bottom of the Timeline View for fine adjustments.

3.3. **Color Code Tasks**:

- Assign colors based on status, priority, or task type.

- This makes it easier to quickly interpret the timeline at a glance.

How to Use the Timeline View Effectively

Once your Timeline View is set up, you can begin leveraging its features to streamline project management. Below are some best practices and tips to maximize its potential:

1. Drag-and-Drop Scheduling

The Timeline View allows you to drag and drop tasks directly on the timeline. This makes rescheduling quick and intuitive. To do this:

- Click on a task in the timeline.

- Drag it to a new start date or extend its end date.

- Watch as the updated schedule reflects in real-time on your board.

Pro Tip: Use this feature to instantly resolve scheduling conflicts or adjust timelines when priorities change.

2. Managing Dependencies

Dependencies are critical for projects with sequential tasks. For instance, Task B may depend on the completion of Task A. Here's how to manage dependencies in the Timeline View:

2.1. **Enable Dependency Column**:

- Add a **Dependency** column to your board.

- Link tasks by specifying which tasks are dependent on others.

2.2. **Visualize Dependencies**:

- In the Timeline View, dependencies are shown as arrows connecting tasks.

- Use these visual cues to identify and adjust dependencies as needed.

3. Monitoring Team Workload

The Timeline View can also help ensure no team member is overburdened. Use the following tips to monitor and balance workload:

3.1. **Group by Assignee**:

- Group tasks by **"Person"** to see each team member's workload.

3.2. **Workload Widget**:

- Add the **Workload Widget** to your timeline to view and adjust task assignments based on capacity.

3.3. **Reassign Tasks**:

- Drag tasks to different team members to redistribute work more evenly.

---

4. Conflict Resolution

Overlapping tasks can create bottlenecks, especially when multiple team members are involved. The Timeline View highlights such overlaps with visual indicators.

4.1. **Identify Overlaps**:

- Look for tasks that are stacked on the timeline.
- Use color coding to distinguish overlapping priorities.

4.2. **Resolve Conflicts**:

- Adjust start and end dates to reduce overlaps.
- Communicate with team members to coordinate shifts in schedules.

Real-Life Use Cases of the Timeline View

Use Case 1: Marketing Campaign Management

- Plan and execute marketing campaigns by visualizing deadlines for deliverables such as social media posts, blog articles, and paid ads.
- Identify potential delays in the campaign timeline and adjust schedules proactively.

Use Case 2: Product Development

- Track the lifecycle of product development, from prototyping to final launch.

- Use dependencies to ensure each development phase progresses sequentially.

Use Case 3: Event Planning

- Coordinate event tasks like venue booking, vendor management, and promotional activities on a single timeline.

Common Challenges and How to Overcome Them

1. Missing Dates

Ensure every task has a start and end date. Missing dates can cause gaps in the timeline.

2. Overwhelming Data

For large projects, break down tasks into smaller groups and filter the timeline to focus on specific projects or team members.

3. Misaligned Dependencies

Regularly review task dependencies to ensure accurate sequencing.

Conclusion

The **Timeline View** is an indispensable tool for organizing and visualizing projects in Monday.com. By effectively utilizing its features—such as drag-and-drop scheduling, dependency management, and workload balancing—you can streamline workflows, avoid bottlenecks, and ensure timely project completion. Whether you're managing simple schedules or complex multi-phase projects, the Timeline View offers the clarity and flexibility you need to stay on top of your tasks.

5.1.3 Calendar View

The **Calendar View** in Monday.com is a powerful visualization tool that helps you see your tasks, projects, and deadlines in a calendar format. This view is particularly useful for time-sensitive tasks, tracking progress on deliverables, or managing schedules across teams. In this section, we will explore the Calendar View in-depth, including how to set it up, navigate its features, and use it effectively for personal and team organization.

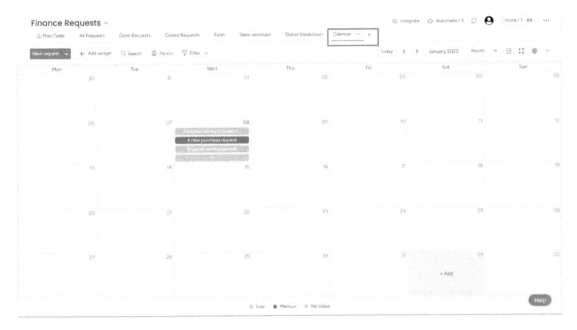

What Is the Calendar View?

The Calendar View displays items from your boards in a date-based format, giving you a clear overview of your timelines. Each task or item that has a date column—such as a due date, start date, or timeline—can be visualized on the calendar. This makes it easy to plan your work, identify overlaps, and ensure you meet deadlines.

Why Use the Calendar View?

The Calendar View is perfect for:

- **Deadline Management:** Quickly see all upcoming deadlines and adjust as needed.

- **Team Coordination:** Ensure team members are aligned by visually identifying key deliverables and shared priorities.

- **Event Planning:** Use the calendar to organize launches, campaigns, or other important dates.

- **Workload Balancing:** Spot overlapping tasks or gaps in schedules to better manage resources.

How to Set Up the Calendar View

To get started with the Calendar View:

1. **Accessing the View:**

    o   Navigate to the board where you want to use the Calendar View.

    o   Click the **"+ Add View"** button located in the top navigation bar of the board.

    o   Select **"Calendar"** from the list of available view options.

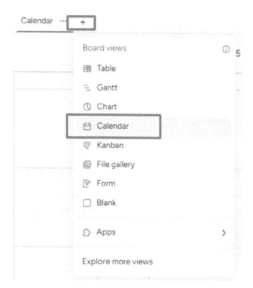

2. **Configuring the Date Column:**

    o   Ensure your board includes at least one **date column**.

    o   If your board does not have a date column, click **"+ Add Column"**, select **"Date"**, and input the relevant dates for each item.

3. **Choosing What to Display on the Calendar:**

    o   In the Calendar settings, select which **date column** you want to visualize.

- For example, you can display due dates, start dates, or any custom date field.

4. **Customizing the View:**

   - Use filters to refine what you see on the calendar (e.g., only display items assigned to specific team members or with certain statuses).

   - Choose a time range, such as a day, week, or month, for better visibility.

Navigating the Calendar View

Once your Calendar View is set up, navigating it is straightforward. Here's how to make the most of its features:

1. **Switching Between Views:**

   - Use the toggle at the top of the Calendar View to switch between **day**, **week**, or **month** views.

   - The **day view** is ideal for focusing on short-term tasks, while the **month view** provides a broader perspective.

2. **Interacting with Items:**

   - Click on any task or item on the calendar to open its details in a pop-up window.

   - From here, you can update information, change dates, or add comments.

3. **Drag-and-Drop Functionality:**

   - Rearrange items on the calendar by dragging them to a new date.

   - This feature automatically updates the associated date column on your board.

4. **Color-Coding and Status Indicators:**

   - Tasks are color-coded based on their status or other custom fields.

   - For example, completed tasks might appear in green, while overdue tasks appear in red.

5. **Synchronizing with External Calendars:**

   o Use the **"Sync"** option to connect your Monday.com Calendar View with Google Calendar, Outlook, or other external calendar apps.

Best Practices for Using the Calendar View

To maximize the benefits of the Calendar View, consider these tips:

1. **Plan Weekly Reviews:**

   o Dedicate time at the start or end of each week to review your calendar.

   o Adjust timelines or priorities as needed to stay on track.

2. **Use Multiple Date Columns:**

   o Boards with both start and end dates can provide a more complete picture of task timelines.

   o Toggle between different date columns to see how they affect your calendar.

3. **Combine with Filters:**

   o Use filters to focus on specific team members, projects, or task statuses.

   o For example, filter for tasks assigned to you or tasks marked as "High Priority."

4. **Integrate with Dashboards:**

   o Embed your Calendar View into a **dashboard** for a high-level overview of multiple boards and timelines.

Common Use Cases for the Calendar View

Here are some examples of how the Calendar View can be used effectively:

1. **Project Deadlines:**

   o Visualize all key milestones and deadlines for a project in one place.

    o   Quickly spot overlapping deadlines and adjust timelines.

2. **Content Planning:**

    o   Marketing teams can use the Calendar View to manage content calendars, ensuring posts, blogs, or campaigns are scheduled appropriately.

3. **Event Management:**

    o   Track important dates for events, such as bookings, rehearsals, or launch days.

    o   Use the drag-and-drop feature to reschedule events with ease.

4. **Personal Productivity:**

    o   Use a personal board with the Calendar View to track meetings, appointments, or deadlines.

Tips for Troubleshooting the Calendar View

If you encounter issues with the Calendar View, try the following:

1. **Items Not Appearing on the Calendar:**

    o   Ensure the board includes a valid date column and that dates are properly entered.

    o   Check your filters to ensure they're not hiding items unintentionally.

2. **Incorrect Dates Displayed:**

    o   Verify that the correct date column is selected in the Calendar settings.

3. **Sync Errors with External Calendars:**

    o   Reconnect your external calendar and ensure the sync settings are correctly configured.

Advanced Features of the Calendar View

1. **Linked Dependencies:**

- o Use Calendar View alongside **dependency columns** to track how task delays impact other tasks.

2. **Timeline Integration:**

   - o Combine the Calendar View with the **Timeline View** for a comprehensive perspective of tasks and deadlines.

3. **Recurring Events:**

   - o Automate recurring tasks, such as weekly meetings or monthly reports, to appear in your Calendar View using **automations**.

Conclusion

The Calendar View is an essential tool in Monday.com for visualizing and managing time-sensitive tasks. Its intuitive interface, customization options, and seamless integration with external tools make it a must-use feature for teams and individuals alike. By effectively leveraging the Calendar View, you can stay organized, meet deadlines, and ensure your projects run smoothly.

5.2 Using Dashboards for Insights

5.2.1 Creating a Dashboard

Dashboards in Monday.com are powerful tools designed to provide a high-level overview of your workflows, projects, and data. They allow you to consolidate information from multiple boards into one visual workspace, enabling you to track progress, monitor key metrics, and make informed decisions at a glance. This section will guide you step-by-step through the process of creating a dashboard in Monday.com, ensuring you maximize its potential to improve your organizational efficiency.

1. Understanding the Purpose of Dashboards

Before creating a dashboard, it's important to identify its purpose. Ask yourself the following questions:

- What information do I need to track?

- Which boards and projects will this dashboard pull data from?

- Who will use this dashboard, and what insights do they need?

Dashboards are flexible and can be tailored to different goals, such as:

- Monitoring project timelines and deadlines.

- Tracking team workload and resource allocation.

- Analyzing data through visual widgets like charts and graphs.

- Summarizing KPIs (Key Performance Indicators) for leadership teams.

2. Step-by-Step Guide to Creating a Dashboard

Step 1: Accessing the Dashboard Creation Tool

1. Navigate to the main menu on the left-hand side of your Monday.com interface.

2. Click on the "+ Add" button at the bottom of the menu.

3. From the dropdown list, select **"Dashboard"**.

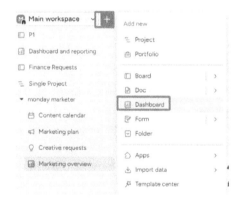

You will be prompted to name your dashboard and choose its type (private, shareable, or main).

- **Private Dashboard**: Accessible only to you or specific team members you invite.

- **Shareable Dashboard**: Ideal for sharing with clients or external stakeholders.

- **Main Dashboard**: Visible to all members of your team.

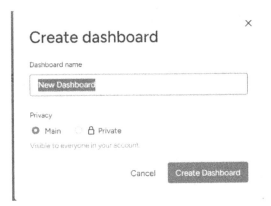

Step 2: Adding Boards to Your Dashboard

After creating your dashboard, you'll need to link it to one or more boards.

1. Click the **"Add Boards"** button.

2. Select the boards you want to include. These boards will serve as the data sources for your dashboard.

3. Confirm your selection by clicking **"Add Boards"**.

Remember, you can always add or remove boards later as your needs evolve.

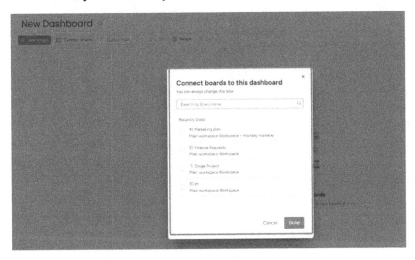

3. Exploring Dashboard Widgets

Widgets are the building blocks of dashboards. They help visualize data in different formats, such as charts, tables, calendars, or workload graphs. To start, you need to add widgets to your dashboard.

Step 1: Adding Your First Widget

1. Click the **"Add Widget"** button at the top of your dashboard.

2. Browse through the available widgets in the widget library or search for a specific one.

3. Select the widget you want to use and click **"Add to Dashboard"**.

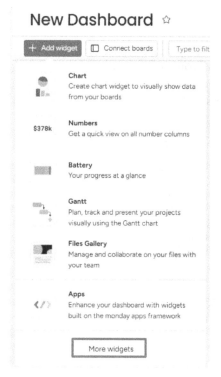

Step 2: Customizing Widgets

Once added, you can configure the widget to display the data you need. For example:

- **Chart Widget**: Select the type of chart (bar, pie, line, etc.), choose the data source, and define parameters such as X-axis and Y-axis values.

- **Timeline Widget**: Link the widget to your project boards to visualize timelines and deadlines.

- **Workload Widget**: Customize this to display team members' task loads and identify potential bottlenecks.

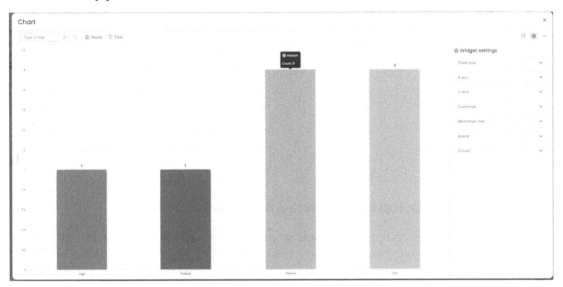

Step 3: Rearranging and Resizing Widgets

You can drag and drop widgets to rearrange their positions on the dashboard. Resize widgets by clicking and dragging their corners to ensure your dashboard is visually organized.

4. Best Practices for Designing an Effective Dashboard

To create a dashboard that truly enhances your organization, keep the following best practices in mind:

1. Prioritize Simplicity
Avoid cluttering your dashboard with too many widgets or data sources. Focus on the most critical metrics and insights. A clean and simple layout ensures the dashboard remains easy to interpret.

2. Use Visual Hierarchy
Position the most important widgets at the top or center of your dashboard, where they are most visible. Use contrasting colors to emphasize key data points.

3. Group Related Information Together
Organize your dashboard so that related widgets are placed near each other. For example, group timeline widgets with workload widgets to get a comprehensive view of project progress and resource allocation.

4. Leverage Color-Coding and Labels
Use consistent color schemes and labels across widgets to make data easier to

understand at a glance. For example, use green for completed tasks, yellow for tasks in progress, and red for overdue tasks.

5. Real-World Use Cases for Dashboards

Use Case 1: Project Progress Tracking
A dashboard for project tracking might include:

- A timeline widget showing key milestones.

- A status widget summarizing tasks as "Done," "In Progress," or "Stuck."

- A workload widget highlighting team members who are over or under capacity.

Use Case 2: Marketing Campaign Dashboard
For marketing teams, a dashboard could include:

- A chart widget displaying campaign performance metrics like click-through rates or ROI.

- A calendar widget to visualize content schedules.

- A table widget summarizing campaign budgets and expenses.

Use Case 3: Executive Overview
An executive dashboard might focus on high-level KPIs:

- A numbers widget showing overall revenue or sales targets.

- A battery widget to visualize progress toward goals.

- A chart widget comparing performance across departments or teams.

6. Sharing and Collaborating on Dashboards

Once your dashboard is set up, you can share it with your team or stakeholders.

Step 1: Sharing a Dashboard

1. Click on the **"Share"** button at the top right corner of your dashboard.

2. Choose who to share it with: specific team members, external collaborators, or the entire organization.

Step 2: Setting Permissions

Define what collaborators can do with the dashboard:

- **View Only**: Users can see the dashboard but cannot make changes.

- **Edit**: Users can customize widgets, add boards, and modify settings.

Step 3: Collaborating in Real-Time

Collaborators can comment on widgets, suggest changes, or provide feedback directly on the dashboard.

7. Troubleshooting Dashboard Issues

Even with a detailed guide, you may encounter some challenges while creating a dashboard. Here are common issues and solutions:

Issue 1: Widgets Not Displaying Data Correctly

- **Solution**: Double-check that the widget is linked to the correct board and columns. Update the filters if necessary.

Issue 2: Dashboard Performance is Slow

- **Solution**: Reduce the number of widgets or limit data sources to essential boards.

Issue 3: Difficulty Sharing Dashboards

- **Solution**: Ensure the dashboard's sharing settings are configured correctly and that collaborators have access to the linked boards.

Conclusion

Creating a dashboard in Monday.com is an essential step in improving organizational visibility and decision-making. By following the steps outlined above and customizing dashboards to your specific needs, you can transform raw data into actionable insights. Whether you're tracking project timelines, analyzing KPIs, or monitoring team workloads, a well-designed dashboard will become a cornerstone of your productivity strategy.

5.2.2 Adding and Customizing Widgets

Dashboards in Monday.com are an incredibly powerful tool that enables you to consolidate and visualize data from various boards in one central location. Widgets are the building blocks of dashboards, and they provide tailored insights into the status of your projects, team workload, and performance metrics. This section will guide you through the process of adding widgets to your dashboards and customizing them to suit your specific needs.

What Are Widgets in Monday.com?

Widgets are mini-tools or modules that display information from your boards in a visual format. They help you track progress, manage timelines, monitor workloads, and make data-driven decisions. Widgets can be customized to present data in a variety of formats, such as charts, graphs, numbers, calendars, or text-based summaries.

Monday.com offers a variety of widget types, such as:

- **Chart Widgets**: Visualize data trends using bar graphs, pie charts, or line graphs.
- **Calendar Widgets**: Display upcoming deadlines and scheduled tasks.
- **Battery Widgets**: Show the overall progress of your projects.
- **Workload Widgets**: Manage and distribute tasks among team members.
- **Number Widgets**: Highlight key metrics like completed tasks or sales figures.
- **Text Widgets**: Add notes or static text for additional context.

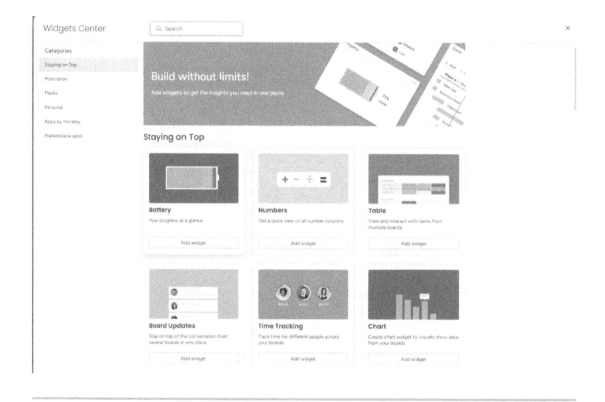

Step-by-Step Guide to Adding Widgets

Step 1: Open Your Dashboard

1. Navigate to the dashboard where you want to add widgets.

2. If you haven't created a dashboard yet, you can do so by clicking the "+" sign in the "Dashboards" section on the left-hand panel, then selecting "New Dashboard."

3. Give your dashboard a name and link it to the boards containing the data you want to visualize.

Step 2: Access the Widget Center

1. Once your dashboard is open, click the **"Add Widget"** button located in the top-right corner of the dashboard.

2. This will open the **Widget Center**, where you can browse through the available widget types.

3. Widgets are categorized for easy navigation, such as "Charts," "Progress," "Time Tracking," and "Team."

Step 3: Select and Add a Widget

1. Choose a widget from the Widget Center that best suits your needs. For example, select the **"Chart Widget"** if you want to create a graph to track task progress.

2. Click on the widget to add it to your dashboard. It will appear as a blank placeholder until you configure it.

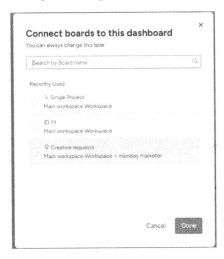

3. Repeat this process to add multiple widgets if necessary.

Customizing Widgets

Once you've added widgets to your dashboard, customization is the key to making them meaningful and relevant. Follow these steps to configure your widgets:

Step 1: Open Widget Settings

1. Hover over the widget you've added, and you'll see a small gear icon (⚙️☐) in the top-right corner. Click on this icon to access the widget's settings.

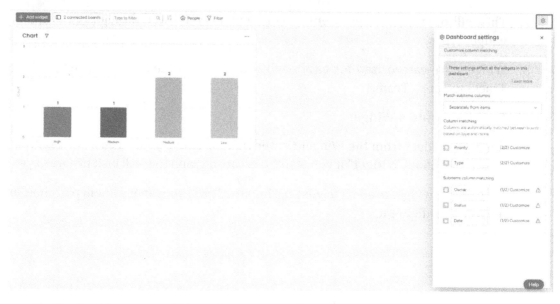

2. Each widget type will have its own set of customization options.

Step 2: Select Data Sources

1. In the settings panel, select the **data source** for the widget.

    o For example, if you're using a Chart Widget, you can choose which board and specific columns (e.g., status, priority, due date) you want the widget to pull data from.

2. You can link data from one or multiple boards, depending on the widget's functionality.

Step 3: Adjust Widget Settings

Each widget has unique settings that allow you to tailor it to your needs:

- **Chart Widget**:

    o Choose the chart type (bar, pie, line, etc.).

    o Select the X-axis and Y-axis data (e.g., X-axis = Task Name, Y-axis = Completion Percentage).

    o Add filters to show specific data (e.g., only "In Progress" tasks).

- **Calendar Widget**:

- Sync columns with dates (e.g., "Deadline" or "Due Date" columns).
- Color-code events based on status or priority.

- **Battery Widget**:
  - Configure it to display progress based on status columns (e.g., "To Do," "In Progress," "Done").
  - Add thresholds for progress indicators (e.g., 50% = yellow, 100% = green).

- **Workload Widget**:
  - Select team members and link tasks to each member.
  - Adjust workload capacity settings to prevent overallocation.

Step 4: Add Filters and Groupings

1. Use the **filter** options to narrow down the data displayed in the widget. For example, you can filter tasks by status (e.g., "Completed") or by assigned user.

2. Group data logically for better visualization. For instance, group tasks by priority levels or project categories.

Step 5: Resize and Rearrange Widgets

1. Resize widgets by dragging their edges to make them larger or smaller.

2. Rearrange widgets by dragging and dropping them within the dashboard. This helps you create a clean and logical layout.

Advanced Tips for Customizing Widgets

1. Combine Multiple Data Sources

Some widgets, like Dashboards and Workload Widgets, allow you to pull data from multiple boards. Use this feature to create a comprehensive view of all your projects in one place.

2. Add Dynamic Widgets

Dynamic widgets, such as Gantt Charts and Timeline Widgets, provide real-time updates on project progress. Use these widgets to track timelines and identify delays quickly.

3. Use Conditional Formatting

Some widgets support conditional formatting. For example, you can configure a widget to highlight overdue tasks in red or to display completed tasks in green.

4. Add Interactive Elements

Enable interactive features where applicable, such as clickable charts that allow you to drill down into specific data points.

5. Test and Refine Widgets

After adding widgets, review your dashboard to ensure it meets your needs. Test different customization options and refine them over time.

Common Use Cases for Customizing Widgets

1. Tracking Team Performance

- Use the **Workload Widget** to monitor each team member's task allocation and prevent burnout.

- Combine with a **Battery Widget** to visualize overall progress on key deliverables.

2. Managing Project Timelines

- Use the **Timeline Widget** to monitor project milestones.

- Pair with a **Calendar Widget** to ensure deadlines are clearly visible.

3. Reporting Key Metrics

- Create a **Chart Widget** to display the number of completed tasks vs. pending tasks.

- Add a **Number Widget** to showcase KPIs like the total number of sales or tickets resolved.

4. Monitoring Client Deliverables

- Use a combination of **Text Widgets** for notes and **File Widgets** for attaching deliverables directly to the dashboard.

Conclusion

Customizing widgets in Monday.com is a straightforward yet powerful way to create dashboards that cater to your unique needs. By understanding the available widget types and leveraging their customization options, you can transform raw data into actionable insights, streamline workflows, and keep your team on the same page. Take time to experiment with different widgets and layouts to maximize the value of your dashboards.

5.2.3 Using Dashboards for Reporting

Dashboards in Monday.com are one of the most powerful tools for reporting, offering users the ability to consolidate, visualize, and analyze data across multiple boards in a single location. Whether you're tracking project progress, managing team workload, or analyzing key performance indicators (KPIs), dashboards provide insights that drive better decision-making. This section will guide you through the process of using dashboards effectively for reporting, from setup to advanced customization.

1. What Are Dashboards in Monday.com?

Dashboards are centralized spaces where you can view and analyze data using a variety of widgets. These widgets pull information from your boards, enabling you to create custom visualizations that suit your reporting needs. For example:

- **Progress Tracking:** Visualize the completion percentage of tasks or projects.

- **Workload Management:** Monitor team members' assignments to avoid overloading.

- **Timeline Overviews:** Gain a clear picture of project schedules and deadlines.

- **Budget Tracking:** Keep tabs on financial metrics such as expenses and revenues.

By consolidating data from multiple boards, dashboards allow you to see the bigger picture and make informed decisions.

2. Setting Up Dashboards for Reporting

2.1 Choosing the Right Data Sources

Before building a dashboard, decide which boards contain the data you want to include. For reporting purposes, consider these steps:

1. Identify the specific goals of your report (e.g., tracking KPIs, monitoring deadlines).

2. Select boards that are relevant to those goals. For instance:

    o Use your **project management board** to track task progress.

    o Include your **budget board** to analyze expenses.

    o Add your **team workload board** to manage resource allocation.

2.2 Creating a New Dashboard

Follow these steps to create your dashboard:

1. Click on the **"Dashboards"** tab on the left-hand navigation panel.

2. Select **"New Dashboard"** and give it a descriptive name (e.g., "Monthly Project Report" or "Team Performance Overview").

3. Choose the boards you want to connect to the dashboard. You can link data from one or multiple boards, depending on your needs.

2.3 Adding Relevant Widgets

Widgets are the building blocks of your dashboard. They enable you to display data in various formats such as graphs, tables, calendars, and charts. Some commonly used widgets for reporting include:

- **The Chart Widget:** Visualize data with bar, pie, or line charts.

- **The Table Widget:** Display raw data in a tabular format.

- **The Numbers Widget:** Highlight key metrics such as total revenue or completed tasks.

- **The Battery Widget:** Track progress toward goals.

- **The Timeline Widget:** Visualize schedules and deadlines.

3. Customizing Dashboards for Reporting

3.1 Configuring Widgets for Clear Insights

Each widget can be tailored to display the exact information you need. Below are some examples of widget configurations:

- **The Chart Widget:**

    - Use this to compare task statuses (e.g., "Completed," "In Progress," "Stuck").

    - Group data by columns such as "Owner" to see performance by team member.

    - Set filters to focus on specific time frames (e.g., "Last 30 Days").

- **The Numbers Widget:**

    - Summarize financial metrics like total expenses or revenues.

    - Track overall project completion percentages.

- **The Table Widget:**

    - Use this widget to show a detailed breakdown of tasks, deadlines, and assignees.

    - Apply filters to display only overdue tasks or items assigned to a specific team member.

3.2 Adjusting Layout and Design

For effective reporting, it's essential that your dashboard is visually clear and well-organized:

- **Rearrange Widgets:** Drag and drop widgets to prioritize important metrics.

- **Resize Widgets:** Adjust the size of each widget to give more space to critical data.

- **Color Coding:** Use color-coded widgets to make the dashboard more intuitive (e.g., green for completed tasks, red for overdue items).

---

4. Filtering Data for Specific Reports

Filters are essential for narrowing down the data displayed in your dashboard. For example:

- **Time-Based Filters:** Show data for a specific period, such as weekly, monthly, or quarterly reports.

- **Status Filters:** Focus on tasks with specific statuses, such as "In Progress" or "Stuck."

- **Board Filters:** If your dashboard pulls data from multiple boards, you can filter by board to isolate certain projects.

Filters can be applied both at the widget level and at the overall dashboard level, depending on your reporting needs.

5. Sharing Dashboards with Stakeholders

5.1 Sharing Permissions

Once your dashboard is ready, you may want to share it with others in your team or organization:

- **Private Dashboards:** Keep your dashboard private if it contains sensitive information.

- **Shareable Dashboards:** Use this option to share dashboards with external stakeholders, such as clients or vendors.

- **Team Dashboards:** Allow all team members to view and interact with the dashboard.

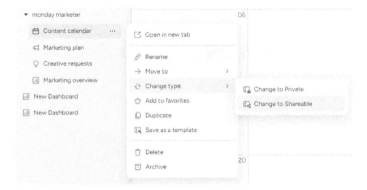

To share a dashboard:

1. Click on the **"Share"** button at the top of the dashboard.

2. Adjust the sharing settings to determine who can view or edit the dashboard.

5.2 Exporting Dashboard Reports

For offline analysis or presentations, dashboards can be exported as PDF files or images:

1. Click the **"…"** menu in the top-right corner of the dashboard.

2. Select **"Export"** and choose your preferred format.

3. Customize the export settings (e.g., include or exclude certain widgets).

Exported dashboards are useful for sharing data with stakeholders who do not have access to Monday.com.

6. Advanced Tips for Reporting with Dashboards

6.1 Combining Multiple Data Sources

To create comprehensive reports, combine data from various boards:

- For a project status report, include task progress, budget metrics, and timeline visualizations in a single dashboard.

- Use the **"Connected Boards"** feature to create relationships between boards and display consolidated data in your widgets.

6.2 Automating Updates

To save time, automate dashboard updates:

- Use Monday.com's automation recipes to trigger data changes (e.g., "When status changes to 'Done,' update progress in the dashboard").

- Enable real-time sync for widgets so that your dashboard reflects the latest data.

6.3 Analyzing Trends Over Time

Dashboards are not only for static reports but also for trend analysis. For example:

- Use line charts to track performance metrics over months.
- Compare data from different time periods using historical snapshots.

7. Real-World Examples of Dashboards for Reporting

Example 1: Marketing Campaign Dashboard

- **Widgets Used:** Progress tracking, budget tracking, and timeline views.
- **Purpose:** Monitor campaign goals, spending, and deadlines.

Example 2: Team Performance Dashboard

- **Widgets Used:** Workload widget, battery widget, and chart widget.
- **Purpose:** Analyze task completion rates and balance team workload.

Example 3: Financial Overview Dashboard

- **Widgets Used:** Numbers widget, table widget, and chart widget.
- **Purpose:** Track expenses, revenue, and budget utilization.

By following the steps and strategies outlined above, you can harness the full power of Monday.com dashboards to create insightful, actionable reports. Dashboards not only provide a clear overview of your data but also empower you to make informed decisions that improve productivity and efficiency.

5.3 Advanced Reporting Tools

5.3.1 Filtering and Sorting Data

When managing large projects or working on multiple boards in Monday.com, it's essential to quickly access relevant information. Filtering and sorting data are powerful tools in Monday.com that help you sift through large amounts of data to find exactly what you need, ensuring that your workflows remain efficient and organized. In this section, we will explore filtering and sorting in detail, covering how to use these tools effectively to improve your project management and organizational efficiency.

1. Why Use Filtering and Sorting in Monday.com?

Filtering and sorting are essential for:

- **Finding Specific Information**: Quickly locate tasks, projects, or team members based on criteria such as status, due date, or assigned person.

- **Streamlining Workflows**: Focus on high-priority items by isolating data that requires immediate attention.

- **Enhancing Team Collaboration**: Ensure everyone sees only the relevant data they need to complete their tasks.

- **Improving Decision-Making**: Sort or filter data to gain insights and make informed decisions.

2. Filtering Data in Monday.com

Filters allow you to display only the items that meet specific criteria, making it easier to focus on what matters most. Here's a step-by-step guide to filtering your data effectively.

2.1 Accessing the Filter Option

1. Open the board you want to filter.

2. Locate the **Filter** button, typically found at the top-right corner of the board. It's represented by a funnel icon.

3. Click on the **Filter** button to open the filtering menu.

2.2 Applying a Filter

1. **Choose a Column to Filter**: Select the column you want to filter by. For example, you can filter by **Status**, **Person**, **Date**, or any custom column you've added.

2. **Set Filter Conditions**: Depending on the column type, you can set specific conditions. For example:

   o **Status Column**: Show items with a status of "In Progress" or "Done."

   o **Date Column**: Filter items by date ranges, such as tasks due this week or overdue tasks.

   o **Person Column**: Display only tasks assigned to a specific team member.

3. As you apply filters, the board will update dynamically to show only the items that match your criteria.

2.3 Combining Multiple Filters

Monday.com allows you to apply multiple filters simultaneously. For example, you can filter for tasks assigned to a specific person that are also due this week.

- After selecting your first filter condition, click **Add Filter** to set another condition.

- Use the **AND/OR Logic** to refine your filters:

  - **AND**: Both conditions must be true.

  - **OR**: Either condition can be true.

2.4 Saving Filters for Reuse

If you frequently use the same filter criteria, you can save it for quick access:

1. Apply your filters.

2. Click the **Save Filter** button (next to the filter menu).

3. Give your filter a name and save it.

4. Access saved filters from the **Saved Filters** dropdown menu in the filter bar.

3. Sorting Data in Monday.com

Sorting allows you to reorder the items on your board based on specific columns. This can be helpful when prioritizing tasks, viewing timelines, or analyzing progress.

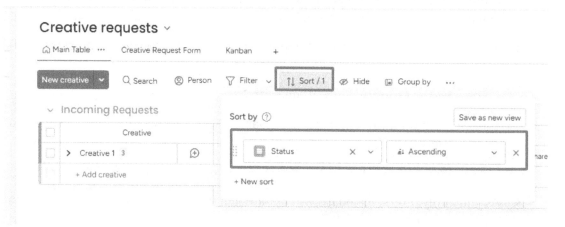

3.1 Accessing the Sorting Feature

1. Open the board where you want to sort data.

2. Locate the column header that you want to sort by.

3. Hover over the column header to reveal the **Sort** button (a small arrow icon).

3.2 Types of Sorting

Monday.com offers two main sorting options:

- **Ascending Order**: Click the arrow pointing upwards to sort items in ascending order (e.g., A–Z, earliest to latest).

- **Descending Order**: Click the arrow pointing downwards to sort items in descending order (e.g., Z–A, latest to earliest).

3.3 Sorting by Multiple Columns

If you need to sort data based on multiple criteria, you can:

1. Apply sorting to the first column.

2. Then, while holding down the **Shift key**, click on another column header to add a secondary sorting level.

For example, you can first sort tasks by **Priority** (High to Low) and then by **Due Date** (Earliest to Latest).

4. Combining Filters and Sorting for Maximum Efficiency

Using filters and sorting together allows you to drill down into your data while also arranging it in a meaningful way. Here are some practical use cases:

- **Prioritize Urgent Tasks**: Filter tasks with a status of "High Priority" and sort them by due date to address the most urgent items first.

- **Analyze Team Performance**: Filter tasks assigned to a specific team member and sort them by completion percentage to track progress.

- **Prepare Reports**: Filter tasks completed within a specific timeframe and sort them alphabetically or by project category for reporting purposes.

5. Advanced Features of Filtering and Sorting

Monday.com offers advanced options to make filtering and sorting even more powerful:

5.1 Conditional Filters

Use advanced conditions such as "contains," "does not contain," or "is empty" to create more nuanced filters. For example:

- Filter items where the title contains "Meeting."

- Exclude items where the status is "Canceled."

5.2 Filter by Subitems

If you use subitems in your boards, you can filter and sort them just like main items. Enable the **Subitems** filter in the filter menu to include or exclude subitems from your view.

5.3 Exporting Filtered and Sorted Data

After applying filters and sorting, you can export the refined data for reporting:

1. Click the three-dot menu in the top-right corner of the board.

2. Select **Export Board to Excel**.

3. Your filtered and sorted data will be exported exactly as displayed on the board.

6. Best Practices for Filtering and Sorting

- **Keep It Simple**: Avoid overcomplicating filters with too many conditions, as it may confuse team members.

- **Name Filters Clearly**: When saving filters, use clear names that indicate their purpose (e.g., "Overdue Tasks for John").

- **Combine with Automations**: Use filters to identify recurring patterns and set up automations to manage them automatically.

- **Educate Your Team**: Ensure all team members understand how to apply filters and sorting to improve collaboration.

By mastering filtering and sorting in Monday.com, you can quickly access the information you need, streamline your workflows, and make data-driven decisions with ease. In the next section, we'll explore how to export these insights into reports for sharing and further analysis.

5.3.2 Exporting Reports

Exporting reports in Monday.com is a powerful feature that allows users to take data from their boards, dashboards, or projects and convert it into formats suitable for offline use or further analysis. Whether you need to share insights with external stakeholders, analyze data in other software like Excel, or simply archive your information, exporting reports is a straightforward process that can enhance your workflow. This section provides a comprehensive, step-by-step guide on how to export reports effectively.

Understanding Export Formats

Monday.com supports exporting data in different formats, depending on your needs. These formats include:

- **Excel (.xlsx):** The most commonly used format for exporting structured data. Ideal for creating pivot tables, performing advanced calculations, and visualizing data in charts.

- **CSV (.csv):** A universal format for data exchange. Perfect for importing data into other systems or software.

- **PDF (.pdf):** Great for creating snapshots of dashboards or static reports to share with stakeholders.

Before exporting, consider your purpose:

- If you need to analyze data or manipulate it further, Excel or CSV is preferable.

- For presentations or sharing polished reports, PDF is the way to go.

Exporting Data from Boards

One of the most common export scenarios is exporting data directly from a board. Follow these steps:

1. **Open the Board You Want to Export**

   o Navigate to the board containing the data you want to export. Ensure all necessary columns, groups, and items are visible.

○ Use the **Filter** and **Sort** options to refine the data as needed before exporting.

2. **Access the Export Option**

○ Click on the three-dot menu (also known as the "More Actions" menu) in the top-right corner of your board.

○ From the dropdown menu, select **Export Board to Excel** or **Export Board to CSV**, depending on your preference.

3. **Download the File**

○ Monday.com will generate the file and download it to your computer automatically.

○ Check your downloads folder or the designated location where your browser saves files.

4. **Open and Review the Exported Data**

○ Open the Excel or CSV file to ensure the data is exported correctly.

○ Verify column headers, item data, and any special fields (e.g., dates, dropdowns, tags).

Exporting Dashboards

Dashboards provide a visual summary of data from multiple boards. Exporting dashboards is especially useful for creating presentations or sharing insights with non-Monday.com users. Here's how to do it:

1. **Navigate to the Dashboard**

   o Open the dashboard you wish to export.

   o Ensure the widgets you want to include are properly configured and displayed.

2. **Export as PDF**

   o Click the three-dot menu in the top-right corner of the dashboard.

   o Select **Export as PDF** from the dropdown menu.

3. **Customize the Export**

   o Some dashboards allow you to customize the export settings, such as selecting specific widgets to include.

   o Preview the export to ensure it captures the necessary data.

4. **Save and Share**

   o The PDF will be downloaded to your computer.

   o Share the file with your stakeholders via email, cloud storage, or other channels.

Exporting Specific Data Segments

Sometimes, you might not want to export an entire board or dashboard but only specific segments of data. Here's how to do it:

1. **Use Filters and Views**

   o Apply filters to your board to narrow down the data to specific groups, statuses, or timeframes.

   o For example, filter tasks marked as "Completed" or items assigned to a particular team member.

2. **Export the Filtered View**

   o Once the data is filtered, proceed with the export process.

- Monday.com will only export the visible data, ensuring irrelevant information is excluded.

3. **Verify the Exported Data**

   - Open the file and check that only the filtered data has been exported.

Automating Exports with Integrations

Monday.com allows users to automate data exports using integrations with external tools. For example:

- **Zapier Integration:** Automate exporting data from Monday.com to Google Sheets, Dropbox, or your email.

- **Power BI or Tableau:** Use these tools to pull data directly from Monday.com and create dynamic reports.

Exporting Reports Best Practices

1. **Review Data Before Exporting**

   - Double-check your board or dashboard for accuracy. Ensure data is up-to-date and no essential fields are missing.

2. **Choose the Right Export Format**

   - For detailed analysis, use Excel or CSV.

   - For sharing visual insights, use PDF.

3. **Secure Your Exported Files**

   - If the data contains sensitive information, ensure the exported files are stored securely.

   - Use password protection or encryption for additional security.

4. **Keep Exports Organized**

   - Label your exported files with clear names, such as "Marketing_Project_Report_Jan2025.xlsx".

   ○   Store files in dedicated folders for easy access later.

Troubleshooting Common Export Issues

- **Export Button Not Visible:** Ensure you have the necessary permissions for the board or dashboard. Contact your admin if needed.

- **Data Format Errors in CSV/Excel:** Check the settings of your file reader (e.g., Excel) to ensure proper encoding (UTF-8) and formatting.

- **Incomplete Data Export:** Verify that no filters are unintentionally applied to the board or dashboard before exporting.

Practical Examples of Export Use Cases

1. **Weekly Team Updates:** Export weekly progress reports in PDF format for team meetings.

2. **Client Deliverables:** Share project status updates in Excel with external clients who do not use Monday.com.

3. **Performance Analysis:** Export raw data to CSV for advanced analysis in tools like Excel or Google Sheets.

By mastering exporting tools in Monday.com, you can unlock the full potential of your data, ensuring it's accessible, shareable, and actionable in any format or context.

CHAPTER VI
Advanced Features for Better Organization

6.1 Customizing Your Workspace

6.1.1 Themes and Layouts

Customizing your workspace in Monday.com allows you to create an environment that is both visually appealing and functionally optimized for your team's needs. By adjusting themes and layouts, you can ensure that the platform aligns with your branding, personal preferences, and workflow requirements. This section will guide you step by step on how to customize your workspace, focusing on themes and layouts.

Understanding Themes in Monday.com

Themes in Monday.com primarily involve the visual elements of your workspace, including colors and display modes. These customizations enhance usability and create a consistent aesthetic for your team.

Light and Dark Modes

Monday.com offers light and dark themes, allowing you to choose the mode that best suits your working style.

1. **Switching Between Light and Dark Modes**

   o   Navigate to your **profile picture** in the bottom-left corner of the screen.

   o   Click on **"My Profile"** to access settings.

- o Under the **"Preferences"** tab, you will find the option to toggle between light and dark modes.

- o Select your preferred mode, and the platform will instantly update its appearance.

2. **Benefits of Using Dark Mode**

- o Reduces eye strain during extended working hours.

- o Saves battery life on devices with OLED or AMOLED screens.

- o Enhances focus by minimizing bright distractions.

3. **Tips for Effective Use**

- o Use light mode in well-lit environments to ensure better visibility.

- o Switch to dark mode in low-light settings to reduce glare.

Branding Your Workspace with Colors

Customizing the colors of your workspace is an excellent way to align Monday.com with your company's branding.

1. **Customizing Board Colors**

    o   Open any board you wish to customize.

    o   Click on the **three-dot menu** in the top-right corner of the board.

    o   Select **"Board Settings"**, and look for options to change the board's theme or color scheme.

    o   Apply your preferred color for a consistent branding experience.

2. **Using Status Colors**
   Status colors are customizable in Monday.com and play a vital role in task management. For example:

    o   Green for tasks marked as **"Done."**

    o   Yellow for tasks labeled as **"In Progress."**

    o   Red for tasks that are **"Stuck."**

How to Customize Status Colors:

- o Click on the **status column** in any board.

- o Select **"Edit Labels"**, and modify the colors and names of each status.

- o Save your changes, and the board will automatically update.

3. **Color Psychology in Workspaces**

- o Use **blue** for calm and focus.

- o Use **green** for success and completion.

- o Avoid overly bright or clashing colors, as they can create visual clutter.

Optimizing Layouts for Better Organization

Layouts in Monday.com determine how information is displayed and accessed. By optimizing layouts, you can ensure that your workspace is both user-friendly and tailored to your team's needs.

Configuring Board Layouts

Boards are the backbone of Monday.com, and their layouts significantly impact how you interact with data.

1. **Choosing the Right View**
   Monday.com offers various board views, including:

- o **Table View:** Best for detailed task tracking.

- o **Kanban View:** Ideal for visualizing workflows.

- o **Timeline View:** Perfect for planning and scheduling.

- o **Calendar View:** Useful for managing deadlines and appointments.

How to Change Board Views:

- o Click on the **"+" button** at the top of the board to add a new view.

- o Select the desired view from the dropdown menu.

- o Customize the view settings to match your workflow.

2. **Grouping Items**

Grouping items allows you to organize tasks and data into manageable sections. For example:

- Group tasks by **project phase** (e.g., "Planning," "Execution," "Review").

- Group tasks by **priority** (e.g., "High," "Medium," "Low").

Steps to Group Items:

- Click on the **"Group Settings"** option in the board menu.

- Create custom groups and drag items into their respective sections.

Customizing Columns for Optimal Functionality

Columns in Monday.com are highly versatile and can be customized to meet specific requirements.

1. **Types of Columns**

- **Text Columns:** Add descriptions or notes.

- **Status Columns:** Track progress with customizable labels.

- **Date Columns:** Manage deadlines and timelines.

- **People Columns:** Assign tasks to team members.

How to Add a Column:

- Click the **"+" button** on the right side of any board.

- Select the column type from the dropdown menu.

- Name the column and adjust its settings as needed.

2. **Customizing Column Order and Width**

- Drag and drop columns to rearrange them.

- Hover over a column header to adjust its width.

3. **Using Formulas and Automations in Columns**

- Add a **Formula Column** to calculate values dynamically.

- Set up **automations** to update columns based on triggers.

Workspace Personalization Tips

Personalizing your workspace ensures that you and your team can navigate it efficiently.

1. **Pinning Favorite Boards**

   - Hover over the name of a board in the sidebar.

   - Click the **star icon** to pin it to your favorites.

2. **Using Widgets for Personal Dashboards**

   - Add widgets like **progress bars**, **to-do lists**, and **calendar views** to create a personalized dashboard.

3. **Archiving Unused Boards**

   - Regularly archive boards that are no longer active to reduce clutter.

Practical Examples of Themes and Layout Customization

1. **For Marketing Teams:**

   - Use vibrant colors to differentiate campaigns.

   - Configure Kanban View to track campaign stages.

2. **For Development Teams:**

   - Set up Timeline View for sprint planning.

   - Use dark mode for coding-friendly environments.

3. **For Personal Productivity:**

   - Customize status labels for personal goals (e.g., "In Progress," "Awaiting Feedback").

   - Group tasks by priority for better time management.

Conclusion

Customizing themes and layouts in Monday.com not only makes your workspace visually appealing but also ensures that it supports your specific workflow needs. By implementing the steps outlined above, you can create a workspace that is both organized and intuitive. This level of personalization will ultimately boost productivity and enhance collaboration for you and your team.

6.1.2 Workspace Templates

When working with Monday.com, one of the most powerful tools at your disposal is **workspace templates**. Workspace templates allow you to set up pre-designed structures tailored to specific use cases, saving time and ensuring consistency across your projects and teams. In this section, we'll dive deep into how to use workspace templates effectively, from understanding what they are, creating your own, customizing existing ones, and leveraging them to optimize your organization.

What Are Workspace Templates?

Workspace templates are predefined frameworks that provide a ready-to-use structure for managing projects, tasks, and workflows. Instead of building boards, columns, and workflows from scratch, you can select a template that fits your needs. These templates are designed to address common use cases, such as project management, HR onboarding, sales pipelines, event planning, and more.

Benefits of Using Workspace Templates

1. **Time-Saving**: Templates eliminate the need to start from scratch, allowing you to jump into work immediately.

2. **Consistency**: Teams across departments can maintain uniformity in how workflows are organized.

3. **Scalability**: Templates can be reused and adapted for different projects, making them ideal for large teams.

4. **Customization**: Pre-designed templates are highly flexible and can be tailored to your unique needs.

Types of Workspace Templates

Monday.com offers several categories of templates designed to suit different industries and functions:

- **Project Management**: Templates for task tracking, milestones, and deliverables.

- **Sales and CRM**: Frameworks for managing sales pipelines, leads, and customer relationships.

- **Marketing**: Campaign planning templates, social media calendars, and content production workflows.

- **HR and Recruitment**: Onboarding checklists, recruitment trackers, and employee feedback systems.

- **Personal Productivity**: To-do lists, goal-setting templates, and personal task organizers.

Each template is designed to be modular and adaptable, ensuring that users from any field can find a structure that works for them.

How to Access Workspace Templates

Step 1: Navigating to the Template Library

1. Open Monday.com and navigate to the workspace where you want to create a new board or structure.

2. Click on the **"+ Add"** button in the workspace sidebar.

3. From the dropdown menu, select **"Choose from Templates"**.

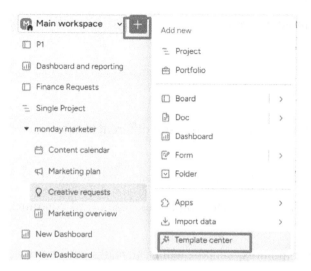

Step 2: Browsing the Template Library

1. You'll see a library of templates organized by category (e.g., Project Management, HR, Sales).

2. Use the **search bar** to look for specific templates based on keywords (e.g., "Event Planning").

3. Preview the templates by clicking on them to see their structure and included features.

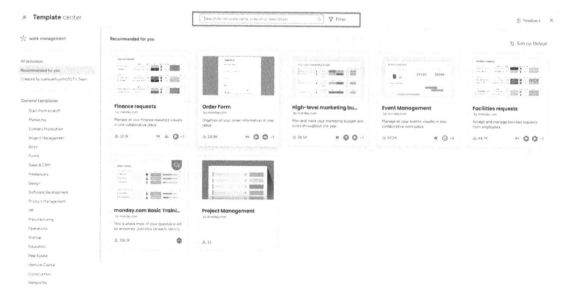

Step 3: Selecting and Applying a Template

1. Once you find a suitable template, click **"Use Template"**.

2. Choose the workspace where the template will be applied.

3. Monday.com will automatically set up the board or workflow based on the template, and you can begin customizing it.

Customizing Workspace Templates

Templates are not rigid structures—they are designed to be customized to fit your needs. Here's how you can adapt a workspace template:

1. Editing Columns

Templates come with predefined columns (e.g., Status, Due Date, Owner). If these don't match your workflow, you can:

- Add new columns by clicking the **"+"** icon.

- Delete unnecessary columns by clicking the column menu and selecting **"Delete Column"**.

- Rename columns to better suit your workflow by clicking the column header and typing a new name.

2. Modifying Item Groups

Most templates are organized into groups (e.g., "To Do," "In Progress," "Completed"). You can:

- Rename groups to match your process.

- Add new groups for additional stages in your workflow.

- Rearrange groups by dragging and dropping them.

3. Adjusting Automations

Many templates include pre-set automations, such as status changes triggering notifications or due date reminders. You can:

- View existing automations by clicking on the **"Automations"** tab.

- Edit automations to align with your processes.

- Add new automations from the automation library.

4. Changing Visualizations

Templates often come with specific board views (e.g., Timeline, Kanban, Calendar). You can:

- Switch between views using the view selector at the top of the board.

- Customize each view to display relevant information.

- Add new views based on your team's needs.

Creating Your Own Workspace Templates

If none of the pre-built templates meet your needs, you can create and save your own custom templates.

Step 1: Build Your Workspace

1. Set up a board with the exact columns, automations, item groups, and views you need.

2. Add any relevant team members and permissions.

Step 2: Save as a Template

1. Once your board is ready, click on the board name at the top.

2. Select **"More Actions"** from the dropdown menu.

3. Click **"Save as Template"**.

Step 3: Reusing Your Template

1. When you want to reuse the template, go to the template library and look under **"My Templates"**.

2. Select your saved template and apply it to a new workspace.

Best Practices for Using Templates

1. **Start Simple**: Begin with a basic template and add complexity as your needs evolve.

2. **Train Your Team**: Ensure all team members understand how to use the template to maximize efficiency.

3. **Review Regularly**: Periodically assess whether your template still meets your needs and update it as necessary.

4. **Combine Templates**: If one template doesn't fully meet your needs, combine elements from multiple templates to create a hybrid solution.

5. **Document Customizations**: Keep a record of any changes you make to a template so new team members can understand the workflow.

Common Challenges and How to Overcome Them

- **Overwhelming Options**: If the number of templates feels overwhelming, focus on your primary goal and filter templates by category.

- **Template Mismatch**: If a template isn't a perfect fit, don't hesitate to customize it extensively or start from scratch.

- **Team Resistance**: Introduce templates gradually and provide training sessions to ensure adoption.

Real-Life Example: Using Templates for Event Planning

Imagine you're planning a company-wide event. You can use Monday.com's Event Planning template, which includes:

- Groups for tasks such as "Venue Selection," "Catering," and "Marketing."

- Columns for task status, deadlines, and assignees.

- Automations to send reminders for critical deadlines.

By customizing the template to include your specific needs (e.g., adding a budget tracking column), you can efficiently manage the entire event from start to finish.

In conclusion, workspace templates are a cornerstone of Monday.com's functionality, offering flexibility, efficiency, and scalability. By mastering how to select, customize, and create templates, you can streamline your workflows and improve organization across your projects. Whether you're a solo user or part of a large team, templates empower you to work smarter, not harder.

6.2 Time Tracking and Workload Management

6.2.1 Setting Up Time Tracking

Time tracking is one of the most powerful features in Monday.com, allowing teams and individuals to monitor how time is spent on tasks, projects, and workflows. This feature not only improves accountability but also helps identify bottlenecks, streamline processes, and optimize resource allocation. In this section, we will walk you through everything you need to know about setting up and using time tracking in Monday.com.

What is Time Tracking in Monday.com?

Time tracking in Monday.com revolves around a specific column type called the **Time Tracking Column**. This column allows you to log the amount of time spent on each item in a board. Team members can start, stop, and manually edit time entries for tasks, making it easy to capture work durations in real time. This data is useful for understanding productivity, tracking project progress, and even creating reports for clients or stakeholders.

Step-by-Step Guide to Setting Up Time Tracking

Step 1: Add a Time Tracking Column to Your Board

1. **Navigate to Your Board**
   Open the board where you want to enable time tracking. Ensure that this board is set up with items (tasks) to which time tracking will be applied.

2. **Add a New Column**

   o Click on the **'+' button** at the top right of your board (next to existing columns).

   o From the dropdown menu, select **'More Column Types'** to open the column library.

3. **Select the Time Tracking Column**

   o Scroll down or use the search bar to find the **Time Tracking Column**.

   o Click on it to add it to your board. This will insert the column into your board and label it as **'Time Tracking'** by default (you can rename it if needed).

Step 2: Configuring the Time Tracking Column

Once the column is added, you can customize its settings to better suit your team's workflow.

1. **Access Column Settings**

   o Hover over the Time Tracking column header.

   o Click the **three-dot menu (•••)** and select **'Settings'**.

2. **Enable Manual Time Adjustments** (Optional)
   If your team needs the flexibility to edit time entries manually, enable the **manual time tracking** option. This is particularly useful for tracking time retrospectively or correcting errors.

3. **Restrict Access (Optional)**
   If you want to limit who can log or edit time, you can set **column permissions**. For instance, only team leaders or specific members can make changes.

Step 3: Starting and Stopping the Timer

With the Time Tracking column in place, you can begin logging time for specific tasks:

1. **Start Tracking Time**

   o Click the **timer icon** within the Time Tracking column of the item you're working on.

   o The timer will start running immediately, and you'll see a visual indicator showing that time is being recorded.

2. **Stop Tracking Time**

- o When you finish the task or take a break, click the timer icon again to stop tracking. The recorded time will be saved automatically.

3. **View Total Time Logged**

- o The total time spent on the item will be displayed in the Time Tracking column.

- o Hover over the recorded time to see a breakdown of each session.

Step 4: Manually Logging or Editing Time Entries

There may be instances where you need to add or adjust time entries manually:

1. **Log Time Manually**

- o Click on the time value in the Time Tracking column of an item.

- o Select **'Add a Time Entry'** to manually input the start and end time of your work session.

2. **Edit Existing Entries**

- o Hover over the time log and click the **edit icon.**

- o Adjust the start or end time as needed, or delete the entry altogether.

Using Time Tracking Data Effectively

1. Analyzing Time Logs at a Task Level

Each task's time log provides insights into the effort required to complete it. By analyzing these logs, you can:

- Identify tasks that take longer than expected.

- Break down complex tasks into smaller, more manageable parts.

- Allocate resources more effectively.

2. Aggregating Time Data at a Board Level

You can aggregate time tracking data for an entire board using Monday.com's **board views and widgets**:

- **Add a Time Tracking Widget to Your Dashboard**

    o Create a dashboard linked to your board.

    o Add the **Time Tracking Widget**, which provides a comprehensive view of how much time is being spent on different tasks or by different team members.

- **Filter by Groups or Team Members**

    o Use filters to break down time data by groups (e.g., project phases) or by team members, giving you a clearer picture of individual and team contributions.

3. Generating Reports

Export time tracking data for external analysis:

- Use the **Export Board to Excel** feature to download time logs.

- Create custom reports to share with stakeholders or clients, showcasing task completion times and overall project effort.

Best Practices for Time Tracking

1. **Encourage Team Members to Track Time Consistently**

    o Make time tracking a habit by integrating it into daily routines. For example, ask team members to start the timer whenever they begin working on a task.

2. **Use Time Tracking Data to Improve Workflows**

    o Analyze patterns to identify inefficiencies and adjust workflows. For instance, if a recurring task consistently takes longer than planned, consider streamlining the process.

3. **Maintain Transparency**

    o   Share time tracking data openly with the team. This fosters accountability and helps everyone stay aligned on goals and deadlines.

4. **Avoid Micromanagement**

    o   Use time tracking as a tool for optimization, not as a means to monitor or pressure team members.

Common Challenges and How to Overcome Them

Challenge 1: Forgetting to Start or Stop the Timer

Solution: Enable manual time adjustments so team members can correct missed entries.

Challenge 2: Resistance to Time Tracking

Solution: Emphasize the benefits of time tracking, such as reducing overtime, improving resource allocation, and streamlining workflows.

Challenge 3: Data Overload

Solution: Use dashboards and widgets to filter and visualize time tracking data, focusing on actionable insights.

Conclusion

Setting up time tracking in Monday.com is a straightforward process, but its impact on productivity and organization can be transformative. By following this guide, you can empower your team to better understand how time is spent, optimize workflows, and deliver projects more efficiently.

6.2.2 Analyzing Workload with the Workload View

One of the most powerful features of Monday.com is its ability to help teams track their workload effectively. The **Workload View** is a critical tool for managers and team leaders who want to ensure that work is distributed evenly and that no team member is overwhelmed. By analyzing workload in this way, you can optimize your team's productivity, improve task management, and make better decisions about resource allocation.

In this section, we'll guide you through how to set up and use the **Workload View** in Monday.com, discuss the features it offers, and explore how it can be used for efficient project and resource management.

What is the Workload View?

The **Workload View** provides a high-level overview of your team's tasks and their distribution. This view helps you understand who is working on what and how much work they have, all in a visually clear and accessible format. It allows you to easily identify potential bottlenecks, resource shortages, or employees who may be overloaded with tasks.

Key Benefits of the Workload View:

- **Visual Overview:** See the total number of tasks assigned to each team member.

- **Balance Workloads:** Quickly spot any team members with too much or too little work.

- **Effective Resource Allocation:** Plan and adjust workloads to ensure no one is overwhelmed or underutilized.

- **Time Management:** Align tasks with deadlines to ensure timely project delivery.

How to Access and Set Up the Workload View

To begin using the **Workload View**, follow these steps:

1. **Navigate to the Board**
   Go to the board you are working with in Monday.com. You should have a project board or workspace that tracks tasks or assignments for your team.

2. **Switch to the Workload View**

   o In the top left of your board, click on the "Views" dropdown menu.

- o From the options, select **Workload**. This will open the Workload View, which shows your team's tasks, allocated dates, and workload distribution.

3. **Configure Columns for Workload View**

   The Workload View requires specific columns to display data effectively. You'll need:

   - o **People Column:** This is where tasks are assigned to specific team members.

   - o **Date Column:** Assign due dates or deadlines to the tasks, so the workload can be calculated over time.

   - o **Time Tracking Column (Optional):** If you're using time tracking, this column will help measure how much time each task requires.

If you haven't yet added these columns to your board, make sure to do so before proceeding.

Understanding the Workload View Interface

Once you've enabled the Workload View, you'll be able to see a visual chart that displays your team's workload across different days or weeks. The Workload View interface has several components that you should familiarize yourself with:

- **Team Member Names (on the left):** The names of all team members are listed on the left side of the view. Each person's assigned tasks will appear next to their name.

- **Task Blocks:** Each task assigned to a team member is represented by a colored block. The length of the block corresponds to the duration of the task, and its placement corresponds to the task's start and due dates.

- **Timeline:** The horizontal timeline allows you to see the distribution of tasks over time. You can zoom in or out to view daily, weekly, or monthly tasks.

- **Filters:** Use the filters at the top to customize what you see. For instance, you can filter by specific people, task status, or project tags to narrow down your view.

Analyzing Workload in the Workload View

Once you have set up the **Workload View**, it's time to start analyzing the data. Here are key features of the Workload View that can help you analyze your team's workload:

1. **Assessing Workload Balance**

   o **Task Distribution:** Look at the number of tasks assigned to each team member. If some team members are assigned a disproportionate number of tasks, it might be time to redistribute work.

   o **Overloaded Employees:** If a person's task blocks are too long, or they have too many tasks on a given day, they may be overloaded. Use the Workload View to visually identify who might need help or support with their tasks.

   o **Team Utilization:** Ideally, you want to distribute tasks evenly. If certain employees consistently have more work, it could lead to burnout. Use the Workload View to manage this imbalance.

2. **Tracking Time and Deadlines**

   o **Visualizing Task Duration:** The blocks in the Workload View show task start and end dates. This feature is especially useful for tracking if tasks overlap or if multiple tasks are due on the same day.

   o **Analyzing Time Management:** If certain team members have too many overlapping tasks, this could cause delays or affect the quality of work. The Workload View helps you visually prioritize tasks to ensure deadlines are met.

3. **Spotting Potential Bottlenecks**

   o By analyzing the timeline and seeing the concentration of tasks on certain days, you can identify potential bottlenecks where multiple tasks are due on the same day. You can move or adjust deadlines within the Workload View to resolve these bottlenecks.

   o Additionally, it's possible to see if any tasks are dependent on other tasks. If the dependencies aren't clearly managed, it might create delays down the line.

4. **Adjusting for Shifting Priorities**

   o The **Workload View** allows for easy adjustments. If priorities shift or new tasks are added, simply drag the task blocks to new dates or assign tasks to different team members to balance out the workload.

   o You can also update task deadlines directly in the Workload View, which is crucial when deadlines are extended or moved forward.

Practical Use Case: Managing a Marketing Campaign

Let's consider a practical example to see how the **Workload View** can help with managing a marketing campaign. Imagine your team is working on a campaign that involves content creation, social media promotion, and email outreach.

1. **Assigning Tasks:**
   In the **Workload View**, you'll see each team member's tasks, such as "Write blog post," "Design graphics," and "Schedule social media posts." Tasks for each employee will be represented with a colored block. You'll be able to see the time allocated for each task and whether it overlaps with other tasks.

2. **Balancing Tasks Across Team Members:**
   As you review the Workload View, you might notice that the graphic designer is overloaded, with too many design tasks scheduled within a short time. You can adjust the timeline by moving some of their tasks to another team member, like a freelancer, or adjusting the deadline to give them more time to complete the tasks.

3. **Identifying Potential Overlaps and Delays:**
   By analyzing the timeline, you spot that the "Schedule social media posts" task is due at the same time as the "Design graphics" task. This could lead to delays in the campaign, as the content won't be ready in time for social media scheduling. You can quickly shift tasks and adjust deadlines to keep the project on track.

Using the Workload View for Resource Planning

The **Workload View** is also an excellent tool for resource planning. You can use it to assess whether your team has the right mix of skills and resources for upcoming projects.

1. **Tracking Resource Availability**
   In the Workload View, the duration of tasks reflects not only the amount of time needed but also the availability of each team member. If you see a shortage in certain areas (e.g., too many tasks are being assigned to a team member with limited availability), you can reassign tasks accordingly.

2. **Proactively Manage Team Capacity**
   Planning ahead is vital for efficient project management. The Workload View can help you predict when resources will be stretched thin, so you can take proactive measures, like hiring temporary staff or using external resources.

Conclusion

The **Workload View** in Monday.com is an indispensable tool for managing your team's tasks and ensuring the efficient use of resources. By providing a clear, visual representation of who is doing what, and when, it helps you prevent overloads, manage priorities, and track deadlines. Whether you are managing a small team or coordinating large projects across multiple departments, the Workload View can transform how you manage tasks and ensure your team stays on track.

6.3 Managing Dependencies and Subitems

6.3.1 Linking Items Across Boards

In today's fast-paced work environment, managing multiple projects, tasks, and teams is crucial. **Monday.com** offers a powerful feature that allows users to **link items across boards** to maintain a connected, organized workflow. This feature enables users to view and update related tasks across multiple boards from a single location. In this section, we will walk you through the importance of linking items across boards, how to set it up, and tips for using this feature efficiently.

Why Link Items Across Boards?

Before diving into how to link items, let's first understand why this feature is so beneficial.

1. **Centralized Information**: When working on complex projects involving multiple departments or teams, having related tasks spread across different boards can make it difficult to get a complete view of the project's status. Linking items across boards allows you to connect related tasks and centralize information in one location.

2. **Improved Workflow**: Linked items act as dependencies, which helps establish relationships between tasks that need to be completed in a specific order. This improves workflow management by ensuring that nothing falls through the cracks.

3. **Streamlined Communication**: When tasks are linked, updates to one item can automatically trigger updates in the linked items. This saves time and improves communication within the team, as everyone stays aligned on progress and changes.

4. **Increased Efficiency**: By linking boards and tasks, users can avoid duplicate data entry and gain more control over managing their projects. This feature reduces manual work and allows for automated processes like status updates and notifications.

How to Link Items Across Boards

Let's explore how to link items across boards step by step.

Step 1: Open the Boards You Want to Link

To begin, you must first ensure that you have access to the boards that you wish to link. You'll need at least two boards: one from which the task is located and another where you want to establish the link. Both boards should be created and contain items that you want to associate.

1. Navigate to the board where the primary task is located (the item that you wish to link from).

2. Also open the board where the related task is located (the item that you wish to link to).

Step 2: Add a Link to Item Column

Next, you will need to add the "Link to Item" column to your board. This column allows you to establish links between items across boards.

1. On the board, click the **Add Column** button (usually located to the right of the last column).

2. From the column options, choose **"Link to Item"**.

3. The "Link to Item" column will be added to your board, allowing you to link it to other items across boards.

Step 3: Linking Items

Once the "Link to Item" column is added, you can start linking your tasks between boards.

1. In the "Link to Item" column, click on the cell next to the task that you want to link.

2. A dialog box will appear asking you to search for an item from another board.

3. Use the search bar to locate the task on the second board that you want to link. Once found, select it.

4. After selecting the item, the link will appear in the cell. The linked item will now be associated with the task, and any updates made to one task can be reflected across both items.

Step 4: Viewing Linked Items

After linking the items, you can easily view the linked task's status without leaving your current board.

1. You can hover over the linked item to preview details, including the item's status and any updates.

2. You can also click on the link to open the linked item directly within the board, allowing for easy navigation and project management.

Step 5: Updating Linked Items

When you update the status or information of a task, the linked item will often reflect the change, depending on the configuration of the board and the automation rules set in place. Here are a few examples:

1. **Updating Status**: When you mark an item as "Done" on one board, the status can automatically update on the linked item. This can be set up through **automations**, which we will discuss later.

2. **Changing Due Dates**: If the due date of one linked item is changed, you can have it automatically push the same change to the linked task to avoid conflicts and ensure timelines remain aligned.

3. **Task Completion**: Linking items helps show dependencies. When one task is completed, linked items can automatically update to show progress. This makes managing project timelines much easier.

Best Practices for Linking Items Across Boards

Linking items across boards is a powerful feature, but using it efficiently requires some best practices. Here are a few tips to make the most of this feature:

1. Use Descriptive Links

When linking items, ensure the link text is clear and descriptive. This way, team members can easily understand what the linked task is about without having to click on it. Descriptive links improve clarity and workflow communication.

2. Leverage Automations for Seamless Updates

Set up automations to keep everything up to date automatically. For example, create an automation rule that changes the status of a linked task when the original task is marked as complete. This reduces manual work and keeps your boards in sync.

3. Be Mindful of Dependencies

Avoid overcomplicating task relationships by linking too many items. It's easy to fall into the trap of linking everything, but too many dependencies can slow down your workflow. Keep your links focused and manageable.

4. Regularly Review Linked Items

Over time, the items linked across boards may change. It's important to regularly review these links to ensure they're still relevant and accurate. As projects evolve, some links may become outdated, so periodic reviews are key.

5. Keep Track of Linked Boards

When you're working on multiple boards and linking tasks, it's easy to lose track of connections. Be sure to use the "Link to Item" column wisely by giving it a clear name or adding notes. Keeping track of linked items will make navigation easier for everyone involved.

6. Don't Over-Link Items

While linking tasks is a great way to manage related work, linking too many items can make your boards more cluttered and harder to follow. Limit links to essential relationships that truly need to be connected for the project's success.

7. Group Linked Tasks for Better Visibility

Organize tasks within linked items by using **groups**. For example, if you are linking marketing and sales tasks, create separate groups like "Marketing Tasks" and "Sales Tasks" for each project, making it easier to navigate and prioritize.

Troubleshooting Common Issues with Linked Items

Despite being a powerful feature, linking items across boards may present some challenges. Here are a few common issues and how to resolve them:

1. Linked Items Not Displaying Correctly

If linked items are not displaying correctly in your "Link to Item" column, it's possible the item has been moved or deleted from the original board. To resolve this, check the board settings to ensure the linked item still exists or is properly moved.

2. Incorrect Item Details

Sometimes, the details of the linked item may not update correctly, particularly when status or due dates are changed. Ensure you have enabled **automations** that trigger updates between linked tasks.

3. Missing Permissions

If you are unable to link to an item, it may be due to insufficient permissions. Ensure you have the correct permissions to access the boards and items you wish to link. Permissions can be adjusted under board settings.

Conclusion

Linking items across boards in Monday.com is an essential feature that allows for streamlined project management and better organization. By creating dependencies between tasks, you can ensure that all related items stay aligned, no matter where they reside on your boards. By following the step-by-step process and applying best practices, you can use this feature to boost efficiency, keep everyone on the same page, and ensure tasks move forward in a well-structured way.

Remember, while linking items can vastly improve your workflow, it's important to do so thoughtfully. Too many links can lead to complexity, so be sure to maintain a balanced, organized approach. By mastering item linking, you'll be well on your way to achieving more with less effort on Monday.com.

6.3.2 Setting Up and Using Subitems

Subitems in Monday.com offer a powerful way to break down larger tasks into smaller, more manageable actions. This feature is particularly useful when a single task is too complex or needs further clarification and steps to be completed. By setting up and using subitems, you can organize your workflow with greater precision and ensure that no detail is overlooked. In this section, we'll guide you step by step through the process of setting up and using subitems on Monday.com.

What are Subitems?

Subitems are essentially tasks or actions that are linked to a parent item. These subitems inherit properties from their parent item but can have their own unique details, such as deadlines, assignees, and statuses. They allow for a granular level of organization within a larger task, making it easier for teams to track progress, collaborate, and manage complex projects.

For example, if the parent item is "Launch Marketing Campaign," the subitems could include tasks like "Design Social Media Graphics," "Write Blog Post," and "Email Newsletter." These tasks are all part of the main campaign but have distinct steps and requirements.

Creating Subitems

Step 1: Navigate to Your Board

To begin creating subitems, start by opening the board where you have the task or item you want to break down into subitems. You can use any type of board such as a project board, task board, or workflow board.

Step 2: Add a Parent Item

If you haven't already created a parent item, click on the "+ Add" button in your desired group or section to create one. This could be any task, project, or to-do list item. Parent items are the main tasks that will hold the subitems.

Step 3: Add Subitems

Once your parent item is created, follow these steps to add subitems:

1. Hover over the parent item in your board.

2. On the far right of the item, you will see a small arrow or a "Subitems" button. Click it.

3. A new area will expand below the parent item, where you can add new subitems.

4. Click the "+ Add Subitem" button to create your first subitem.

5. Enter the title or task description for the subitem.

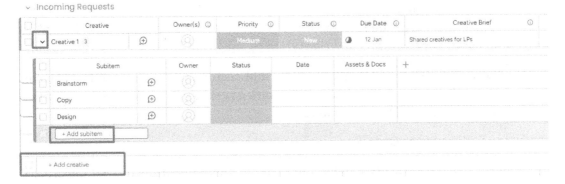

Step 4: Customize Subitem Details

After creating a subitem, you can customize its details just like any other item in Monday.com. You can:

- **Assign team members** to the subitem by clicking the "People" column.

- **Set deadlines** for each subitem to ensure timely completion.

- **Use status columns** to track the progress of each subitem (e.g., Not Started, In Progress, Done).

- **Add text or notes** to provide additional instructions or context for the subitem.

- **Attach files** directly to each subitem for easy access.

Managing Subitems Effectively

Once subitems are created, managing them effectively is essential for keeping your projects organized and ensuring that all tasks are completed on time.

Organizing Subitems

You can keep your subitems organized in several ways:

1. **Reordering Subitems:** If the order of the tasks changes, you can simply drag and drop subitems to rearrange them within the parent item. This is especially useful for keeping tasks in a logical sequence.

2. **Grouping Subitems by Category:** Within the subitems section, you can group them by category or type of work. For example, if you're planning an event, your subitems could include groups like "Pre-Event," "Event Day," and "Post-Event." This helps with organization and clarity.

3. **Using Labels and Columns:** You can add custom labels or use different column types (e.g., text, date, numbers) to track specific details like costs, priority, or resources needed for each subitem.

Updating Subitem Statuses

It's important to regularly update the status of your subitems to ensure that the project is progressing smoothly:

1. **Status Tracking:** Use the status column to indicate whether the subitem is "Not Started," "In Progress," or "Completed." This is crucial for tracking the overall progress of your project.

2. **Setting Dependencies:** If the completion of one subitem depends on another, you can set up dependencies to visually track which subitems need to be completed first. You can do this by linking the subitems to other tasks within the board.

Filtering and Sorting Subitems

As your list of subitems grows, it's crucial to filter and sort them to stay on top of tasks:

1. **Filtering Subitems:** Use the filtering options in Monday.com to view only subitems that meet specific criteria. For example, you can filter subitems by assignee, due date, or status to prioritize tasks.

2. **Sorting Subitems:** Sort your subitems based on different columns (e.g., by due date, priority, or assignee) to ensure that your most urgent tasks are highlighted.

Viewing Subitems Across Different Views

Monday.com offers various views that allow you to manage and view subitems in different ways:

1. **Kanban View:** In the Kanban view, you can visually organize your subitems by moving them between columns that represent different stages (e.g., To Do, In Progress, Done). This is perfect for teams that need to track tasks in a more visual way.

2. **Timeline View:** Use the Timeline view to view your subitems along with their deadlines. This helps you to see the overall project timeline and identify bottlenecks or delays.

3. **Calendar View:** The Calendar view displays subitems with their due dates, helping you see which tasks need to be completed each day or week.

Subitems Best Practices

To make the most of subitems, follow these best practices:

1. **Use Subitems for Task Breakdown:** Subitems are best used when tasks need to be broken down into smaller, manageable actions. If your parent item is too general (e.g., "Create Marketing Plan"), break it down into subitems like "Conduct Market Research," "Design Visuals," "Write Content," etc.

2. **Avoid Overcomplicating:** While subitems are great for managing details, try not to go overboard by creating too many levels of subitems. Too many layers can make things more difficult to manage. Stick to what's necessary for the task at hand.

3. **Delegate Tasks Clearly:** When assigning team members to subitems, be clear about the specific responsibilities. Each subitem should have one or more team members assigned, so there's no confusion about who is responsible for what.

4. **Track Dependencies:** If some subitems are dependent on the completion of others, be sure to set up dependencies to prevent bottlenecks. This allows you to manage the flow of work more effectively.

5. **Use Subitems for Detailed Reporting:** If you need to generate reports or track progress on complex tasks, subitems can provide the level of detail needed to make informed decisions.

Advanced Features for Subitems

Linking Subitems Across Boards

Sometimes, a subitem may need to be linked to another task on a different board. This is especially useful if a task spans across multiple departments or teams. Monday.com allows you to create dependencies and link subitems across boards so that all related work is connected. You can do this by:

1. **Creating Linked Items:** In the subitem's column, you can add a "Link to Item" column. Here, you can link a subitem from one board to an item in another board.

2. **Tracking Cross-Board Progress:** This feature helps teams track cross-board dependencies and ensures that nothing falls through the cracks.

Automating Subitem Management

Automation is a key feature of Monday.com that can save you a lot of time when managing subitems:

1. **Creating Automation Rules:** You can set up automation to trigger actions on subitems. For example, when a subitem's status changes to "Completed," you can automatically change the status of the parent item.

2. **Notifying Team Members:** Use automation to notify team members when a subitem is due or when an update occurs. This keeps everyone on track and ensures timely communication.

Conclusion

Subitems are a powerful feature within Monday.com that help break down complex tasks into manageable actions. By following the steps outlined in this section, you can set up subitems efficiently and use them to streamline your workflows, improve task management, and increase productivity. With the ability to track progress, assign tasks, and automate processes, subitems provide the granularity needed to stay on top of every detail, ensuring that nothing is left behind.

Whether you're managing a large-scale project or handling multiple smaller tasks, subitems will make your workflow more organized and effective. Keep experimenting with their features and capabilities to unlock the full potential of Monday.com for your team and projects.

CHAPTER VII
Troubleshooting and Best Practices

7.1 Common Issues and How to Solve Them

7.1.1 Connectivity and Sync Problems

Connectivity and synchronization issues can disrupt your workflow on Monday.com and negatively impact your team's productivity. Understanding how to diagnose, troubleshoot, and prevent these problems is essential for maintaining a seamless experience. This section provides detailed guidance on identifying common connectivity and sync problems, resolving them effectively, and implementing preventative measures to avoid future issues.

Understanding Connectivity and Sync Problems

Monday.com is a cloud-based platform, which means it heavily relies on an internet connection to function properly. Connectivity and sync issues typically arise due to:

- **Weak or unstable internet connections**
- **Problems with Monday.com's servers**
- **Device or browser compatibility issues**
- **Network security settings, such as firewalls or VPNs**
- **Outdated software or plugins**

These issues may manifest as:

- Slow-loading boards or dashboards

- Delayed updates or missing changes in shared workspaces

- Error messages during login or while accessing boards

- Trouble syncing Monday.com with third-party integrations

Step-by-Step Troubleshooting for Connectivity and Sync Problems

Step 1: Check Your Internet Connection

The first step in resolving connectivity issues is to ensure that your internet connection is stable and meets the minimum requirements for Monday.com.

- **Run a Speed Test:** Use online tools like Speedtest.net to verify your upload and download speeds. For optimal performance, Monday.com recommends a connection speed of at least 5 Mbps.

- **Switch to a Wired Connection:** If you are using Wi-Fi, try switching to a wired Ethernet connection for greater stability.

- **Restart Your Router:** A simple router restart can often resolve network glitches that cause slow or intermittent connections.

- **Avoid High Bandwidth Usage:** Ensure that other devices or applications on the same network are not consuming excessive bandwidth (e.g., video streaming or large file uploads).

Step 2: Confirm Monday.com's Server Status

Sometimes, the issue may not be on your end but rather with Monday.com's servers.

- **Visit Monday.com's Status Page:** Monday.com provides a real-time status page (status.monday.com) where you can check for server outages, scheduled maintenance, or performance issues.

- **Contact Support:** If the status page confirms a server issue, you can report the problem to Monday.com's support team to get updates on the resolution timeline.

Step 3: Update Your Browser or App

Outdated browsers or mobile applications can cause compatibility problems with Monday.com.

- **Update Your Browser:** Ensure you're using the latest version of Google Chrome, Mozilla Firefox, or any other recommended browser.

- **Clear Browser Cache and Cookies:** Old cache and cookies can interfere with Monday.com's performance. Clear these files from your browser's settings.

- **Switch Browsers:** If the problem persists, try accessing Monday.com on a different browser to determine if the issue is browser-specific.

- **Update the Mobile App:** For users accessing Monday.com on mobile devices, ensure the app is updated to the latest version via the App Store or Google Play.

Step 4: Disable VPNs, Firewalls, or Security Software

Network security configurations can occasionally block Monday.com or its associated services.

- **Disable VPN Temporarily:** VPNs can interfere with Monday.com's ability to sync data. Temporarily disable your VPN and check if the issue persists.

- **Check Firewall Settings:** Ensure your firewall allows connections to Monday.com's IP addresses and ports. Consult your IT department if you're on a corporate network.

- **Whitelist Monday.com:** Add Monday.com and its related services to your antivirus or security software's whitelist to prevent blocking.

Step 5: Verify Integration Sync Settings

If you're experiencing sync issues with third-party integrations, such as Google Calendar, Slack, or Dropbox:

- **Reconnect the Integration:** Go to your account's integration settings, disconnect the problematic app, and reconnect it.

- **Check API Permissions:** Ensure that Monday.com has the necessary permissions to access and modify data in the integrated app.

- **Test the Integration:** Use test cases to verify if the integration is syncing correctly after reconnection.

Step 6: Monitor Team Activity and Account Settings

In some cases, syncing problems arise due to conflicting updates made by multiple users or incorrect account settings.

- **Check User Permissions:** Ensure that all team members have the appropriate permissions to make updates to shared boards.

- **Avoid Simultaneous Edits:** Inform your team to avoid making simultaneous edits to the same board, as this can lead to sync conflicts.

- **Review Account Settings:** Go to your Monday.com account settings and check for misconfigurations, such as time zone mismatches or language settings, that may cause syncing issues.

Preventing Future Connectivity and Sync Problems

1. Regularly Update Software and Systems

- Keep your browser, Monday.com app, and any integrated tools updated to their latest versions.

- Schedule periodic system maintenance for team devices to ensure compatibility and performance.

2. Maintain Network Stability

- Upgrade your internet plan if your team frequently experiences bandwidth limitations.

- Use Quality of Service (QoS) settings on your router to prioritize traffic for Monday.com and related applications.

3. Implement Clear Team Practices

- Create a team protocol for managing updates on shared boards to prevent sync conflicts.

- Educate your team on basic troubleshooting steps to minimize downtime caused by connectivity issues.

4. Optimize Integrations

- Limit the number of active integrations to reduce sync overhead.

- Regularly review and update integration settings to maintain compatibility with Monday.com updates.

5. Utilize Monday.com Support Resources

- Bookmark Monday.com's help center for quick access to troubleshooting articles and video tutorials.

- Attend Monday.com's webinars or training sessions to stay informed about new features and best practices.

Case Study: Resolving Connectivity Issues for a Marketing Team

A marketing team using Monday.com experienced frequent sync delays with their Google Calendar integration. After identifying the root cause (an outdated API token), they resolved the issue by:

- Reconnecting the Google Calendar integration with updated permissions.

- Implementing a team protocol to avoid overlapping calendar edits.

- Upgrading their office network for better connectivity.

This proactive approach not only resolved the issue but also improved the team's overall efficiency.

Conclusion

Connectivity and sync problems can be frustrating, but with a structured approach, they are often easy to resolve. By understanding common causes, applying troubleshooting steps, and implementing preventative measures, you can ensure a smooth and reliable Monday.com experience for your team.

7.1.2 Permissions and Access Errors

Permissions and access control are crucial for ensuring that your team members have the appropriate level of access to boards, workspaces, and data in Monday.com. Misconfigurations or misunderstandings in permissions settings can lead to disruptions in workflow, unintentional data exposure, or even frustration among team members. In this section, we will explore common permission and access-related issues in Monday.com, their potential causes, and detailed step-by-step solutions to resolve them effectively.

Understanding Permissions in Monday.com

Permissions in Monday.com are the rules that determine who can view, edit, or manage specific boards, items, or workspaces. Understanding these permissions is the first step toward resolving access-related issues. Here are the main levels of permissions:

1. **Workspace Permissions**: Control access to entire workspaces.

     o **Owners**: Full access to manage settings and members.

     o **Members**: Access based on the permissions set for specific boards.

     o **Guests**: Limited access to shareable boards only.

2. **Board Permissions**: Control who can view or edit a board.

     o **Private Boards**: Only invited members can access.

     o **Shareable Boards**: Access is shared with specific external users.

     o **Main Boards**: Visible to all workspace members by default.

3. **Column and Item Permissions**: Fine-tune permissions at a granular level.

     o Example: Restrict editing of specific columns to certain users.

4. **Automation Permissions**: Define who can create or modify automations within boards.

Common Permissions and Access Issues

Let's examine some of the most common issues related to permissions and access:

Issue 1: Team Members Cannot Access a Board

- **Symptoms**:
    - A team member reports they cannot view or access a board.
    - They receive an error message like "You do not have permission to access this board."

- **Potential Causes**:
    - The board is set to private, and the user is not invited.
    - The user is a guest and the board is not shareable.
    - The user was removed from the workspace or board accidentally.

Issue 2: Users Cannot Edit Items or Columns

- **Symptoms**:
    - A team member can view a board but cannot make edits to items or columns.
    - They report that the "Edit" button or field is greyed out.

- **Potential Causes**:
    - The board's permissions are set to "View Only."
    - The user's role is restricted (e.g., guest or viewer).
    - Column permissions restrict editing for specific users.

Issue 3: Unintended Data Access

- **Symptoms**:
    - A guest or member sees sensitive data they should not have access to.

- **Potential Causes**:

- o A shareable board was mistakenly shared with too many people.

- o Permissions were not set correctly for sensitive columns.

Step-by-Step Solutions for Permissions and Access Errors

1. Resolving "Cannot Access Board" Issues

Step 1: Verify the Board Type

- Navigate to the board in question and check if it's set as **Private, Shareable,** or **Main**.

- Go to the board settings (three dots in the top-right corner) > **Board Permissions.**

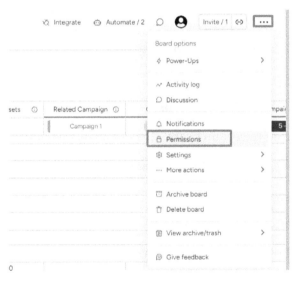

Step 2: Add the User to the Board

- If it's a private or shareable board:

  - o Click the "Share" button at the top right.

  - o Search for the user's name or email address.

  - o Assign them a role (Editor, Viewer, etc.) and click **Invite.**

Step 3: Check Workspace Membership

- Ensure the user is a member of the workspace.

  - Go to **Admin Settings** > **Users**.

  - If they are not listed, click **Invite Members** to add them.

Step 4: Share Board Link (Optional)

- If appropriate, share a direct board link via email or chat for quick access.

---

2. Fixing "Cannot Edit Items or Columns" Errors

Step 1: Check Board Permission Settings

- Open the board settings and ensure the permission is set to **Edit Content** for the user role.

  - Navigate to **Board Permissions** > Select **Edit** or **Custom**.

Step 2: Review Column Permissions

- Right-click on the column header > **Column Permissions**.

  - Check if the column is restricted to certain users.

  - Adjust the settings to allow the necessary team members to edit.

Step 3: Grant Editor Role to the User

- Go to **Board Settings** > **Manage Users**.

  - Verify that the user is set to **Editor** rather than **Viewer**.

  - Change the role if necessary.

---

3. Preventing and Resolving Unintended Data Access

Step 1: Audit Board Sharing Settings

- Review which users have access to shareable boards.

  - Navigate to **Board Permissions** and look for external guests or unintended members.

    o Remove unauthorized users immediately.

Step 2: Use Private Boards for Sensitive Information

- Move sensitive data to a **Private Board** to restrict access.

Step 3: Restrict Access to Specific Columns

- For sensitive columns (e.g., salary or financial details):

      o Right-click the column > **Column Permissions**.

      o Choose "Restrict editing to specific users."

Step 4: Use Dashboards for Secure Reporting

- Instead of sharing raw boards, create **Dashboards** with limited widgets.

      o Customize widgets to display only the necessary information.

Proactive Tips for Managing Permissions

1. **Regularly Audit Access**

       o Schedule monthly reviews of board and workspace permissions.

       o Remove inactive users or guests no longer associated with the project.

2. **Educate Team Members**

       o Host training sessions to familiarize team members with permission levels.

       o Share best practices for sharing boards and workspaces securely.

3. **Set Default Permissions**

       o In workspace settings, define default permissions for new boards (e.g., all new boards are private by default).

4. **Use Guest Access Wisely**

       o Limit guest access to specific shareable boards only.

       o Avoid granting access to entire workspaces for external users.

5. **Leverage Admin Tools**

    o   Use admin controls to monitor activity and identify potential access issues early.

Troubleshooting Permissions Issues: A Quick Checklist

If you're still facing permissions-related challenges, here's a quick checklist to guide your troubleshooting:

- **Is the user invited to the workspace?**

- **Is the board type (Private/Main/Shareable) appropriate for the user's role?**

- **Are the user's permissions set correctly (Editor, Viewer, etc.)?**

- **Are column or item permissions restricting access?**

- **Are there any automations that override default permissions?**

By systematically addressing these questions, you can quickly identify and resolve most permissions and access errors.

7.2 Tips for Effective Team Collaboration

7.2.1 Setting Clear Goals and Expectations

Effective team collaboration begins with clarity—clarity in goals, responsibilities, deadlines, and expected outcomes. Without this foundational clarity, even the most advanced tools like Monday.com may fail to deliver the desired results. This section explores the critical importance of setting clear goals and expectations when using Monday.com for team collaboration, along with actionable tips and best practices to implement this effectively.

Why Setting Clear Goals and Expectations Matters

When goals and expectations are ambiguous, team members often feel confused or overwhelmed, which leads to inefficiency, missed deadlines, and reduced morale. Setting clear goals and expectations ensures that every team member:

- Understands their role and responsibilities.

- Knows the overarching objectives of the project or task.

- Has visibility into the progress of other team members.

- Feels empowered to contribute effectively.

With Monday.com, you can leverage features like boards, timelines, and automations to make these goals and expectations visible and actionable.

Steps to Set Clear Goals and Expectations on Monday.com

1. Define Your Goals

Before diving into Monday.com, define what your team is working toward. Clear goals should be:

- **Specific**: Clearly articulate the objective.

- **Measurable**: Define how success will be quantified.

- **Achievable**: Ensure the goal is realistic given the team's resources.

- **Relevant**: Align the goal with broader organizational objectives.

- **Time-Bound**: Set a deadline to create a sense of urgency.

For example, instead of saying, "Improve team efficiency," a clear goal might be, "Reduce task completion time by 20% over the next three months."

2. Translate Goals into Monday.com Boards

Once you've defined your goals, use Monday.com boards to break them into actionable tasks. Here's how:

- **Create a New Board**: Name it based on your project or goal, e.g., "Marketing Campaign Q1."

- **Define Groups**: Use groups to represent different phases of the project or key deliverables. For example, "Research," "Execution," and "Reporting."

- **Add Columns**: Use columns to track key information, such as:

    o **Task Owner**: Assign the responsible person.

    o **Deadlines**: Set due dates for tasks.

    o **Status**: Use status labels like "Not Started," "In Progress," and "Completed."

    o **Priority**: Indicate whether a task is low, medium, or high priority.

3. Assign Clear Responsibilities

Use Monday.com's "People" column to assign tasks to team members. Ensure responsibilities are explicitly defined by:

- **Clarifying Roles**: In the task description, explain what is expected. For example: "Research five competitor campaigns and upload findings to the board."

- **Using Subitems**: For complex tasks, break them into subitems to make responsibilities more granular.

- **Setting Accountability**: Use the "Updates" section to request progress reports or additional clarification.

4. Communicate Expectations

In addition to setting goals, it's vital to outline how tasks should be completed and the quality standards expected. Use Monday.com's tools for transparency:

- **Team Updates**: Use the "Updates" section to post detailed instructions or best practices.

- **Templates**: Create and share templates for repetitive tasks to ensure consistency.

- **Pinned Notes**: Use the "Info Boxes" feature to pin guidelines, checklists, or other important information at the board level.

5. Visualize Progress with Views and Dashboards

Track progress against goals by using Monday.com's visualization tools:

- **Timeline View**: Monitor deadlines and identify potential bottlenecks.

- **Kanban View**: See task progress in a visual flow.

- **Dashboards**: Create widgets that display metrics like task completion rates, overdue tasks, and team workload.

By consistently visualizing progress, you reinforce accountability and keep everyone aligned.

Best Practices for Setting Goals and Expectations with Monday.com

1. Involve the Entire Team in Goal Setting

Goals should not be dictated top-down. Involve the team in the goal-setting process to ensure buy-in and alignment. Use Monday.com to facilitate brainstorming sessions:

- Create a shared board for ideas and feedback.

- Use the voting column to prioritize the most important objectives.

- Consolidate the feedback into a finalized plan.

2. Use Automations to Reinforce Expectations

Automations in Monday.com are a powerful way to reinforce expectations without micromanaging. For example:

- Send reminders when deadlines are approaching.

- Notify managers when a task status changes to "Stuck."

- Automatically assign follow-up tasks once a key milestone is completed.

3. Review Goals Regularly

Goals and expectations should be dynamic, not static. Schedule regular check-ins (weekly or bi-weekly) to review:

- Progress toward goals.

- Challenges or blockers faced by the team.

- Opportunities to improve workflows.

Use Monday.com's "Recurring Tasks" automation to schedule these reviews and ensure they happen consistently.

4. Celebrate Milestones

Acknowledging achievements boosts morale and reinforces the importance of meeting goals. Use Monday.com to celebrate milestones by:

- Creating a "Celebrations" column to track accomplishments.

- Sharing updates in the "Updates" section with team-wide recognition.

- Using the "High-Five" automation to send congratulatory messages automatically when tasks are completed.

Common Challenges and How to Overcome Them

Even with clear goals and expectations, teams may encounter obstacles. Below are common challenges and solutions:

1. Lack of Clarity in Goals

- **Problem**: Team members misunderstand what success looks like.

- **Solution**: Use the "Info Boxes" to add detailed descriptions for each board or group.

2. Unclear Deadlines

- **Problem**: Tasks are delayed because deadlines are not well-communicated.

- **Solution**: Use the "Timeline View" to map deadlines and share the view with the team.

3. Overlapping Responsibilities

- **Problem**: Multiple team members assume the same task, causing confusion.

- **Solution**: Assign clear owners using the "People" column, and use subitems for additional roles if needed.

4. Lack of Accountability

- **Problem**: Tasks remain incomplete because no one is held responsible.

- **Solution**: Use dashboards to track task completion and publicly display progress during team meetings.

Conclusion: Aligning Your Team for Success

Setting clear goals and expectations is the cornerstone of effective team collaboration. By leveraging Monday.com's robust features—like boards, automations, and dashboards—you can ensure every team member understands their role, works toward shared objectives, and stays accountable.

Consistency is key. Make goal-setting and progress reviews an integral part of your Monday.com workflow. With clear communication, transparency, and the right tools, your team will not only meet its goals but exceed them.

7.2.2 Maintaining Board Cleanliness

Maintaining board cleanliness in Monday.com is critical for fostering a productive, organized, and efficient work environment. A clean board ensures that information is easily accessible, tasks are clearly defined, and team members can focus on their responsibilities without unnecessary confusion. Below is a detailed guide on how to maintain board cleanliness effectively.

1. Why Board Cleanliness Matters

Before diving into the practical steps, it's essential to understand why maintaining cleanliness on your boards is crucial:

- **Improves Clarity:** A well-organized board allows team members to quickly locate tasks and understand their priorities.

- **Reduces Errors:** Clean boards reduce the risk of missed deadlines or overlooked items.

- **Saves Time:** Teams can focus on their work instead of spending time searching for information or deciphering messy structures.

- **Boosts Team Morale:** A clear and structured workspace promotes a sense of professionalism and encourages better collaboration.

2. Practical Tips for Maintaining Board Cleanliness

2.1 Use Consistent Naming Conventions

Adopting a standardized naming convention for boards, groups, items, and columns ensures that everyone understands the structure of the board.

- **Examples of Naming Conventions:**
  - For Boards: "Marketing Campaign Q1 2025" or "Product Launch – Development Tasks."

- o   For Groups: "To Do," "In Progress," "Completed."

- o   For Items: "Design Website Mockups" or "Submit Budget Proposal."

- **Best Practices:**

  - o   Avoid overly long names.

  - o   Use abbreviations sparingly and only if they are universally understood by the team.

2.2 Limit the Number of Columns

Too many columns can clutter your board and overwhelm team members.

- **Essential Columns:** Focus on the most critical columns, such as **Status**, **Due Date**, and **Owner**.

- **Combine Similar Columns:** If multiple columns serve the same purpose, merge them into one. For instance, instead of separate "Start Date" and "End Date" columns, consider using a "Timeline" column.

- **Archive Unused Columns:** If certain columns are no longer relevant, archive or delete them.

2.3 Regularly Archive Completed Tasks

Keeping completed tasks visible on the board can clutter the workspace and make it harder to find active tasks.

- **How to Archive Items:**

  - o   Move completed tasks to a separate "Completed" group before archiving them.

  - o   Use Monday.com's archiving feature to store old items that may need to be referenced later.

- **Schedule Archiving Sessions:** Assign a team member to archive items at the end of each week or project.

2.4 Organize Items into Logical Groups

Grouping related items together helps maintain structure and clarity.

- **Examples of Logical Groups:**
    - By Status: "To Do," "In Progress," "Done."
    - By Priority: "High Priority," "Medium Priority," "Low Priority."
    - By Department: "Marketing," "Sales," "Development."
- **Keep Groups Balanced:** Avoid overloading any single group with too many items. Split large groups into smaller, more manageable ones.

2.5 Standardize the Use of Colors and Labels

Colors and labels are powerful tools for visual organization but can create chaos if used inconsistently.

- **Set a Team-Wide Color Scheme:** Assign specific colors to statuses or labels and ensure the team adheres to them.
    - Example: Green = Completed, Yellow = In Progress, Red = High Priority.
- **Avoid Overuse of Labels:** Only use labels that add value or provide clarity to the board.

3. Tools and Features to Help Maintain Cleanliness

Monday.com offers several built-in features that make it easier to keep your boards tidy and organized.

3.1 Filters and Search Bar

- **Filters:** Use filters to display only the relevant information, such as tasks assigned to a specific team member or tasks due within a particular timeframe.
- **Search Bar:** Quickly locate items, groups, or boards without scrolling through cluttered content.

3.2 Automations

Automations can help clean up your board automatically.

- **Examples of Useful Automations:**
    - Move items to the "Completed" group when their status changes to "Done."
    - Notify team members if an item has been inactive for a specified period.
- **How to Set Up Automations:**
    - Go to the "Automations Center" and select a pre-made recipe or create a custom one.

3.3 The Dashboard Feature

Dashboards provide a summarized view of data, reducing the need for team members to navigate through cluttered boards.

- **Widgets for Cleanliness:**
    - Use the "Status Overview" widget to track progress at a glance.
    - Use the "Tasks by Owner" widget to ensure task distribution is clear and balanced.

3.4 The Archive Function

The archive function is ideal for decluttering boards while preserving information for future reference.

- **Accessing Archived Items:**
    - Navigate to the "Archive" section in the board settings.
    - Restore items when needed.

4. Team Responsibilities and Best Practices

Maintaining board cleanliness is a team effort. Assigning clear responsibilities and establishing best practices ensures everyone contributes to a tidy workspace.

4.1 Assign a Board Owner

- Designate one person as the board owner to oversee organization and cleanliness.

- Responsibilities include:
  - Archiving old tasks.
  - Merging duplicate items.
  - Monitoring for clutter or inconsistencies.

4.2 Encourage Regular Updates

- Team members should update their tasks regularly to keep the board current.
- Create a habit of reviewing the board during daily or weekly team meetings.

4.3 Provide Training for New Users

- Ensure new team members understand your board structure and organizational rules.
- Offer training sessions or create a short guide to explain naming conventions, color schemes, and archiving processes.

4.4 Conduct Routine Clean-Up Sessions

- Schedule regular clean-up sessions where the team reviews and tidies up the board together.
- Focus on archiving completed tasks, merging duplicate items, and removing irrelevant columns.

5. Long-Term Benefits of a Clean Board

Maintaining board cleanliness is not just about aesthetics—it directly impacts productivity and team performance. Clean boards lead to:

- **Faster Decision-Making:** Clear information helps leaders make quicker, more informed decisions.
- **Improved Accountability:** Everyone knows their responsibilities and can track their progress.

- **Higher Team Morale:** A well-organized workspace boosts team confidence and reduces stress.

By following these strategies, your team can create a Monday.com workspace that is not only visually appealing but also functional and efficient. Regular maintenance, clear guidelines, and the use of Monday.com's powerful features will help ensure your boards remain clean and productive.

7.3 Scaling Monday.com for Large Teams

7.3.1 Organizing Workspaces for Big Projects

Managing large-scale projects using Monday.com requires careful organization to ensure efficiency, collaboration, and timely completion. This section will guide you step-by-step on how to set up and manage your workspaces effectively when dealing with big projects or large teams.

Understanding the Challenges of Large Projects

Large projects often involve multiple teams, complex workflows, and a large volume of tasks. Without a structured approach, it can lead to:

- Overlapping responsibilities.

- Miscommunication between teams.

- Difficulty tracking progress and deadlines.

- Inefficient allocation of resources.

Monday.com offers a variety of tools to tackle these challenges. By leveraging features like boards, automations, and dashboards, you can ensure your workspace is organized, scalable, and optimized for collaboration.

Step 1: Define the Scope of Your Project

Before diving into Monday.com, start by defining the project's scope:

1. **Break the Project into Phases**

   o Divide your project into clear, manageable phases (e.g., planning, execution, review).

   o Each phase can be represented as a separate board in Monday.com.

2. **Identify Key Objectives and Deliverables**

   o Write down the project's main goals and deliverables.

   o Use these as the foundation for structuring your boards and tasks.

3. **Map Out Team Roles**

   o Determine which teams and individuals will handle specific parts of the project.

   o Assign clear roles and responsibilities to avoid duplication of effort.

Step 2: Create and Organize Your Workspaces

Workspaces are the top-level structure in Monday.com and can represent different departments, teams, or projects.

1. **Set Up a Dedicated Workspace for the Project**

   o Create a new workspace for your project by clicking on **+ Add Workspace** from the main menu.

   o Name the workspace clearly, such as "Marketing Campaign 2025" or "Product Launch Initiative."

2. **Group Boards by Project Phases or Departments**

   o Use separate boards for each phase of the project. For example:

     ▪ **Board 1: Planning** (tasks related to research, strategy, and approvals).

     ▪ **Board 2: Execution** (tasks related to implementation).

     ▪ **Board 3: Review** (tasks related to feedback and optimization).

   o Alternatively, group boards by departments or teams (e.g., Design Team, Marketing Team, Operations).

3. **Utilize Folders for Additional Organization**

- Create folders within the workspace to categorize boards further (e.g., "Internal Processes," "Client Deliverables").

- Drag and drop boards into relevant folders for a cleaner structure.

Step 3: Customize Boards for Scalability

Each board in Monday.com should be optimized to handle the complexities of a large project.

1. **Use Columns Strategically**

   - Add columns that reflect the specific needs of your project:

     - **Status Column:** Track task progress (e.g., "Not Started," "In Progress," "Completed").

     - **Timeline Column:** Assign start and end dates to tasks.

     - **People Column:** Assign tasks to team members.

     - **Priority Column:** Indicate task urgency (e.g., High, Medium, Low).

2. **Group Tasks by Categories**

   - Create groups within the board to categorize tasks. For example:

     - In a Marketing Campaign board, groups could include "Social Media," "Email Campaigns," and "Event Planning."

     - In a Product Development board, groups could include "Prototype," "Testing," and "Launch."

3. **Set Up Subitems for Complex Tasks**

   - For tasks with multiple steps, use subitems to break them down further.

   - Example: For the task "Create Social Media Content," subitems could include "Design Graphics," "Write Captions," and "Schedule Posts."

4. **Add Custom Views**

- o Use different views to suit your project's needs:
    - **Kanban View:** Ideal for agile workflows.
    - **Gantt View:** Helps visualize timelines and dependencies.
    - **Workload View:** Ensures tasks are evenly distributed among team members.

Step 4: Utilize Dashboards for Oversight

Dashboards consolidate information from multiple boards, making it easier to monitor progress across the entire project.

1. **Create a Master Dashboard**
    - o Go to the Dashboard section and create a new dashboard.
    - o Name it something descriptive, like "Project Overview Dashboard."

2. **Add Key Widgets**
    - o **Table Widget:** Display data from multiple boards in one place.
    - o **Timeline Widget:** Track deadlines and milestones.
    - o **Chart Widget:** Visualize task completion rates and team performance.

3. **Customize Dashboard Permissions**
    - o Ensure that only project leads or managers can edit the dashboard to maintain consistency.

Step 5: Leverage Automations for Efficiency

Automations can save time by reducing manual work.

1. **Set Up Task Notifications**
    - o Use automations like: "When a due date arrives, notify [assignee]."

2. **Automate Status Updates**

   ○ Example: "When a subitem's status changes to 'Done,' update the parent item's status to 'In Progress.'"

3. **Streamline Task Assignments**

   ○ Example: "When a new item is created, assign it to [team member]."

Step 6: Managing Resources Across Teams

For large projects, resource management is critical.

1. **Use the Workload View**

   ○ Visualize team members' workloads to avoid overloading anyone.

   ○ Reassign tasks as necessary to balance workloads.

2. **Monitor Time Tracking**

   ○ Add a Time Tracking column to boards.

   ○ Analyze how much time tasks are taking and identify bottlenecks.

Step 7: Establish Communication Protocols

Clear communication ensures that large projects run smoothly.

1. **Use Comments and Updates**

   ○ Encourage team members to leave updates directly on items.

   ○ Use @mentions to tag relevant people.

2. **Set Up Weekly Check-Ins**

   ○ Use Monday.com's "Recurring Tasks" feature to schedule weekly team check-ins.

Best Practices for Organizing Workspaces for Big Projects

- **Keep Boards Clean and Consistent**: Use clear naming conventions for boards, groups, and items.

- **Train Your Team**: Provide training sessions to ensure everyone understands how to use Monday.com effectively.

- **Review and Optimize Regularly**: Periodically review your boards and workflows to ensure they align with project goals.

- **Encourage Feedback**: Ask team members for feedback on the workspace setup and make adjustments as needed.

Illustrative Example for Organizing Workspaces for Big Projects

Let's consider an example of a large-scale project: launching a **new product**. This project involves multiple teams, various deliverables, and strict deadlines. Below, we'll walk through how to organize and manage this project in Monday.com using the strategies outlined earlier.

Scenario Overview: New Product Launch

Project Goal: Successfully launch "EcoBottle 2.0," a sustainable water bottle, within six months.

Teams Involved:

- **Marketing Team**: Responsible for branding, campaigns, and outreach.

- **Product Development Team**: Designs and tests the product.

- **Operations Team**: Manages manufacturing and logistics.

Step-by-Step Implementation in Monday.com

Step 1: Define the Scope of the Project

- **Phases**:
  - **Phase 1: Research and Development**
  - **Phase 2: Marketing Strategy**
  - **Phase 3: Manufacturing and Distribution**
  - **Phase 4: Product Launch Event**
- **Key Objectives**:
  - Complete product testing within three months.
  - Develop a marketing campaign within two months.
  - Ensure production and distribution readiness by the fifth month.
- **Team Roles**:
  - Marketing Team: Campaign ideation and execution.
  - Product Development Team: Prototyping and testing.
  - Operations Team: Production planning and logistics.

Step 2: Create and Organize Workspaces

1. **Create a Workspace**:
   - Name it **"EcoBottle 2.0 Launch."**

2. **Set Up Boards for Each Phase**:
   - **Board 1: Research and Development**
     - Groups: "Initial Prototyping," "Product Testing," "Design Finalization."
   - **Board 2: Marketing Strategy**
     - Groups: "Campaign Planning," "Content Creation," "Execution."

- o **Board 3: Manufacturing and Distribution**
    - Groups: "Raw Material Procurement," "Production," "Logistics."
- o **Board 4: Product Launch Event**
    - Groups: "Event Planning," "Media Invitations," "Day-of Coordination."

3. **Folder Organization**:
    - o Create a folder called **"EcoBottle 2.0 Project"** and place all boards within it for easy access.

Step 3: Customize Boards

Example: Marketing Strategy Board

Columns for the board:

- **Task Name (Item Name)**: Name of the task, e.g., "Design Social Media Graphics."
- **Status Column**: Progress status (e.g., "Not Started," "In Progress," "Completed").
- **People Column**: Assign tasks to team members (e.g., John Smith for graphic design).
- **Priority Column**: High, Medium, Low.
- **Timeline Column**: Start and end dates for each task.

Groups in the board:

- **Group 1: Campaign Planning**
    - o Example Task: "Develop campaign strategy document."
    - o Assigned to: Marketing Lead.
    - o Status: Completed.
- **Group 2: Content Creation**

- o Example Task: "Write blog post for EcoBottle launch."

- o Assigned to: Content Writer.

- o Status: In Progress.

- **Group 3: Execution**

  - o Example Task: "Schedule Instagram posts."

  - o Assigned to: Social Media Manager.

  - o Status: Not Started.

Views:

- **Kanban View**: Visualize task progress across groups.

- **Timeline View**: See deadlines and avoid overlaps.

Step 4: Create Dashboards for Oversight

1. **Master Dashboard**: Name it **"EcoBottle 2.0 Overview."**

   - o Widgets:

     - **Timeline Widget**: Display tasks and milestones for all phases.

     - **Progress Tracking Widget**: Show the percentage of tasks completed in each phase.

     - **Workload Widget**: Monitor team member assignments to ensure balanced workloads.

Step 5: Automations for Efficiency

Example Automations:

- **Task Notifications**:

  - o "When a status changes to 'Completed,' notify [Marketing Lead]."

- **Recurring Tasks**:
    - "Every Monday, create a new task in 'Content Creation' titled 'Weekly Social Media Review.'"

- **Status Updates**:
    - "When the subitem 'Design Instagram Post' changes to 'Done,' update the parent item 'Social Media Campaign' to 'In Progress.'"

Step 6: Resource Management Across Teams

Using Workload View:

In the **Workload View**, the team realizes that the Product Development team lead is overbooked with testing tasks. To address this:

- Reassign some testing tasks to the assistant team lead.

- Move the deadline for "Finalize Prototype" by one week to give the team additional time.

Step 7: Establish Communication Protocols

1. **Comments and Updates**:
    - For the task "Confirm Influencers for Campaign," the Marketing Lead comments:

"@John, please finalize the influencer list by Thursday. Let me know if you need any help!"

2. **Weekly Check-Ins**:
    - The Operations Team sets up a recurring task for a weekly progress meeting on Fridays.
    - The update in the meeting task reads:

"This week's focus: Confirming shipping routes for distribution. @Anna, can you share the latest updates?"

Final Workspace Structure

Here's how the workspace might look after implementation:

Workspace: EcoBottle 2.0 Launch

- **Boards**:
    - Research and Development
    - Marketing Strategy
    - Manufacturing and Distribution
    - Product Launch Event

Dashboard: EcoBottle 2.0 Overview

Widgets to track overall progress, timelines, and workloads.

Conclusion

By following this structure, the **EcoBottle 2.0 Launch** workspace is now:

- **Organized**: Teams and tasks are clearly structured.
- **Scalable**: Additional phases or tasks can easily be added.
- **Collaborative**: Everyone knows their roles, responsibilities, and deadlines.

This approach ensures that the project is completed on time while maintaining transparency and effective communication across teams.

7.3.2 Training and Onboarding New Users

As your organization scales and more team members start using Monday.com, effective training and onboarding become crucial to ensure consistency, efficiency, and full utilization of the platform. This section will guide you through a structured approach to onboard new users and provide them with the knowledge and skills they need to maximize Monday.com's capabilities.

Step 1: Prepare a Structured Onboarding Plan

A clear onboarding plan ensures that new users receive consistent information and know exactly where to begin. Here's how to create one:

1. **Define Training Goals:** Identify the core competencies new users need to develop. For example:

   o Understanding the Monday.com interface.

   o Navigating workspaces, boards, and items.

   o Using essential features such as automations and integrations.

2. **Create a Timeline:** Break down onboarding into phases (e.g., Day 1: Introduction; Week 1: Basic Usage; Month 1: Advanced Features).

3. **Prepare Training Materials:** Develop resources such as:

   o Written guides or handbooks specific to your organization's workflows.

   o Pre-recorded video tutorials demonstrating key processes.

   o FAQ documents for common questions.

4. **Assign a Mentor:** Pair new users with experienced team members to provide personalized guidance.

Step 2: Introduce Monday.com in Context

Help new users understand how Monday.com fits into the broader organizational workflow.

1. **Explain the Purpose:** Start by describing how your team uses Monday.com to achieve goals. For example:

   - "Monday.com is our central hub for tracking projects, tasks, and deadlines."

   - "We use Monday.com to improve collaboration across departments."

2. **Show Real-World Examples:** Walk them through actual boards and workflows already in use by your team. Focus on key use cases relevant to their role, such as:

   - Project timelines for project managers.

   - Campaign calendars for marketing teams.

3. **Provide Role-Specific Context:** Customize the onboarding experience for different roles. For instance:

   - A project manager may need to learn about dependencies and timeline views.

   - A team member working on deliverables may focus on item updates and notifications.

Step 3: Hands-On Training

The best way to learn Monday.com is by using it. Organize interactive sessions to help users practice key features.

1. **Start with the Basics:** Guide users through:

   - Logging in and navigating the dashboard.

   - Creating and customizing boards.

   - Adding and managing items and groups.

2. **Simulate Real Scenarios:** Set up training boards where new users can practice real tasks, such as:

   - Assigning tasks to team members.

   - Changing item statuses.

     o   Attaching files and sharing updates.

3. **Encourage Experimentation:** Allow new users to explore advanced features like automations and integrations in a safe environment. Provide a "sandbox" workspace where they can try out ideas without affecting live projects.

Step 4: Focus on Key Features

Make sure users understand the core features of Monday.com that are critical to your workflows:

1. **Automations:**

   o   Teach users how to set up basic automation recipes, such as sending reminders or updating statuses.

   o   Emphasize the time-saving benefits of automations.

2. **Integrations:**

   o   Highlight integrations your team relies on (e.g., Google Drive, Slack, or Zoom).

   o   Show how to connect and manage integrations within a board.

3. **Views and Dashboards:**

   o   Demonstrate how to switch between Kanban, Timeline, and Calendar views.

   o   Show how to create and use dashboards for tracking progress.

Step 5: Build a Culture of Continuous Learning

Training doesn't end after onboarding. Encourage users to continuously learn and improve their skills.

1. **Schedule Regular Training Sessions:**

- ○ Host monthly or quarterly workshops to introduce new features and best practices.
- ○ Focus on specific topics, such as advanced reporting or scaling automations.

2. **Provide Ongoing Support:**

- ○ Create a dedicated Slack channel or forum for Monday.com questions.
- ○ Encourage users to share tips and tricks they've discovered.

3. **Encourage Certification:**

- ○ Recommend Monday.com's official training and certification programs.
- ○ Recognize team members who complete certifications.

Step 6: Address Common Onboarding Challenges

Be prepared to overcome obstacles that may arise during onboarding:

1. **Resistance to Change:**

- ○ Explain the benefits of using Monday.com, such as increased efficiency and collaboration.
- ○ Highlight success stories from other teams in your organization.

2. **Overwhelm with Features:**

- ○ Focus on teaching essential features first.
- ○ Gradually introduce advanced tools as users become more comfortable.

3. **Lack of Engagement:**

- ○ Use gamification to make training sessions fun and interactive.
- ○ Recognize and reward users who actively participate in onboarding.

Step 7: Measure the Success of Your Onboarding Program

To ensure your onboarding process is effective, track its success using the following strategies:

1. **Survey New Users:**

   o   Ask for feedback on the onboarding experience.

   o   Identify areas where users feel confident and where they need more help.

2. **Monitor Usage Metrics:**

   o   Use Monday.com's activity logs and reporting tools to track user engagement.

   o   Look for signs of active participation, such as board updates and task completions.

3. **Collect Success Stories:**

   o   Gather testimonials from new users about how Monday.com has improved their workflow.

   o   Use these stories to refine your onboarding program and motivate others.

Step 8: Create a Scalable Onboarding System

As your organization grows, you'll need to onboard multiple users at once. Make your process scalable by:

1. **Developing Online Resources:**

   o   Host pre-recorded training videos and guides on an internal knowledge base.

   o   Use Monday.com's Help Center to supplement your materials.

2. **Using Templates:**

   o   Create board templates for common workflows, such as project management or task tracking.

   o   Teach new users how to duplicate and customize templates.

3. **Empowering Team Leaders:**

   o   Train team leaders to onboard their own teams.

   o   Provide them with resources to ensure consistency across departments.

Conclusion

Training and onboarding new users for Monday.com is essential for ensuring that everyone on your team is equipped to contribute to your organization's success. By preparing a structured onboarding plan, providing hands-on training, and encouraging continuous learning, you can create a scalable system that helps users at all levels maximize the value of Monday.com. As your team grows, a strong onboarding program will ensure that Monday.com continues to be a central tool for collaboration and organization.

Illustrative Scenario: Training and Onboarding New Users in a Growing Marketing Team

Context

Imagine you are managing the onboarding process for a growing marketing department within a mid-sized company. Your team has recently adopted Monday.com to centralize project management and improve collaboration. You need to onboard five new hires who will be handling content creation, campaign planning, and analytics.

Step-by-Step Example for Onboarding

Step 1: Preparing the Onboarding Plan

- **Goal:** Train new hires to navigate Monday.com, use campaign boards, and automate repetitive tasks within their first month.

- **Timeline:**

   o   **Week 1:** Introduction to the interface, personal dashboard setup, and basic board navigation.

- **Week 2:** Hands-on practice with creating items, assigning tasks, and updating statuses.

- **Week 3:** Advanced topics like automations and integrating tools like Google Drive.

- **Week 4:** Review progress, answer questions, and provide personalized tips.

Step 2: Introducing Monday.com in Context: You begin the onboarding session with a 15-minute presentation:

- "Monday.com will be the backbone of our marketing team. It keeps track of all ongoing campaigns, ensures everyone knows their responsibilities, and provides transparency on deadlines."

- Show a campaign board for an upcoming product launch. Explain how the board is structured with groups for "Planning," "Execution," and "Post-Launch Analysis."

Step 3: Hands-On Training Example

1. **Training Task:**

   - Assign each new hire to create a "Campaign Plan" board.

   - Include groups for tasks like "Social Media," "Email Campaigns," and "Paid Ads."

2. **Step-by-Step Exercise:**

   - Add five items to each group (e.g., "Write social media copy," "Schedule email blasts").

   - Assign tasks to team members and set deadlines.

   - Practice updating item statuses like "In Progress" or "Done."

Advanced Feature Training: Automations Example

Scenario: One of your team members is responsible for scheduling social media posts. Automating repetitive tasks can save them hours of work.

1. **Demonstration:**

   ○ Open the "Social Media" group on a board.

   ○ Create an automation: "When a status changes to 'Done,' notify the Social Media Manager."

2. **Practice:**

   ○ Ask the new hire to replicate this automation in their own board.

   ○ Show them how to test the automation by changing item statuses.

Scaling Onboarding for Future Growth

Example: You're anticipating hiring 10 more team members in the next quarter. To make onboarding scalable, you:

1. **Develop a Video Tutorial:** Record a 10-minute video showing how to:

   ○ Set up a personal dashboard.

   ○ Join a workspace and view shared boards.

   ○ Update statuses and add comments.

2. **Create a Board Template:** Save the "Campaign Plan" board as a template. When new hires join, they can duplicate this board and practice customizing it for their own projects.

Real-World Application Example: Resolving Onboarding Challenges

Challenge 1: Overwhelmed by Features: During the second week, a new hire mentions feeling overwhelmed by the number of buttons and views in Monday.com.

- **Solution:** Schedule a 30-minute one-on-one session to focus on the features they'll use most often. For example, demonstrate how to filter items to see only their tasks and deadlines.

Challenge 2: Resistance to Change: Another new team member prefers their previous task management tool and hesitates to adopt Monday.com.

- **Solution:** Share success stories from other departments. For example, "The Sales team reduced their time spent on reporting by 30% after switching to Monday.com."

- Offer additional support, like pairing them with an experienced mentor for the first month.

Practical Example: Continuous Learning and Improvement

Scenario: After one month, you conduct a review session to address questions and refine workflows.

- **Feedback:** A team member suggests adding a "Campaign Approval" step before marking items as "Done."

- **Action:** Use the suggestion to create a new group on the campaign board called "Approval Needed." Train users on how to move items between groups to reflect this new process.

Success Story: One of the new hires, initially unfamiliar with Monday.com, shares their experience:

- "At first, it was overwhelming, but the onboarding videos and hands-on practice helped me feel confident. Now, I can manage all my campaigns without juggling multiple tools."

Sample Board Visualization

Campaign Plan Board Example (After Onboarding):

Group	Task	Assignee	Deadline	Status
Social Media	Write Instagram Captions	Alex	Jan 10	In Progress
Social Media	Schedule Facebook Posts	Jamie	Jan 12	Not Started

Email Campaigns	Draft Newsletter Copy	Mia	Jan 14	Done
Paid Ads	Launch Google Ads Campaign	Chris	Jan 15	Approval Needed

This board structure, built during onboarding, serves as a practical and replicable example for the team to follow.

Conclusion

By integrating real-world examples and hands-on exercises into the onboarding process, you create an engaging and effective learning experience. These scenarios ensure that every new user feels confident in their ability to use Monday.com effectively, setting the stage for better organization and collaboration at scale.

CHAPTER VIII
Real-Life Use Cases

8.1 Project Management with Monday.com

Project management is at the heart of Monday.com. It helps streamline communication, track progress, and manage tasks more effectively. Whether you're managing a small team or a large enterprise, Monday.com can be a game-changer in how you plan and track deliverables. By using the platform's various features, you can ensure your project is on track, resources are allocated efficiently, and team members stay aligned with project goals.

8.1.1 Planning and Tracking Deliverables

Planning and tracking deliverables is the foundation of successful project management. Deliverables represent the key outcomes or outputs of a project and must be well-defined, tracked, and completed on time. Monday.com offers a wide array of tools to help manage these deliverables, ensuring that every step in the project lifecycle is clearly mapped out.

Step 1: Define the Deliverables

Before you can track deliverables, it's essential to define what they are. This means understanding the end goals of the project and breaking them down into manageable, measurable outputs. Deliverables might include anything from the completion of a report, product launch, marketing campaign, or the final implementation of a system.

In Monday.com, you can create a **Board** specifically for your project and list all the deliverables as **Items** within that Board. Each deliverable can be tracked through various stages using **Columns** and **Views**.

For instance, let's imagine you are managing a software development project with the goal of releasing a new app. Some key deliverables might include:

- **Designing UI/UX mockups**

- **Developing the backend system**

- **Testing the app for bugs**

- **Marketing the app for launch**

Once these deliverables are identified, you can begin setting them up in Monday.com. Each of these tasks will become an **Item** on your Board.

Step 2: Break Deliverables Into Tasks and Subtasks

Once you have your deliverables outlined, the next step is to break them down into smaller, actionable tasks and subtasks. Monday.com's flexibility allows you to add as many layers of detail as needed, which ensures that nothing is overlooked.

For example, under the deliverable "Designing UI/UX mockups," you might break it down into the following tasks:

- **Research user preferences**

- **Sketch initial designs**

- **Create wireframes**

- **Get feedback from stakeholders**

Each of these tasks can then be listed under the primary deliverable item in Monday.com, and each task can be assigned to a specific team member, with a due date, priority, and status.

Step 3: Set Clear Deadlines and Timelines

One of the most important elements of project management is ensuring that deadlines are met. Monday.com helps you visually plan and track your deliverables with its **Timeline View** and **Due Date** columns. By setting clear due dates and using dependencies between tasks, you can create a project schedule that everyone can follow.

For instance, you could create a timeline for the "Developing the backend system" deliverable. The timeline view would allow you to visualize the tasks involved in the backend development and ensure that each subtask is completed on time for the next phase to begin.

You can also use the **Gantt Chart View** to see how different tasks are interdependent. This is helpful in managing the timeline of deliverables and ensuring that all team members are aligned with the project schedule. For example, "Marketing the app" can't begin until the backend development is completed, so you can set a dependency to ensure that tasks are automatically adjusted based on changes in deadlines.

Step 4: Track Progress Using Status Columns

Tracking the progress of deliverables is essential to understand where the project stands at any given time. Monday.com's **Status Column** is perfect for monitoring the stage of each deliverable or task.

In our software development example, you can use different status labels like:

- **Not Started**: Task has not yet begun.

- **In Progress**: Task is actively being worked on.

- **Waiting on Feedback**: Task is pending input from stakeholders.

- **Completed**: Task has been finished.

These labels give you a quick snapshot of the project's health and provide a visual cue for the team and stakeholders. As tasks move through the pipeline, the status will be updated accordingly. This helps ensure that nothing falls through the cracks.

Step 5: Automate Notifications and Reminders

Monday.com also allows you to set up **Automations** that trigger reminders and notifications when a task is nearing its deadline or when it requires attention. For instance, you can automate reminders for deliverables that are approaching their due date, or send notifications to a team member when their task status changes.

For example, if a task labeled "Sketch initial designs" is approaching its deadline, you can set an automation to send an email reminder to the team member responsible. You can even create a recurring reminder for daily or weekly progress updates, which helps keep everyone on track.

Step 6: Collaborate on Deliverables

Effective collaboration is vital to the successful completion of deliverables. Monday.com allows you to collaborate directly on each item with built-in communication tools. You can:

- **Leave comments** on tasks to ask questions, provide updates, or give feedback.

- **Tag team members** using @mentions, ensuring that relevant people are notified immediately.

- **Attach files** and links to relevant documents, designs, or resources to ensure that everyone has access to the necessary information.

For example, if a task such as "Create wireframes" is complete, the designer can tag the product manager in the comments section to review the work. The product manager can then leave feedback, and the designer can make any necessary adjustments directly in the system.

Step 7: Review and Report on Deliverables

At the end of the project or at specific milestones, it's important to review the progress and the results of the deliverables. Monday.com's **Dashboards** are great for this. Dashboards allow you to collect data from multiple boards and present them visually in charts, graphs, and widgets.

For example, you could create a Dashboard that pulls data from the project's board and shows:

- The percentage of tasks completed for each deliverable.

- The number of overdue tasks.

- Team members' workloads.

This helps identify any areas that require attention and ensures that the project stays on track.

Example: Real-Life Use Case

To further illustrate the steps outlined above, let's look at a real-life use case of a marketing agency launching a new campaign.

Project: New Marketing Campaign for Client X

- **Deliverable 1: Concept Development**
  Tasks: Research trends, Create concepts, Get client approval

- **Deliverable 2: Content Creation**
  Tasks: Write blog posts, Design graphics, Produce video content

- **Deliverable 3: Campaign Launch**
  Tasks: Set up ads, Monitor performance, Report results

In Monday.com, the team can create a Board with these deliverables as Items. Each task can be assigned to team members, with due dates set for each stage of the deliverable. Using the Timeline View, the marketing manager can track when content creation should start, how long it will take, and ensure that it aligns with the campaign launch date.

Throughout the project, team members can communicate directly within the platform, share files, and update the status of tasks as they progress. Automations can be used to remind content creators of deadlines, and a final dashboard will help the project manager monitor progress and adjust timelines as needed.

8.1.2 Collaborating Across Departments

Collaboration is at the heart of any successful project, especially when multiple departments need to work together seamlessly. Monday.com provides the tools and flexibility to ensure cross-departmental collaboration is not just efficient but also enjoyable. This section explores how teams from different departments can align their efforts, stay informed, and achieve shared goals using Monday.com.

The Challenge of Cross-Departmental Collaboration

Cross-departmental collaboration often presents challenges such as communication gaps, misaligned priorities, and inconsistent workflows. For example:

- **Marketing teams** may require design assets from the **Creative team**, while simultaneously waiting on budget approvals from the **Finance team**.

- **Sales teams** might depend on deliverables from the **Product team** to meet client expectations.

Without a centralized platform, these dependencies can lead to delays, missed deadlines, and frustration among team members.

How Monday.com Solves This Problem

Monday.com acts as a centralized hub where all departments can collaborate in real-time, share updates, and align their workflows. It eliminates silos by:

1. **Providing a Single Source of Truth**: All teams have access to the same information, reducing misunderstandings.

2. **Streamlining Communication**: Teams can communicate directly within the platform, keeping conversations contextually relevant.

3. **Customizing Workflows for Each Department**: Boards can be tailored to meet the unique needs of every team while still being interconnected.

Step-by-Step Guide to Collaborating Across Departments

1. Create a Shared Board

The first step to fostering cross-departmental collaboration is to set up a **Shared Board**. For example, let's imagine a scenario where the **Marketing**, **Creative**, and **Product** teams are collaborating on a product launch campaign.

1. **Create a Board** titled "Product Launch Campaign."

2. Add relevant stakeholders from all departments as board members.

3. Divide the board into **Groups** such as:

   o **Marketing Tasks**

   o **Creative Assets**

   o **Product Development Updates**

2. Define Clear Tasks and Ownership

Each department's responsibilities should be clearly outlined. On the shared board:

- **Marketing Tasks Group** might include:

   o Writing the product announcement email (Owner: Marketing Team Lead).

   o Planning the social media campaign (Owner: Social Media Manager).

- **Creative Assets Group** might include:

   o Designing promotional graphics (Owner: Graphic Designer).

- o Creating a product explainer video (Owner: Video Editor).

- **Product Development Updates Group** might include:

  - o Finalizing product features (Owner: Product Manager).

  - o Testing product functionality (Owner: QA Lead).

3. Use Status Columns to Track Progress

Each task should have a **Status Column** to indicate progress, such as:

- **Not Started**

- **In Progress**

- **Waiting on Approval**

- **Done**

This ensures that all stakeholders can instantly see the status of every task without needing to send follow-up emails or messages.

Example: Collaborating on a Product Launch

Let's break this down into a practical example.

Scenario: A company is launching a new app, and the **Marketing, Creative**, and **Product** teams need to work together to meet the launch deadline.

1. **Marketing Team** creates a content calendar for social media, outlining post topics, dates, and platforms.

2. They request graphics and videos from the **Creative Team**, tagging the Creative Team Lead on the board with specific deadlines.

3. The **Product Team** updates the board with the app's finalized features and provides demo screenshots for the Creative Team to include in their designs.

On Monday.com:

- The **Marketing Team** uses the **Timeline View** to visualize the campaign schedule.

- The **Creative Team** uses the **Files Column** to upload drafts of graphics for approval.

- The **Product Team** uses the **Checklist Feature** to break down app testing tasks and ensure everything is ready for launch.

By centralizing these tasks, all three teams can see how their work fits into the larger picture, avoiding duplication and miscommunication.

4. Enhance Communication with Updates and Tags

One of Monday.com's standout features is the ability to add **Updates** directly to items. Instead of long email threads, team members can:

- Leave comments on specific tasks.

- Tag colleagues using **@Mentions** to request input or feedback.

- Attach files, screenshots, or links for reference.

For example:

- The **Marketing Team Lead** tags the **Graphic Designer** in an update:

    o "@JohnSmith Can you provide the Instagram carousel design by Wednesday? Here's the copy we'll be using (attached)."

- The **Graphic Designer** responds with a draft and tags the **Social Media Manager**:

    o "@EmilyJones Here's the draft. Let me know if any adjustments are needed before finalizing."

5. Automate Workflow Dependencies

Automations on Monday.com can significantly reduce manual follow-ups. For example:

- When the **Creative Team** marks a task as "Done," an automation can notify the **Marketing Team** that the design is ready for review.

- If a **deadline approaches**, Monday.com can automatically send reminders to ensure tasks stay on track.

Example Automation Recipe:

- **Trigger**: Status changes to "Waiting on Approval."

- **Action**: Notify the "Marketing Team Lead" via an in-app message and email.

6. Visualize Progress with Dashboards

Dashboards provide a bird's-eye view of the project. For cross-departmental collaboration:

- Add a **Workload Widget** to see if any team members are overloaded with tasks.

- Use the **Timeline Widget** to track if any deadlines are at risk.

- Include a **Chart Widget** to visualize the percentage of tasks completed by each department.

For example, the dashboard might show that the **Creative Team** is 80% done with their deliverables, while the **Product Team** is only 50% complete. This insight allows teams to allocate resources or adjust priorities as needed.

Best Practices for Cross-Departmental Collaboration on Monday.com

1. **Schedule Regular Check-Ins**: Use Monday.com to schedule weekly updates where all departments review progress and discuss roadblocks.

2. **Standardize Naming Conventions**: To keep boards organized, establish a naming convention for tasks and items, such as "Team Name – Task Description."

3. **Encourage Transparency**: Ensure all team members update task statuses promptly to keep everyone informed.

4. **Celebrate Wins Together**: Use Monday.com to track milestones and celebrate when key goals are achieved, fostering a sense of shared accomplishment.

By leveraging the tools and strategies outlined above, Monday.com can become a powerful ally in fostering collaboration across departments. Whether it's a product launch or an internal initiative, the platform ensures that every team member has the tools, clarity, and support they need to succeed.

8.2 Using Monday.com for Marketing Teams

Marketing teams thrive on collaboration, structured workflows, and clear communication. Monday.com provides the flexibility and tools necessary to handle complex campaigns, from brainstorming ideas to delivering measurable results. This section will explore how marketing teams can utilize Monday.com for efficient **campaign planning**, with real-world examples to illustrate its capabilities.

8.2.1 Campaign Planning

Introduction to Campaign Planning with Monday.com

Campaign planning is at the heart of any successful marketing strategy. It involves defining objectives, assigning tasks, tracking progress, and ensuring team alignment throughout the project lifecycle. Monday.com provides marketing teams with a centralized hub to streamline this process, offering custom boards, automations, integrations, and visual tracking tools.

Let's break down how to effectively plan marketing campaigns using Monday.com, step by step.

Step 1: Create a Campaign Planning Board

The first step in organizing your marketing campaign is to create a dedicated board.

1. **Set Up Columns for Key Campaign Details:**

   - **Campaign Name:** Add a text column to list the names of campaigns.

   - **Goals/Objectives:** Use a text or long-text column to specify campaign objectives. For example: *"Increase social media engagement by 20% over 3 months."*

   - **Status:** Add a status column with labels like *Not Started, In Progress, Completed, Stuck.*

- o **Assigned Team Members:** Use a people column to assign tasks to team members.

- o **Due Dates:** Include a date column to track deadlines.

Example:

Imagine your marketing team is launching a new product. You can create a board titled *"New Product Launch Campaign"* and populate it with tasks like *Create a product teaser video*, *Design launch email templates*, and *Schedule social media posts*.

Step 2: Break the Campaign into Phases

Marketing campaigns often consist of multiple phases, such as research, content creation, execution, and analysis. Monday.com allows you to group these phases as separate *Groups* on your board.

- **Group 1: Research Phase**

  - o Tasks might include competitor analysis, identifying target audience demographics, and keyword research.

  - o Example: Assign *Competitor Analysis* to Sarah, with a deadline of January 15, and mark its status as *In Progress*.

- **Group 2: Content Creation Phase**

  - o Tasks in this group could include copywriting, video production, and graphic design.

  - o Example: Assign *Write blog posts for campaign* to Alex, with a status of *Not Started*.

- **Group 3: Execution Phase**

  - o This group includes scheduling posts, launching email campaigns, and running ads.

  - o Example: Assign *Schedule social media ads on Facebook and Instagram* to Taylor.

- **Group 4: Analysis Phase**

- Tasks such as monitoring key performance indicators (KPIs) and reporting on results go here.

- Example: Create a task titled *Analyze campaign engagement metrics* and set its due date for the end of the campaign.

Step 3: Utilize Templates for Consistency

Monday.com offers pre-built templates for marketing campaigns, which can save time and ensure consistency across projects.

- Use the **"Marketing Campaign Template"** to quickly populate your board with essential columns, sample groups, and tasks.

- Customize the template to fit your campaign's unique needs. For example, add a column for *Estimated Budget* or *Priority Level*.

Example: For a *Holiday Sale Campaign*, you can use the template to structure tasks like *Design holiday-themed graphics* or *Send Black Friday promotional emails*.

Step 4: Assign Responsibilities and Deadlines

Clear task assignment and deadline tracking are critical to keeping campaigns on schedule.

- Use the **People Column** to assign team members to each task.

- Set specific **Due Dates** for every task using the date column.

- Turn on **Deadline Notifications** so that team members receive reminders as deadlines approach.

Example: Assign *Create landing page for holiday sale* to the web design team with a deadline of November 10. Enable notifications so the team receives a reminder one week prior to the due date.

Step 5: Visualize Campaign Progress with Views

Monday.com offers multiple views to help marketing teams visualize campaign progress:

- **Kanban View:** Ideal for tracking tasks by status (e.g., To Do, In Progress, Completed).

- **Timeline View:** Provides a Gantt-style chart to ensure deadlines don't overlap.

- **Calendar View:** Displays tasks with deadlines on a calendar for easy scheduling.

- **Dashboard:** Combine data from multiple boards to create a high-level overview of all campaigns.

Example: Use the Timeline View to ensure that the *Social Media Post Schedule* doesn't overlap with the *Email Blast Launch*.

Step 6: Automate Repetitive Tasks

Marketing teams often perform repetitive tasks, such as sending follow-up emails or updating task statuses. Monday.com's automation recipes can handle these processes, freeing up time for creative work.

- **Example Automation Recipes:**

    o When the status changes to *Completed*, notify the campaign manager.

    o Every Monday at 9 AM, create a task for *Weekly Campaign Update Meeting*.

    o When a task is overdue, send an alert to the assigned team member.

Example: For the *New Year's Campaign*, you can automate task creation for weekly status check-ins with the team.

Step 7: Integrate Marketing Tools

Monday.com integrates seamlessly with many marketing tools to centralize workflows.

- **Google Drive or Dropbox:** Store and link campaign assets like images, videos, or presentations.

- **Mailchimp:** Sync email campaigns and monitor performance metrics directly within Monday.com.

- **Hootsuite or Buffer:** Schedule and track social media posts without switching platforms.

Example: Connect Monday.com to Google Drive to upload campaign graphics and share them directly with your design team.

Step 8: Monitor Campaign Performance

After launching your campaign, use Monday.com's reporting tools to analyze its performance:

- Add widgets to your dashboard for metrics like *Engagement Rate, Click-Through Rate (CTR),* and *Budget vs. Spend.*

- Track KPIs in real-time and make data-driven adjustments to improve results.

Example: For a *Spring Sale Campaign,* use a dashboard widget to monitor CTR from social media ads and adjust targeting if engagement is low.

Conclusion

Campaign planning with Monday.com transforms complex marketing projects into manageable workflows. By creating organized boards, breaking tasks into phases, leveraging automations, and integrating essential tools, marketing teams can focus on creativity and strategy rather than administration.

In the next section, we'll explore how Monday.com can be used for **Social Media Calendar Management** to streamline daily social media operations and maximize engagement.

8.2.2 Social Media Calendar Management

Introduction

Social media marketing is a critical component of modern marketing strategies. For marketing teams, staying organized and consistent with social media posts is essential to maintain engagement and build a strong online presence. Monday.com provides a robust platform for managing social media calendars, allowing teams to plan, schedule, and track campaigns efficiently. In this section, we will explore how to use Monday.com for social media calendar management with real-life examples, detailed instructions, and practical tips.

1. Setting Up a Social Media Calendar Board: The foundation of managing a social media calendar in Monday.com starts with creating a dedicated board. Here's how:

1. **Create a New Board**:

    o Name your board "Social Media Calendar."

    o Choose the type of board: A **main board** if it's an internal project or a **shareable board** if you collaborate with external partners or clients.

2. **Add Relevant Columns**: Customize your columns to include essential details for each social media post:

    o **Post Title** (Text column): Briefly describe the content, e.g., "New Product Launch Teaser."

    o **Platform** (Dropdown column): Specify where the post will be published (e.g., Instagram, Facebook, LinkedIn, TikTok).

    o **Publish Date** (Date column): Add the scheduled publishing date.

    o **Status** (Status column): Track the progress (e.g., "Draft," "Scheduled," "Published").

    o **Owner** (People column): Assign team members responsible for creating or approving the post.

- o **Assets** (File column): Attach images, videos, or graphics for the post.

3. **Group Items by Week or Campaign**: Structure your board by grouping posts by week, month, or campaign to keep everything organized and visually clear. For example:

   - o Group 1: "January 2025: New Year Campaign"

   - o Group 2: "February 2025: Valentine's Day Specials"

---

2. Planning Your Social Media Content: Effective planning ensures your social media strategy aligns with your marketing goals. Monday.com allows teams to collaborate and brainstorm content ideas within the board.

1. **Brainstorm Content Ideas**: Use the **Updates** section within each item to collaborate. For example:

   - o Post Title: "Behind-the-Scenes Video of Our New Product."

   - o Updates: "Let's include a time-lapse of production and a short interview with the team."

2. **Use the Timeline View**: Switch to the **Timeline View** to visualize the distribution of your posts over the month. This helps ensure posts are spaced appropriately and avoid gaps or overlaps in content.

3. **Set Deadlines for Team Members**: Use the **Date Column** and automation to remind team members of upcoming deadlines. For example:

   - o Automation: "When a Publish Date arrives, notify the Owner."

---

3. Scheduling and Tracking Posts: Once the content is planned, it's time to schedule and track your posts. Monday.com provides tools to streamline this process.

1. **Link with Publishing Tools**:

   - o Integrate Monday.com with tools like Hootsuite, Buffer, or HubSpot. For example:

- Automation: "When a Status changes to Scheduled, create a new post in Buffer."
  - This integration ensures seamless scheduling of posts across platforms.

2. **Add Checklists for Quality Control**: Use the **Checklist Widget** within each item to ensure all steps are completed before publishing. For example:

  - Checklists:
    - Proofread captions.
    - Approve graphics.
    - Test all links.

3. **Track Performance Metrics**:

  - Add columns for metrics like **Engagement Rate** or **Impressions** after the post is published.
  - For example:
    - Post Title: "Valentine's Day Promo Video."
    - Engagement Rate: 12%.
    - Impressions: 20,000.

4. Managing Campaigns Across Teams: Collaboration is key to running successful social media campaigns. Monday.com makes it easy for multiple teams to work together.

1. **Use Subitems for Campaign Breakdown**:

  - For larger campaigns, break down tasks into subitems.
  - Example:
    - Item: "Valentine's Day Promo Campaign."
    - Subitems:
      - "Create Instagram Story Graphics" (Owner: Designer).

- ▪ "Write Post Captions" (Owner: Copywriter).

    - ▪ "Approve Final Drafts" (Owner: Marketing Lead).

2. **Communicate in Real-Time**: Use the **Updates** section to keep discussions centralized. For example:

    - o Designer: "Here's the final version of the Instagram graphic."

    - o Marketing Lead: "Looks great! Let's move this to the 'Approved' status."

3. **Track Campaign Progress with Dashboards**:

    - o Create a dashboard to monitor the status of all campaign tasks.

    - o Add widgets like **Progress Bars** and **Pie Charts** to visualize completion rates.

---

5. Practical Example: Managing a Monthly Social Media Calendar

Let's consider a real-life scenario where a marketing team is managing a monthly calendar for February 2025.

- • **Campaign Name**: Valentine's Day Specials

- • **Platforms**: Instagram, Facebook, Twitter

- • **Goals**: Increase engagement by 20% and drive traffic to the website.

Steps in Monday.com:

1. **Create a Group**: "February 2025: Valentine's Day Specials."

2. **Add Items**:

    - o Post Title: "Valentine's Day Promo Video."

    - o Platform: Instagram, Facebook.

    - o Publish Date: February 10, 2025.

    - o Status: Scheduled.

- o Owner: Social Media Manager.

- o Assets: Attach the promo video and graphic designs.

3. **Set Automations**:

- o Automation: "When Status changes to Published, notify the Marketing Lead."

4. **Monitor Engagement Metrics**: After publishing, add columns for metrics:

- o Engagement Rate: 15%.

- o Website Traffic: 1,200 clicks.

6. Tips for Effective Social Media Calendar Management

1. **Consistency is Key**: Schedule posts at optimal times for each platform based on audience insights.

2. **Leverage Analytics**: Use performance data from Monday.com integrations to refine future campaigns.

3. **Collaborate with Transparency**: Ensure all team members are aligned on goals, deadlines, and deliverables by maintaining an updated board.

Conclusion

Managing a social media calendar with Monday.com simplifies collaboration, streamlines planning, and provides a clear overview of campaigns. By following the steps and tips in this section, marketing teams can maximize their efficiency and deliver consistent, impactful content.

8.3 Managing Personal Productivity

8.3.1 Using Monday.com as a To-Do List

Managing personal productivity effectively is a critical aspect of success, whether you're working on professional goals or organizing your personal life. Monday.com, with its user-friendly interface and customizable tools, serves as an excellent platform for creating and managing a digital to-do list. This section will guide you through the process of setting up a personalized to-do list on Monday.com, demonstrate how to utilize its features for optimal organization, and provide real-life examples of practical usage.

Why Use Monday.com as a To-Do List?

Traditional to-do lists—whether on paper or in a basic app—often lack flexibility and fail to provide the level of customization and tracking that modern professionals need. Monday.com takes the concept of a simple checklist to the next level by offering:

- **Customizable layouts** for tracking different types of tasks.

- **Status updates** to reflect progress at a glance.

- **Integration with other tools** to streamline workflows.

- **Automation features** to reduce repetitive tasks.

- **Accessibility across devices**, ensuring your to-do list is always within reach.

Step-by-Step Guide to Setting Up a To-Do List on Monday.com

Step 1: Create a New Board

Begin by creating a new board dedicated to your to-do list.

1. Go to the workspace of your choice and click on the **"+ Add"** button.

2. Select **"Board"**, and name it something like "My To-Do List" or "Daily Tasks."

3. Choose a template (optional) or start from scratch.

Step 2: Add Columns to Organize Your Tasks

Columns in Monday.com allow you to structure your tasks in a way that suits your needs. For a to-do list, consider adding the following columns:

- **Item Name (Task Title):** List the name of the task.

- **Status Column:** Use this to mark tasks as "To Do," "In Progress," or "Done."

- **Due Date Column:** Set deadlines to keep track of time-sensitive tasks.

- **Priority Column:** Label tasks as High, Medium, or Low to prioritize effectively.

- **Person Column (optional):** Assign tasks to yourself or others if working collaboratively.

Step 3: Input Tasks

Start populating the board with your tasks. Each row represents a single task. For instance:

- **"Write draft for client proposal"** (High Priority, Due by Thursday).

- **"Respond to project emails"** (Medium Priority, Due today).

- **"Book flights for conference"** (Low Priority, Due next Monday).

Step 4: Organize Tasks by Groups

Monday.com allows you to create groups within your board to further segment tasks. Examples include:

- **"Daily Tasks":** Short-term tasks you need to complete today.

- **"Weekly Goals":** Broader tasks or projects to accomplish within the week.

- **"Long-Term Goals":** Tasks with flexible deadlines.

Using Advanced Features to Enhance Your To-Do List

1. Status Updates for Progress Tracking

The **status column** enables you to track the progress of each task in real-time. Examples of statuses include:

- "To Do" for tasks not yet started.

- "In Progress" for tasks currently being worked on.

- "Stuck" for tasks requiring assistance or additional information.

- "Done" for completed tasks.

For instance, if you're working on a presentation, you could update the status as follows:

- **"Create slide outline"** → "Done."

- **"Design slides"** → "In Progress."

- **"Review presentation"** → "To Do."

2. Deadlines and Notifications

Setting deadlines in the **Due Date column** ensures you never miss an important task. You can also enable notifications to remind you about upcoming or overdue tasks.

For example:

- **Task:** Submit project report.

- **Deadline:** Friday, 3 PM.

- **Notification:** Set a reminder for Thursday at 5 PM to review and finalize.

3. Prioritization for Better Focus

Use the **Priority column** to decide which tasks deserve immediate attention. By filtering your to-do list by High, Medium, or Low priority, you can focus on what matters most.

For example:

- **High Priority:** Prepare client pitch (due tomorrow).

- **Medium Priority:** Organize files in Google Drive.

- **Low Priority:** Research new productivity apps.

4. Automations for Routine Tasks

Automations on Monday.com can save time by handling repetitive tasks. Examples include:

- Automatically marking a task as "Done" when the deadline is reached.

- Sending you a notification if a high-priority task is still "To Do" one day before its deadline.

Real-Life Examples of Using Monday.com as a To-Do List

Example 1: Daily Task Management for a Freelancer

As a freelancer, John uses Monday.com to manage his daily tasks:

- **Morning Routine:** John sets up tasks such as "Check emails" and "Plan the day."

- **Client Work:** Tasks like "Write blog post for Client A" and "Submit invoice for Client B" are added with specific deadlines.

- **Admin Work:** Ongoing tasks like "Track expenses" and "Update portfolio" are assigned medium priority.

By the end of the day, John checks off all completed tasks and updates statuses, ensuring nothing is overlooked.

Example 2: Personal Productivity for a Student

Sophia, a university student, uses Monday.com to balance her academic and personal responsibilities:

- **Academic Tasks:** Sophia tracks assignments like "Finish biology paper" and "Study for chemistry exam" in her "Weekly Goals" group.

- **Personal Goals:** Her to-do list includes "Meal prep for the week" and "Call mom."

- **Hobby Projects:** She also tracks tasks for her blog, such as "Write draft for new post" and "Edit photos."

With Monday.com, Sophia stays organized and meets her deadlines effortlessly.

Example 3: Managing a Household To-Do List

Emma, a busy parent, uses Monday.com to manage her family's to-do list:

- **Household Chores:** Tasks like "Clean the kitchen" and "Water the plants" are assigned to family members.

- **Family Activities:** Tasks like "Plan weekend picnic" and "Buy birthday gift for Dad" are added to the board.

- **Recurring Tasks:** Automations remind Emma to "Pay electricity bill" and "Order groceries" every week.

Tips for Maximizing Efficiency

- **Use Color Coding:** Assign colors to priority levels or statuses for quick visual cues.

- **Leverage Filters:** Filter tasks by priority or due date to focus on what's most urgent.

- **Keep It Simple:** Avoid overloading your board with unnecessary columns or details.

By following these steps and utilizing the features discussed, Monday.com can transform a simple to-do list into a powerful productivity tool. Whether you're managing daily chores, personal goals, or complex projects, this platform ensures you stay on top of everything with ease and efficiency.

8.3.2 Setting Personal Goals and Deadlines

Monday.com is not just a powerful tool for teams and organizations; it can also be an excellent platform for managing personal productivity. Setting personal goals and deadlines in Monday.com allows you to stay organized, prioritize effectively, and ensure accountability for achieving your objectives. Whether you're planning your career, improving personal habits, or managing a side project, Monday.com provides the structure and tools to make your plans actionable.

1. Why Personal Goals and Deadlines Matter

Before diving into the "how," let's explore the importance of setting goals and deadlines:

- **Clarity and Focus:** Personal goals help you define what you want to achieve and provide a clear roadmap. Deadlines ensure you stay on track.

- **Accountability:** Setting goals in a system like Monday.com creates a sense of commitment, especially when deadlines are in place.

- **Measurable Progress:** By breaking goals into manageable tasks, you can track your progress and celebrate small wins along the way.

Let's now look at how you can leverage Monday.com to set and manage personal goals and deadlines effectively.

2. Step-by-Step Guide to Setting Personal Goals in Monday.com

Step 1: Create a Dedicated Goal-Tracking Board

Start by creating a board specifically for personal goals.

- **Board Name:** "My Personal Goals" or "2025 Goals Tracker."

- **Columns to Use:**

  - **Goal Name:** A clear, concise title for each goal (e.g., "Write a Book," "Learn Python," "Run a Marathon").

  - **Description:** A short explanation of what the goal entails and why it matters.

  - **Status:** Use statuses like "Not Started," "In Progress," and "Completed."

  - **Deadline:** Add a date column for the target completion date.

  - **Progress:** Use a numeric column or progress bar to measure completion percentage.

  - **Priority:** Label tasks as "High," "Medium," or "Low" priority.

Example Board Layout:

Goal Name	Description	Status	Deadline	Progress	Priority
Write a Book	Finish my first novel	In Progress	March 31, 2025	45%	High
Learn Python	Complete an online course	Not Started	June 15, 2025	0%	Medium
Run a Marathon	Train for a 5k run	In Progress	December 31, 2025	30%	High

Step 2: Break Goals into Manageable Tasks

Breaking a goal into smaller, actionable tasks makes it less overwhelming and easier to track.

- **Subitems in Monday.com:** Use the subitem feature to list specific tasks under each goal.

- **Example for the Goal "Write a Book":**

    o   Subitem 1: Outline book chapters.

    o   Subitem 2: Write 1,000 words per week.

    o   Subitem 3: Edit chapters 1–5 by February 15, 2025.

This structured breakdown ensures that each step feels achievable and provides a clear path forward.

Step 3: Set Realistic Deadlines for Each Task

Deadlines are essential for staying motivated and avoiding procrastination.

- Use Monday.com's **Deadline Mode** to assign due dates to each task.

- Enable deadline notifications to receive reminders as a task's due date approaches.

- Prioritize flexibility: If unexpected delays occur, adjust the deadlines to remain on track.

Example of a Goal with Deadlines:

Task	Deadline	Status
Outline book chapters	January 10, 2025	Completed
Write 1,000 words weekly	Weekly (Recurring)	In Progress
Edit chapters 1–5	February 15, 2025	Not Started

3. Using Views to Stay Organized

Monday.com offers various views to help you visualize and manage your goals and deadlines:

Kanban View for Prioritization

The Kanban view allows you to drag and drop goals or tasks between status columns like "Not Started," "In Progress," and "Completed." This method is ideal for visualizing progress.

Calendar View for Deadlines

With the calendar view, you can see all your deadlines in one place. This is particularly useful for long-term planning, as it ensures no tasks or goals are overlooked.

Timeline View for Task Dependencies

For more complex goals with interdependent tasks, the timeline view helps you schedule and manage overlapping deadlines.

4. Tips for Staying on Track with Personal Goals

1. **Set SMART Goals:** Goals should be Specific, Measurable, Achievable, Relevant, and Time-bound.

2. **Use Automations:** Automate reminders or notifications to stay on top of deadlines. For instance, set up an automation to notify you one week before a task is due.

3. **Track Weekly Progress:** Schedule a weekly review to update the status of your goals and adjust deadlines if necessary.

4. **Celebrate Milestones:** Mark key milestones as "Complete" and celebrate small wins to stay motivated.

5. **Reflect and Adjust:** Use Monday.com's data analysis tools to identify patterns (e.g., recurring delays) and improve your approach to goal setting.

5. Real-Life Example: Managing a Fitness Goal

Imagine you want to train for a marathon using Monday.com:

1. **Goal:** "Run a Marathon by December 31, 2025."

2. **Tasks and Subitems:**

   o Research marathon training plans (Deadline: January 15, 2025).

   o Register for a marathon event (Deadline: February 1, 2025).

   o Follow a weekly training schedule (Subitems: "Run 5k by March," "Run 10k by May").

   o Track progress using Monday.com's time tracking column.

3. **Tools:**

   o Add a column for tracking weekly mileage.

   o Use automations to receive reminders for upcoming runs.

   o Visualize the training schedule in the calendar view.

6. Benefits of Using Monday.com for Personal Productivity

- **Customizable Features:** Tailor boards to suit your specific goals and habits.

- **Increased Accountability:** Deadlines and progress tracking keep you committed to your plans.

- **Cross-Device Access:** Work on your goals from your computer, phone, or tablet.

- **Integration with Other Tools:** Sync Monday.com with Google Calendar or other apps to centralize your productivity efforts.

By leveraging Monday.com for personal goals and deadlines, you not only gain clarity and organization but also increase your chances of success. With consistent effort and effective use of the platform's features, your goals become achievable milestones on your journey to personal growth.

CHAPTER IX
Continuous Learning and Resources

9.1 Monday.com Help Center and Community

The **Monday.com Help Center and Community** serve as invaluable resources for users at all levels of experience. Whether you're a beginner just starting out or a seasoned pro looking to fine-tune your workflows, Monday.com provides a robust platform for continuous learning and collaboration. These resources are designed to help users maximize the platform's potential, solve problems, and connect with other professionals using the tool.

9.1.1 Accessing Online Tutorials

Introduction to Online Tutorials

Monday.com offers a wide array of online tutorials that cater to users with varying levels of expertise. These tutorials are accessible through the **Monday.com Help Center** and are structured to provide step-by-step guidance on key features, functionalities, and best practices. Whether you're learning how to create a basic board or exploring advanced automation techniques, these tutorials are the foundation for building your Monday.com skills.

Online tutorials are typically delivered in three formats:

- **Video Tutorials**: Short and focused videos that demonstrate specific features visually.

- **Written Guides**: Detailed articles and how-tos with screenshots for users who prefer reading.

- **Interactive Webinars**: Live or recorded sessions where users can interact with trainers and ask questions.

Step-by-Step Guide to Accessing Tutorials

Here is how you can access and utilize the tutorials effectively:

Step 1: Navigating to the Help Center

1. **Log into your Monday.com Account**: Start by logging into your Monday.com account.

2. **Click the Help Icon**: On the bottom right corner of your workspace, click the "Help" button (usually represented by a question mark icon).

3. **Choose "Help Center"**: In the dropdown menu, select **"Help Center"** to open the resource hub.

Alternatively, you can directly visit the Monday.com Help Center by going to support.monday.com in your web browser.

Step 2: Searching for Relevant Tutorials

Once in the Help Center, use the search bar to look for specific tutorials. For example:

- **Search "Creating a New Board"** to find beginner-level tutorials.

- **Search "Setting Up Automations"** for advanced workflows. The Help Center categorizes articles and videos by topic, such as Boards, Views, Automations, Integrations, and more, making it easy to navigate.

Step 3: Watching Video Tutorials

Video tutorials are ideal for visual learners. For instance, if you're interested in automating recurring tasks, you can search for the tutorial titled **"How to Set Up Automations."** A short 3-5 minute video will walk you through the process, including:

- How to create automation recipes.

- Real-life examples of task automation (e.g., automatically assigning team members when a status changes).

Step 4: Exploring Written Guides

If you prefer written instructions, click on a guide like **"Using Views to Visualize Your Workflows."** These articles include:

- Screenshots to illustrate each step.

- Troubleshooting tips for common errors.

Step 5: Attending Webinars

Webinars provide a hands-on learning experience. Monday.com frequently hosts live sessions, such as **"Monday.com for Marketing Teams"** or **"Using Dashboards for Data-Driven Insights."** By attending these webinars, you can:

- Watch live demonstrations of advanced features.

- Participate in Q&A sessions with Monday.com experts.

Examples of Tutorials for Different Use Cases

Example 1: Beginner User - Setting Up a Simple Board

A beginner user, Emma, wants to set up a task board for her small business. She accesses the tutorial **"How to Create Your First Board"** in the Help Center.

1. The tutorial guides her to create a blank board.

2. It explains how to add columns such as **Status**, **Due Date**, and **Assigned To.**

3. Emma learns how to customize item names to match her team's workflow (e.g., Tasks: "Design Logo," "Create Website Content").

4. The tutorial suggests using the **Timeline View** to track deadlines visually.

Emma finishes the tutorial in 15 minutes and now has a fully functional board that her team can use immediately.

Example 2: Advanced User - Setting Up Dependencies

An advanced user, James, wants to set up dependencies between tasks in his project. He watches the tutorial **"How to Use Dependencies in Monday.com."**

1. The video explains how to enable the **Dependencies Column** in board settings.

2. James learns how to link tasks (e.g., Task B starts only after Task A is completed).

3. The tutorial provides tips for using the **Gantt Chart View** to visualize task dependencies.

After following the tutorial, James successfully automates his project timeline and ensures that deadlines are realistic and sequential.

Tips for Getting the Most Out of Tutorials

1. **Start with Your Goals**: Identify what you want to achieve before diving into tutorials. For example, are you trying to improve team collaboration, automate tasks, or track progress more efficiently?

2. **Bookmark Useful Tutorials**: Save links to tutorials that you find particularly helpful for future reference.

3. **Practice as You Learn**: Open your Monday.com workspace and apply what you're learning in real time.

4. **Engage with the Community**: After completing a tutorial, visit the **Monday.com Community Forum** to ask questions or share your experience with others.

Benefits of Online Tutorials

1. **Self-Paced Learning**: Tutorials allow you to learn at your own speed, pausing and rewinding videos as needed.

2. **Immediate Problem Solving**: You can find solutions to common challenges, such as setting up complex workflows or troubleshooting integrations.

3. **Access Anytime, Anywhere**: Whether you're at your desk or on the go, tutorials are always available through the Help Center or Monday.com's mobile app.

4. **Stay Updated**: With Monday.com frequently releasing new features, tutorials are often updated to reflect the latest functionality.

By consistently utilizing the online tutorials in Monday.com's Help Center, users can confidently build their skills, solve problems efficiently, and take full advantage of the platform's powerful tools. The next section, **9.1.2 Joining Monday.com User Forums**, will explore how to connect with a vibrant community of users for even deeper learning and collaboration.

9.1.2 Joining Monday.com User Forums

Monday.com's user forums are an invaluable resource for users looking to deepen their understanding of the platform, troubleshoot issues, and connect with a community of like-minded professionals. These forums are designed to facilitate collaboration, share best practices, and provide a space for users to learn from each other's experiences. In this section, we'll explore what these forums offer, how to access and navigate them, and ways to make the most out of your participation.

What Are Monday.com User Forums?

Monday.com user forums are online communities where users come together to discuss the platform, share ideas, and solve problems. These forums are hosted by Monday.com and are accessible to all registered users. Whether you're a beginner or an advanced user, the forums provide opportunities to:

- **Ask Questions:** Get help from other users or Monday.com experts.

- **Share Solutions:** Contribute your knowledge and help others solve their problems.

- **Learn Best Practices:** Discover tips and tricks to optimize workflows.

- **Network:** Connect with professionals in your industry using Monday.com.

The forums are categorized into various topics, including specific features like automations, integrations, and templates, as well as broader discussions about project management or team collaboration.

How to Access the Forums

To join the Monday.com user forums, follow these steps:

1. **Log in to Your Monday.com Account:** Open Monday.com in your browser and log in using your account credentials.

2. **Navigate to the Help Center:** From your Monday.com dashboard, click the question mark icon (?) located in the bottom-left corner. Select **"Help Center"** from the menu.

3. **Locate the Forums Link:** In the Help Center, you'll find a section labeled **"Community."** Click the link to access the user forums.

4. **Sign Up for the Forums (If Required):** While you can browse some topics as a guest, creating a forum account allows you to post questions, reply to threads, and personalize your profile.

5. **Start Exploring Topics:** Use the search bar or navigate through categories to find discussions that interest you.

Navigating the Forums

Once you've accessed the forums, it's important to understand how to navigate them effectively:

- **Search Functionality:** Use the search bar to find topics, keywords, or specific features you're looking for. For example, searching "automations for recurring tasks" will yield threads related to that topic.

- **Categories and Tags:** Forums are organized into categories like **Getting Started**, **Troubleshooting**, **Feature Requests**, and more. Tags like "Automations," "Templates," or "Integrations" help you quickly identify relevant discussions.

- **Pinned Posts:** Moderators often pin important posts, such as announcements or FAQs, to the top of each category. Make sure to review these for valuable insights.

- **Active Threads:** Look for threads with recent activity. These often provide the most up-to-date solutions or ideas.

Making the Most of User Forums

To get the best experience out of Monday.com's forums, follow these tips:

1. **Ask Clear Questions:** When posting a question, be specific about your issue or what you're trying to achieve. Include details like:

   o The type of board or workflow you're using.

   o Steps you've already tried.

   o Screenshots (if allowed) for better clarity.

Example:
"I'm trying to create an automation where a status change triggers an email to my team. I've set up the automation, but the emails are not sending. Does anyone know how to fix this?"

2. **Engage in Discussions:** Contribute to ongoing threads by sharing your experiences or providing solutions. Even if you're new, your insights might help someone else.

Example Response: *"I had a similar issue with email automations not sending. It turned out I had to enable the integration permissions in my account settings. Hope that helps!"*

3. **Follow Thought Leaders:** Many experienced users or Monday.com representatives frequently contribute to the forums. Following their posts can provide a wealth of knowledge and inspiration.

4. **Use Feedback Loops:** If you find a solution to your problem through the forums, return to your thread and share what worked for you. This helps other users who might face the same issue.

5. **Participate in Community Events:** Monday.com often hosts community challenges, webinars, or Q&A sessions. Engaging in these events can enhance your learning and expand your professional network.

Real-Life Example: Problem Solved Through Forums

Scenario:

Emma, a project manager at a marketing agency, faced a challenge when her team needed to integrate Monday.com with Slack for real-time updates. Although she had set up the Slack integration, notifications weren't being sent for some board changes.

Emma's Forum Post: *"I've set up the Slack integration for my project board, but notifications aren't being sent for 'Task Completed' updates. I've double-checked the integration settings and triggers. Any ideas on what might be wrong?"*

Forum Response: Several users replied with suggestions:

- **User 1:** "Check if the Slack channel permissions allow messages from Monday.com."

- **User 2:** "Make sure the automation trigger matches the exact column name. I had a similar issue when the column name was slightly different."

- **Moderator:** "If none of these work, try reconnecting the Slack integration under Admin > Integrations. Sometimes resetting the connection solves the problem."

Outcome:
By following these suggestions, Emma identified the issue—her automation trigger didn't match the exact column name—and successfully resolved the problem. She updated her thread with the solution, which later helped several other users facing similar challenges.

Building Connections Through Forums

The Monday.com user forums aren't just a place to troubleshoot—they're a platform for networking and collaboration. You can connect with professionals from various industries, share insights, and even discover opportunities for partnerships or mentorship.

Pro Tip: If you find a user whose insights you value, consider sending them a private message to discuss your challenges in more detail. Many users are happy to mentor or collaborate outside of the forums.

Conclusion

Joining and participating in Monday.com's user forums can transform the way you use the platform. By leveraging the collective knowledge of the community, you'll not only solve problems more efficiently but also discover innovative ways to optimize your workflows. Whether you're troubleshooting an issue, exploring advanced features, or simply seeking inspiration, the forums provide a wealth of resources to enhance your Monday.com experience.

9.2 Exploring Advanced Tutorials

9.2.1 Advanced Automation Techniques

Automation is one of the most powerful features in Monday.com, allowing teams to save time, reduce errors, and maintain consistency in their workflows. While basic automation recipes like due date reminders and status changes are useful, advanced automation techniques take your project management and organizational capabilities to a whole new level. In this section, we'll explore the nuances of creating complex automation workflows and demonstrate how you can optimize Monday.com to its fullest potential.

What are Advanced Automations?

Advanced automations are sophisticated, multi-step workflows that combine multiple triggers, conditions, and actions to handle complex processes. Unlike basic automations that execute a single action based on a single trigger, advanced automations allow you to:

- Handle conditional logic (e.g., "If A happens, then do X; if B happens, then do Y").

- Automate multi-board dependencies.

- Create cascading workflows with multiple layers of actions.

- Integrate third-party applications seamlessly to automate cross-platform processes.

By implementing advanced automations, you can ensure that your team spends less time on repetitive tasks and more time on strategic work.

Building Advanced Automation Recipes

Let's break down the steps to create advanced automation recipes in Monday.com:

1. Using Multiple Triggers and Conditions

A single trigger might not always capture the complexity of your workflow. For example, you may want a task's priority to update only if both the deadline is approaching **and** its status is still "Not Started."

- **Step-by-Step Example:**
    - Go to the **Automations Center** on your board.
    - Choose the "When" trigger, such as "When a date arrives."
    - Add an additional condition using the "And" logic, such as "And status is Not Started."
    - Set the action: "Change priority to High."

This allows you to address conditional scenarios and streamline decision-making for your team.

2. Cross-Board Automations

Managing dependencies across multiple boards is a common challenge for teams with interconnected projects. Monday.com enables you to automate actions between boards.

- **Example Use Case:** A marketing team's campaign board is linked to a content calendar board. When a campaign's status is marked as "Ready to Launch" on the campaign board, you can automatically add the task to the content calendar board.
    - Trigger: "When status changes to Ready to Launch."
    - Action: "Create an item in the content calendar board."
    - Additional customization: Sync the due dates between the two boards.

3. Automating Subitems

Subitems are great for breaking down tasks into smaller steps, but they can become challenging to manage manually. Advanced automations let you handle subitems efficiently.

- **Example:**
    - Trigger: "When a subitem's status changes to Done."

- o   Action: "Change the parent item's progress to reflect the completed percentage of subitems."

This ensures that the parent item always displays an accurate status based on its subitems, giving your team better visibility.

Combining Automations for Complex Scenarios

Scenario 1: Multi-Step Approval Processes

Imagine your team needs to approve a project proposal before moving to execution. You can create an automated multi-step approval process:

1. **Trigger 1:** "When a proposal is submitted (status changes to Submitted), assign it to the manager for review."

2. **Trigger 2:** "When the manager approves (status changes to Approved), assign the task to the execution team and notify them."

3. **Trigger 3:** "If the manager rejects (status changes to Rejected), notify the proposal owner with feedback."

This eliminates the need for manual follow-ups and ensures that each step in the approval process is automatically tracked.

Scenario 2: Escalation Workflows

In time-sensitive situations, you can automate escalation workflows to alert higher-level team members if tasks are delayed.

- Trigger: "When a due date passes and status is not Done."

- Action 1: "Notify the task owner."

- Action 2: "If still not resolved in 2 days, notify the department head and change the task priority to Critical."

This keeps the team accountable and ensures that important tasks are not overlooked.

Using Third-Party Integrations in Automations

1. Integrating with Slack

Automations can be enhanced by integrating Slack for real-time notifications. For example:

- Trigger: "When a project's status changes to Blocked."

- Action: "Send a message in the #team-alerts Slack channel with task details."

This ensures that urgent updates are communicated instantly to the right stakeholders.

2. Integrating with Zapier

Zapier expands Monday.com's automation capabilities by allowing you to connect with thousands of apps. For example:

- Trigger: "When an item's status changes to Completed in Monday.com."

- Action: "Create an invoice in QuickBooks automatically."

3. Connecting with Google Calendar

Sync your boards with Google Calendar to automate scheduling.

- Trigger: "When a due date is set in Monday.com."

- Action: "Add the task to the team's shared Google Calendar."

Best Practices for Advanced Automations

1. **Start Small and Build Gradually**

   o Begin with simple automations and layer complexity as your team becomes more comfortable.

   o Test new automations thoroughly before applying them to critical workflows.

2. **Avoid Automation Overload**

   o Too many overlapping automations can create confusion and lead to errors.

- o Regularly review and clean up outdated or unnecessary automations.

3. **Involve Your Team in the Process**

- o Gather feedback from your team to ensure the automations meet their needs.

- o Train team members on how to manage and modify automations.

4. **Monitor Automation Performance**

- o Use Monday.com's activity logs to track automation performance and resolve any issues.

Real-Life Examples of Advanced Automations

1. **E-commerce Order Fulfillment**

- o Automate the process of tracking online orders from placement to delivery.

- o Example Workflow:

  - Trigger: "When a new order is added to the board."

  - Action 1: "Assign the order to the warehouse team."

  - Action 2: "Send an email notification to the customer with order details."

  - Action 3: "When the status changes to Shipped, update the delivery board."

2. **Software Development Bug Tracking**

- o Automate bug tracking and resolution workflows.

- o Example Workflow:

  - Trigger: "When a bug is reported (item added to the bug tracking board)."

  - Action: "Notify the developer assigned to the project."

- Action: "If the bug is not resolved within 3 days, escalate to the project manager."

Conclusion

Advanced automation techniques are a game-changer for teams looking to optimize their workflows and improve efficiency. By leveraging conditional logic, cross-board automations, subitem management, and third-party integrations, you can handle even the most complex processes with ease. As you continue to explore and refine your automations, you'll unlock new possibilities to make Monday.com an indispensable tool for your team.

9.2.2 Advanced Integration Workflows

In today's interconnected world, seamless integration between tools is essential for maximizing efficiency and productivity. Monday.com offers a robust ecosystem of integrations that allow you to connect with various applications, creating advanced workflows that meet the unique needs of your organization. This section delves into how to set up and optimize advanced integration workflows to streamline your processes and enhance collaboration.

Understanding Advanced Integration Workflows

An advanced integration workflow is more than a simple connection between two tools. It involves automating complex, multi-step processes that save time, reduce manual effort, and eliminate the risk of errors. These workflows combine multiple applications and Monday.com features to create a cohesive system that works together harmoniously.

For example:

- Automatically syncing data between your CRM and Monday.com boards.

- Triggering email campaigns in Mailchimp based on status changes in Monday.com.

- Generating reports in Google Sheets whenever a task is marked as "Complete."

By leveraging advanced integrations, you can build workflows that bridge gaps across teams, departments, and tools.

Step 1: Identifying Your Workflow Needs

Before diving into setup, start by analyzing your team's existing workflows. Identify:

- **Repetitive Tasks**: Which tasks are time-consuming and can be automated?

- **Manual Processes**: Are there processes that require switching between multiple tools?

- **Integration Gaps**: Are there data silos preventing smooth communication across platforms?

By mapping your workflow, you can identify areas where integrations will have the most impact.

Example: If your marketing team uses Monday.com to manage campaigns and Google Analytics to track performance, an integration could automate the collection of analytics data directly into a Monday.com dashboard.

Step 2: Choosing the Right Tools to Integrate

Monday.com supports integrations with a variety of tools across categories such as communication, file management, CRM, and analytics. Some of the most popular integrations for advanced workflows include:

- **Slack**: Automate notifications for specific updates.

- **Google Workspace**: Sync tasks with Google Calendar or import Sheets data into boards.

- **Zapier**: Connect Monday.com with thousands of apps like Trello, Asana, and Salesforce.

- **Integromat**: For building more complex automation workflows.

Choose tools that are essential to your workflow and offer integration support via Monday.com or third-party connectors like Zapier.

Step 3: Setting Up Advanced Integration Workflows

Once you've identified your needs and selected the tools, follow these steps to set up advanced workflows:

3.1 Enabling the Integration

1. Navigate to the **Integrations Center** in Monday.com.

2. Search for the app you want to integrate (e.g., Slack, Google Sheets, HubSpot).

3. Click **Add to Board** and follow the setup instructions to authenticate the connection.

3.2 Configuring Multi-Step Workflows

Multi-step workflows involve combining several actions across tools. Here's an example:

Scenario: A sales team wants to automate their lead management process.

1. **Step 1**: When a new lead is added to the CRM (e.g., HubSpot), it automatically creates an item on a Monday.com board.

2. **Step 2**: A notification is sent to the sales team in Slack with the lead's details.

3. **Step 3**: Once the lead's status changes to "Won," the data is updated in Google Sheets for reporting purposes.

3.3 Using Third-Party Tools for Complex Integrations

If the integration you need isn't available in Monday.com's native options, use third-party tools like Zapier or Integromat. These platforms allow you to build advanced workflows by connecting multiple applications. For example:

- Zapier can trigger a sequence where completing a task in Monday.com sends an invoice via QuickBooks.

- Integromat can synchronize tasks between Monday.com and Microsoft Teams, while simultaneously archiving completed tasks in Dropbox.

Step 4: Testing and Optimizing Workflows

Before rolling out advanced workflows, always test them thoroughly to ensure they function as expected.

4.1 Testing Your Workflow

- Use sample data to simulate real-world scenarios.
- Verify that triggers and actions occur as intended.
- Check for errors or delays in execution.

4.2 Monitoring Workflow Performance

Once live, monitor the performance of your workflows:

- Are tasks being completed faster?
- Are team members engaging with the integrations?
- Is there any downtime or failed automations?

4.3 Refining Your Workflow

Periodically review your workflows to identify improvements. As your team's needs evolve, your workflows should adapt. Update triggers, actions, or even the integrated tools to maintain relevance.

Advanced Use Cases for Integration Workflows

Here are some examples of how businesses use advanced workflows with Monday.com:

1. E-commerce Workflow

- Integrate Monday.com with Shopify to track orders.
- Automatically update inventory levels on Monday.com when a sale is made.

- Send alerts to the shipping team when orders are ready to dispatch.

2. Marketing Campaigns

- Use Monday.com with Google Ads to track campaign performance.

- Create a new task in Monday.com whenever an ad is approved or rejected.

- Generate automated weekly reports with Google Sheets.

3. HR Onboarding

- Connect Monday.com with DocuSign to send and track employment contracts.

- Automate reminders for pending HR tasks in Slack.

- Sync new hire data with a payroll system via Zapier.

Tips for Building Advanced Integration Workflows

1. **Start Small**: Begin with basic workflows before moving to more complex setups.

2. **Collaborate with Teams**: Involve your team members to ensure workflows align with their needs.

3. **Document Processes**: Keep a record of workflows for training and troubleshooting.

4. **Stay Updated**: Keep track of new integration features released by Monday.com and third-party tools.

5. **Use Templates**: Leverage pre-built automation recipes or templates to save time.

Conclusion

Advanced integration workflows are a game-changer for teams looking to optimize their productivity and streamline their processes. By thoughtfully combining Monday.com with the right tools, you can create a system that eliminates inefficiencies and fosters better collaboration. With proper planning, testing, and refinement, your workflows will become a key driver of success for your organization.

9.3 Staying Up-to-Date with Monday.com Updates

Monday.com is a dynamic and ever-evolving platform. The development team continuously enhances its functionality, introduces new features, and improves existing ones to ensure users get the most out of their experience. Staying up-to-date with these updates is crucial for maximizing your efficiency and ensuring you are leveraging the platform's full potential. This section will explore the different ways you can stay informed about Monday.com updates, why it's important, and how to incorporate these updates into your workflows effectively.

Why Staying Updated Matters

In a fast-paced work environment, keeping up with the latest tools and features ensures that you and your team can work smarter, not harder. Here's why staying updated on Monday.com is essential:

1. **Improved Productivity:** New features and enhancements often address common pain points or automate repetitive tasks, making your workflows more efficient.

2. **Enhanced Collaboration:** Updates may include new ways for teams to interact or share information, fostering better collaboration.

3. **Security Enhancements:** Software updates often include important security patches that protect your data and ensure compliance with the latest standards.

4. **Access to Cutting-Edge Tools:** Monday.com frequently introduces innovative tools, such as AI-driven automations or advanced reporting dashboards, that can give your team a competitive edge.

5. **Ease of Use:** Updates can simplify complex processes or improve the user interface, making it easier for your team to adopt and use Monday.com effectively.

Where to Find Update Information

Monday.com provides several channels to keep users informed about updates, ensuring you never miss important news or changes. Below are the key resources to monitor:

1. **Official Monday.com Blog:** The Monday.com blog is a valuable source of information about new features, product launches, and updates. Posts are written in an easy-to-understand format and often include examples, screenshots, and use cases. Bookmarking the blog or subscribing to its newsletter can help you stay in the loop.

2. **In-App Notifications:** Monday.com sends in-app notifications whenever significant updates are rolled out. These notifications typically include a brief summary of the update and a link to learn more. To ensure you don't miss these, check your notifications regularly or enable email alerts.

3. **What's New Page:** The "What's New" section within Monday.com's Help Center consolidates all recent updates in one place. It includes release notes, detailed explanations, and links to resources.

4. **Email Newsletters:** Monday.com regularly sends newsletters to registered users, highlighting key updates, new features, and tips for using the platform more effectively.

5. **Social Media Channels:** Monday.com maintains active profiles on platforms like LinkedIn, Twitter, and YouTube. Following these accounts can keep you updated on announcements and tutorials.

6. **Community Forums:** The Monday.com Community Forums often discuss updates and their implications. Experienced users and Monday.com staff frequently provide insights on how to use new features effectively.

Best Practices for Adopting New Features

While staying informed about updates is important, adopting them effectively is just as critical. Here are some best practices to ensure smooth integration of new features into your workflows:

1. **Review Update Details:** Always read the release notes or blog posts accompanying an update. This ensures you understand the purpose and scope of the change, as well as any potential impact on existing workflows.

2. **Communicate with Your Team:** Share information about updates with your team and explain how they can benefit from the new features. Hosting a brief meeting or sharing an email summary can help everyone get on the same page.

3. **Experiment in a Test Workspace:** Before implementing major changes in your primary workspace, test new features in a separate board or workspace. This allows you to understand their functionality without disrupting ongoing projects.

4. **Update Training Materials:** If your organization relies on training documents or videos to onboard new users, ensure these materials reflect the latest features. Keeping resources up to date minimizes confusion for new and existing team members.

5. **Attend Webinars and Tutorials:** Monday.com often hosts webinars or releases video tutorials to demonstrate how to use new features effectively. Participating in these sessions can provide valuable insights.

6. **Gather Feedback:** After introducing a new feature, collect feedback from your team to identify any challenges or opportunities for improvement. Use this feedback to refine your processes.

Anticipating Future Updates

Being proactive about updates can help your team prepare for changes before they happen. Here are ways to anticipate future updates:

1. **Follow Monday.com's Product Roadmap:** The product roadmap, often shared on their website or community forums, provides a sneak peek into features currently under development. This allows you to plan ahead and align your workflows with upcoming enhancements.

2. **Participate in Beta Testing:** Monday.com sometimes invites users to participate in beta testing for new features. This not only gives you early access but also allows you to provide feedback that can shape the final product.

3. **Engage with the Community:** Active participation in community forums and discussions can provide insights into upcoming features. Other users may share experiences or predictions about future updates.

9.3.5 Overcoming Challenges with Updates

While updates are generally beneficial, they can occasionally cause disruptions if not handled properly. Here's how to address common challenges:

1. **Adjustment Period:** Team members may need time to adapt to new features. Provide them with clear instructions, training sessions, and time to explore the changes.

2. **Compatibility Issues:** Updates might occasionally cause compatibility issues with integrations or workflows. Report any problems to Monday.com's support team promptly and explore temporary workarounds.

3. **Resistance to Change:** Some team members may be reluctant to adopt new features. Address this by highlighting the benefits of the update and providing examples of how it can simplify their work.

Real-Life Examples of Benefiting from Updates

Many organizations have leveraged Monday.com updates to enhance their productivity. Here are a few examples:

- **Automations Upgrade:** A marketing team reduced manual follow-ups by implementing advanced automations introduced in a recent update. This saved hours of repetitive work and improved campaign tracking.

- **Improved Dashboard Widgets:** A project management team used new reporting widgets to gain better insights into team performance, allowing them to identify bottlenecks and optimize workflows.

- **Enhanced Integration with Slack:** A sales team streamlined communication by using the updated Slack integration, enabling real-time updates for deal tracking.

Conclusion

Staying up-to-date with Monday.com updates is essential for maintaining a competitive edge and ensuring your team's workflows are as efficient as possible. By leveraging the resources provided by Monday.com, adopting best practices for integrating new features, and anticipating future updates, you can ensure your organization gets the most out of this powerful platform.

Conclusion

10.1 Recap of Key Features and Benefits

Monday.com has revolutionized the way individuals and teams approach project management and workflow organization. As we conclude this guide, it's important to revisit the key features and benefits that make Monday.com a powerful and versatile tool. Whether you're managing large-scale projects, working with a remote team, or simply organizing your daily tasks, Monday.com provides tools and functionalities that simplify and enhance your workflow.

Key Features of Monday.com

1. Intuitive and Flexible Interface

The heart of Monday.com lies in its user-friendly and highly customizable interface. The platform is designed for users of all levels, ensuring that even those without a technical background can navigate and set up their boards effortlessly. Key aspects include:

- **Drag-and-Drop Functionality:** Simplifies organizing items, tasks, and columns.
- **Customizable Columns:** Allows you to tailor your boards to specific project needs, such as adding status, text, date, or formula columns.
- **Color-Coded Labels:** Helps visually organize tasks and priorities for easy reference.

The flexibility of the interface ensures it can adapt to a wide range of industries, from marketing and sales to IT and human resources.

2. Powerful Collaboration Tools

Monday.com excels at fostering team collaboration, regardless of location. Its real-time features promote seamless communication and teamwork:

- **Comments and Updates:** Every item has a dedicated space for comments, enabling team members to share updates, ask questions, and provide feedback directly within the platform.

- **@Mentions:** Notify team members instantly by tagging them in updates, ensuring that everyone stays informed.

- **File Attachments:** Upload files directly to tasks, making it easy to centralize resources and eliminate the need for external file-sharing platforms.

These tools ensure that conversations are tied to actionable items, reducing miscommunication and improving accountability.

3. Advanced Automations

One of Monday.com's standout features is its automation capabilities, which save time and reduce repetitive manual tasks. Users can create workflows that trigger actions based on specific conditions, such as:

- **Recurring Task Creation:** Automatically generate tasks on a regular schedule.

- **Status-Based Notifications:** Send alerts to team members when the status of an item changes.

- **Dependency Automations:** Adjust deadlines for dependent tasks when one task is delayed.

By streamlining processes, automations free up time for more strategic work.

4. Versatile Integrations

Monday.com integrates with a variety of popular tools, making it a hub for all your work-related needs. Key integrations include:

- **Google Workspace:** Sync Google Drive files, Calendar events, and Gmail communications.

- **Slack:** Receive project updates and reminders directly in Slack channels.

- **Zoom:** Schedule and join meetings without leaving the Monday.com interface.

- **CRM Tools:** Integrate with Salesforce or HubSpot to manage sales pipelines.

These integrations ensure that Monday.com works seamlessly with your existing tech stack, enhancing productivity and reducing context switching.

5. Diverse View Options

Monday.com provides multiple ways to visualize your data, catering to different work styles and preferences:

- **Kanban View:** Ideal for agile workflows, allowing teams to track tasks visually through columns.

- **Timeline View:** A Gantt chart-style view that helps with planning and managing deadlines.

- **Calendar View:** Displays tasks and deadlines in a calendar format for easy scheduling.

- **Dashboard View:** Offers high-level insights with widgets that summarize key metrics, such as task completion rates, workload distribution, and deadlines.

These views ensure that users can find the most effective way to manage their projects.

6. Scalability and Adaptability

Whether you're a solo entrepreneur or part of a large enterprise, Monday.com grows with your needs. Features that support scalability include:

- **Multiple Workspaces:** Organize projects for different teams or departments under one account.

- **Templates for Any Use Case:** Start with pre-built templates for marketing campaigns, event planning, recruitment processes, and more.

- **Enterprise-Grade Security:** Ensure data protection with advanced security measures like two-factor authentication and SOC 2 compliance.

This adaptability makes Monday.com a go-to tool for businesses of all sizes and industries.

Key Benefits of Using Monday.com

1. Increased Productivity

By consolidating tools and streamlining processes, Monday.com eliminates time wasted on switching between platforms or searching for information. Automations, integrations, and intuitive features help teams work smarter, not harder.

2. Improved Transparency

Monday.com promotes accountability and transparency by making project details accessible to all stakeholders. With shared boards, real-time updates, and progress tracking, everyone knows exactly what needs to be done and when.

3. Enhanced Collaboration

With centralized communication, file-sharing capabilities, and collaborative tools, Monday.com ensures that team members are always on the same page. Remote teams, in particular, benefit from its seamless integration of communication and task management.

4. Customization for Any Workflow

From tracking sales leads to managing creative projects, Monday.com's customizable boards and columns allow teams to tailor the platform to their unique workflows. The ability to create templates and automate tasks further enhances efficiency.

5. Visual and Data-Driven Insights

Dashboards and visual tools make it easy to track progress, monitor performance, and make informed decisions. Teams can quickly identify bottlenecks, allocate resources, and adjust priorities based on data insights.

6. Better Work-Life Balance

By simplifying task management and automating repetitive work, Monday.com reduces stress and helps users maintain a better work-life balance. With clear priorities and deadlines, users can focus on what matters most.

Final Thoughts on Key Features and Benefits

As we've seen, Monday.com is more than just a project management tool—it's a comprehensive solution for organizing, streamlining, and enhancing workflows. Its flexibility, powerful features, and user-centric design make it a valuable asset for individuals, teams, and organizations looking to stay ahead in a fast-paced world.

In the next section, we'll provide final tips to help you maximize the potential of Monday.com in your day-to-day operations.

10.2 Final Tips for Better Organization

Monday.com is a versatile and powerful platform that can transform the way you and your team manage tasks, projects, and workflows. While mastering its core features is essential, applying smart strategies and adopting best practices can significantly improve your organization and productivity. Below are some final tips to help you optimize your use of Monday.com and take your organizational skills to the next level.

1. Simplify Your Boards for Clarity

A cluttered board can be overwhelming and counterproductive. To maintain clarity:

- **Keep Your Boards Focused:** Avoid cramming too many tasks or unrelated items into a single board. Instead, create separate boards for distinct projects or departments.

- **Use Groups Effectively:** Break tasks into logical groups to make them easier to track. For example, you might use groups for stages of a project (e.g., "To-Do," "In Progress," "Completed") or for team members responsible for different parts of the workflow.

- **Archive Old Items:** Regularly archive or delete completed items and outdated boards. This keeps your workspace clean and ensures that team members focus on current priorities.

2. Create and Use Templates

Templates are a game-changer for repetitive tasks or projects. They save time and ensure consistency across boards.

- **Start with Built-in Templates:** Monday.com offers many pre-designed templates for various workflows, such as project management, marketing campaigns, and event planning. Explore these options to get a head start.

- **Design Custom Templates:** If you have unique workflows, create custom templates tailored to your needs. For example, if you run weekly team meetings, create a template with pre-set columns for agenda items, discussion points, and action items.

- **Share Templates with Your Team:** Ensure all team members have access to shared templates to promote standardized processes and reduce setup time.

3. Leverage Automations Thoughtfully

Automations can save time, reduce errors, and improve efficiency. However, using too many automations or poorly planned ones can complicate your workflows.

- **Start Small:** Introduce basic automations, such as reminders for due dates or notifications for status changes. Gradually expand as your team becomes comfortable.

- **Focus on High-Impact Automations:** Identify repetitive tasks that consume significant time and automate them. For example, automatically assign tasks to team members based on status changes.

- **Test and Review Automations:** Regularly review your automation settings to ensure they align with your workflow and don't create unnecessary complexity.

4. Use Views to Visualize Workflows

Monday.com offers various views that cater to different working styles and needs.

- **Default Table View:** Great for detailed task management and tracking individual items.

- **Kanban View:** Perfect for visualizing workflows in a column-based layout. Ideal for agile project management or tracking tasks by stages.

- **Timeline View:** Useful for project managers who need to see how tasks overlap or track deadlines over time.

- **Calendar View:** Best for scheduling tasks, events, and milestones. Ideal for managing deadlines or planning campaigns.

- **Dashboard Widgets:** Use widgets to monitor metrics, team performance, and progress across multiple boards. Customize dashboards to reflect KPIs or other important data.

5. Foster Collaboration with Clear Communication

Effective collaboration is a cornerstone of successful project management. Monday.com's communication tools can help streamline team interaction.

- **Use the Updates Section:** Encourage team members to document progress, share updates, and provide feedback directly on task items.

- **@Mentions for Clarity:** Use @mentions to direct messages to specific individuals or groups. This ensures everyone knows who's responsible for what.

- **Centralize File Sharing:** Upload all relevant files and documents directly to task items to keep resources organized and accessible.

- **Set Communication Norms:** Establish team guidelines for how and when to use Monday.com versus other communication tools like email or chat apps.

6. Organize Workspaces for Teams and Departments

As your team grows, structuring your Monday.com workspaces effectively becomes increasingly important.

- **Departmental Workspaces:** Create separate workspaces for each department (e.g., marketing, operations, HR) to reduce clutter and improve focus.

- **Cross-Functional Boards:** For projects that require collaboration across departments, create shared boards with clearly defined roles and responsibilities.

- **Permission Levels:** Use Monday.com's permission settings to restrict access to sensitive information or limit editing rights for certain users.

7. Track and Analyze Performance

Tracking progress and analyzing performance can help you identify bottlenecks and improve workflows.

- **Set Milestones:** Break down larger projects into milestones and track their completion to measure progress.

- **Monitor KPIs:** Use dashboard widgets to track key performance indicators, such as task completion rates or time spent on tasks.

- **Conduct Regular Reviews:** Schedule weekly or monthly reviews to assess what's working and what needs improvement. Use insights from these reviews to refine workflows and processes.

8. Stay Organized with Time Management Tools

Monday.com offers features to help you and your team stay on top of deadlines.

- **Due Dates and Deadlines:** Assign due dates to tasks and use calendar views to monitor upcoming deadlines.

- **Time Tracking:** Use the time tracking column to monitor how long tasks take. This can help with future project planning and resource allocation.

- **Set Priorities:** Use status columns to label tasks as "High Priority," "Medium Priority," or "Low Priority." This helps team members focus on what's most important.

9. Train Your Team and Encourage Adoption

Even the best tool won't be effective if your team doesn't know how to use it.

- **Provide Onboarding:** Use Monday.com's tutorials or create your own training sessions to onboard new team members.

- **Share Best Practices:** Encourage team members to share tips and tricks they discover while using Monday.com.

- **Promote Consistency:** Standardize how your team uses boards, columns, and automations to avoid confusion.

10. Experiment and Evolve

Monday.com is constantly updating with new features and improvements. Stay flexible and open to experimenting with new tools and workflows.

- **Test New Features:** Regularly explore Monday.com's updates and test out new features that may benefit your team.

- **Seek Feedback:** Encourage team members to share feedback on what's working and what could be improved.

- **Iterate Your Processes:** Use feedback and performance data to refine workflows and adapt to changing needs.

Final Thoughts

The key to better organization lies in using Monday.com not just as a tool, but as a central hub for collaboration, communication, and productivity. By simplifying your boards, leveraging automations, encouraging teamwork, and continuously evolving your processes, you can unlock the full potential of this platform. With these tips, you're well-equipped to organize your work more effectively, achieve your goals, and empower your team to succeed.

10.3 Where to Go Next

As you wrap up your journey through this book, it's important to consider what's next. Learning to use Monday.com is a significant step toward better organization and productivity, but there's always room to grow, adapt, and explore further. This chapter is designed to guide you on the path forward, offering insights on how to continue developing your skills, discovering advanced features, and unlocking Monday.com's full potential for both personal and professional use.

Deepening Your Knowledge

Now that you've mastered the fundamentals of Monday.com, the next step is to expand your understanding by diving into its advanced features. Here are a few ways to deepen your knowledge:

1. **Experiment with Advanced Automations**: Automations are one of the most powerful features in Monday.com. While this book has covered the basics, there's an entire world of advanced automation recipes waiting to be explored. Take some time to experiment with custom triggers, multi-step automations, and integration-specific workflows to streamline even the most complex processes.

2. **Explore New Integrations**: Monday.com supports a growing list of integrations with tools like Salesforce, HubSpot, Jira, and more. Research which tools are most relevant to your work or industry and learn how to connect them seamlessly with Monday.com. The possibilities are endless, from syncing your CRM data to automating marketing campaigns.

3. **Master Board Templates**: Templates are an excellent way to save time and maintain consistency across projects. If you haven't explored Monday.com's extensive template library, now is the time. Look for industry-specific templates, or create your own reusable templates to standardize your workflows.

4. **Take Advantage of the Monday.com Academy**: Monday.com offers an online learning platform called the Monday.com Academy. This free resource includes video tutorials, certifications, and best practices for using the platform effectively.

Enrolling in these courses can help you stay ahead of the curve and maximize your productivity.

Joining the Monday.com Community

One of the best ways to grow as a Monday.com user is by connecting with other users. The Monday.com community is a vibrant, global network of professionals who share tips, use cases, and innovative ideas.

1. **Participate in the Monday.com Forum**: The community forum is an invaluable resource for troubleshooting, learning, and networking. Whether you're looking for answers to specific questions or sharing your own expertise, the forum is a space to engage with like-minded individuals.

2. **Attend Webinars and Live Events**: Monday.com regularly hosts webinars and live events, where experts demonstrate new features, share success stories, and provide hands-on training. These events are an excellent opportunity to stay up-to-date with the latest developments.

3. **Join Local User Groups**: Many cities have local Monday.com user groups where professionals gather to discuss strategies and solutions. Joining these groups can help you build meaningful connections and learn from others' experiences.

4. **Contribute to the Knowledge Base**: If you've developed unique solutions or workflows, consider contributing to the community knowledge base. Sharing your expertise not only helps others but also positions you as a leader in your field.

Scaling Monday.com for Your Organization

If you've been using Monday.com for personal or small team projects, now might be the time to scale it across your entire organization. Implementing Monday.com at a larger scale requires careful planning, but the benefits are well worth the effort.

1. **Onboarding and Training**: Rolling out Monday.com to a larger team or department involves onboarding new users and ensuring they understand how to use the platform effectively. Create comprehensive training sessions or provide resources like this book to help your team get up to speed.

2. **Customizing Workspaces for Departments**: Different teams within an organization have unique needs. For instance, the marketing team might use Monday.com for campaign planning, while the HR department could use it for recruitment tracking. Work closely with each department to customize workspaces and boards that align with their specific workflows.

3. **Measuring Success with Dashboards**: As you scale, it's essential to track the effectiveness of your workflows. Use Monday.com dashboards to monitor key performance indicators (KPIs) across projects, teams, and departments. Regularly reviewing these metrics ensures that your organization remains aligned and efficient.

Exploring Monday.com's Roadmap

Monday.com is constantly evolving, with new features, integrations, and updates being released regularly. Staying informed about these developments can help you leverage the latest tools to enhance your workflows.

1. **Follow Product Announcements**: Monday.com frequently shares updates and announcements about upcoming features. Subscribe to their newsletter or follow them on social media to stay in the loop.

2. **Test Beta Features**: If you're an adventurous user, consider joining Monday.com's beta testing program. This allows you to try out new features before they're widely released and provide feedback to the development team.

3. **Plan for Upgrades**: As new features are introduced, evaluate how they can improve your existing workflows. For example, if Monday.com releases a new integration or view, experiment with it to see how it fits into your processes.

Adapting Monday.com to Your Evolving Needs

As your projects, teams, and goals evolve, so should your use of Monday.com. Flexibility is one of the platform's greatest strengths, so don't be afraid to adapt your workflows as needed.

1. **Reassess Your Workflows Regularly**: Set aside time every quarter to review your boards, automations, and integrations. Identify areas where you can simplify, improve, or expand your processes.

2. **Gather Feedback from Your Team**: If you're using Monday.com with a team, gather regular feedback from your colleagues. Understanding their pain points and suggestions can help you refine your workflows for better collaboration.

3. **Experiment with New Use Cases**: Think outside the box and explore how Monday.com can support different aspects of your life or work. From managing personal goals to planning events, the platform is versatile enough to handle it all.

Inspiring Stories from Other Users

Finally, draw inspiration from how other individuals and organizations are using Monday.com. Case studies and success stories can spark ideas for improving your own workflows.

1. **Learn from Industry-Specific Use Cases**: Many companies share their Monday.com success stories, particularly within industries like marketing, construction, or IT. Research how others in your field are leveraging the platform.

2. **Adopt Best Practices**: Look for best practices from power users and experts. Whether it's organizing complex projects or managing remote teams, these tips can save you time and effort.

3. **Find Inspiration Beyond Work**: Some users employ Monday.com for personal projects, such as planning vacations or organizing hobbies. These creative approaches might inspire you to think differently about how you use the platform.

Closing Thoughts

As you move forward, remember that Monday.com is more than just a tool—it's a powerful ally in achieving your goals, improving collaboration, and staying organized. Whether you're managing small projects or scaling operations across an entire organization, Monday.com offers endless opportunities to optimize and grow.

Your journey doesn't end here. Instead, it's the beginning of a dynamic process of learning, adapting, and succeeding with Monday.com by your side. Keep exploring, experimenting, and pushing the boundaries of what's possible—you'll be amazed at what you can achieve!

Acknowledgments

Dear Reader,

*Thank you for choosing to purchase and read **Monday.com: A Step-by-Step Guide to Better Organization**. Your trust and investment in this book mean more to me than words can express. I am truly grateful for the opportunity to share this journey with you and to help you unlock the potential of Monday.com for better organization and productivity in your personal and professional life.*

Writing this guide has been a labor of love, inspired by the desire to make complex tools accessible and empower people like you to achieve more with less stress. My goal was to create a resource that is both practical and approachable, and I hope it has served as a valuable companion on your path toward greater efficiency and success.

I want to acknowledge the time, effort, and energy you've dedicated to learning and growing through this book. Your commitment to improving your organizational skills and embracing new tools is inspiring, and it's a privilege to be a part of that journey.

If this book has helped you, even in a small way, then it has accomplished its purpose. Please know that your feedback, thoughts, and experiences are always welcome. Your voice matters, and it helps me continue to improve and create resources that truly meet your needs.

Once again, thank you for your support and for taking the time to explore this book. May it guide you to greater clarity, collaboration, and success in all your endeavors.

Wishing you all the best,